W9-BVU-657

At Home and Abroad

Patrick Lennox

At Home and Abroad
The Canada-US Relationship and Canada's Place in the World

UBCPress · Vancouver · Toronto

20 19 18 17 16 15 14 13 12 11 10 09   5 4 3 2 1

Printed in Canada on ancient-forest-free paper (100% post-consumer recycled) that is processed chlorine- and acid-free.

Library and Archives Canada Cataloguing in Publication

Lennox, Patrick
    At home and abroad : the Canada-US relationship and Canada's place in the world / Patrick Lennox.

Includes bibliographical references and index.
ISBN 978-0-7748-1705-9

    1. Canada – Foreign relations – United States. 2. United States – Foreign relations – Canada. 3. Canada – Foreign relations – 1945-. I. Title.

FC249.L435 2009   327.71073   C2009-905200-8

Canada

UBC Press gratefully acknowledges the financial support for our publishing program of the Government of Canada through the Book Publishing Industry Development Program (BPIDP), and of the Canada Council for the Arts and the British Columbia Arts Council.

This book has been published with the help of a grant from the Canadian Federation for the Humanities and Social Sciences, through the Aid to Scholarly Publications Programme, using funds provided by the Social Sciences and Humanities Research Council of Canada.

UBC Press
The University of British Columbia
2029 West Mall
Vancouver, BC V6T 1Z2
604-822-5959 / Fax: 604-822-6083
www.ubcpress.ca

Contents

Acknowledgments

A number of fine scholars made significant contributions to this book at various stages of its development. Stephen Clarkson, Abraham Rotstein, John Kirton, Lou Pauly, Kim Richard Nossal, Brian Bow, and the two anonymous UBC Press reviewers all provided thorough and insightful comments and suggestions. For all the time and care they invested in me and in this work, I am sincerely thankful. For institutional support, I must thank the Munk Centre for International Studies at the University of Toronto, the Centre for Foreign Policy Studies at Dalhousie University, and the Centre for Military and Strategic Studies at the University of Calgary. For financial support in the form of generous postdoctoral fellowships, I am grateful to the Security and Defence Forum of the Department of National Defence (2006-7) and the Centre for Military and Strategic Studies (2007-9). Finally, I must give thanks and praise to the family, friends, colleagues, and students that kept me strong and inspired me over the period of years it took to complete this book. Peace be with you all.

Introduction

All too often we hear the Canada-US relationship described as "special." It is a partnership between friends, allies, neighbours, even family members. There is, obviously, a grain of truth to these platitudinous assessments that often spill from the mouths of politicians and the pens of pundits. Two more culturally similar states have rarely, if ever, coexisted side by side on this planet. More often than not, however, as most serious observers would be quick to point out, Canada and the United States find themselves at odds on the international stage. The chapters that follow demonstrate consistently and in the most critical of cases the discrepancy between the rhetoric that has traditionally described the "special relationship" and its practice. Canada itself has *also* been endowed with something of an exceptional status in the international community. Deemed a peacekeeper, a helpful fixer, an honest broker, and now even a "model citizen,"[1] Canada has an international reputation – however homegrown, contrived, and mythological – that suggests that it is somehow above the dark, incendiary fray of power politics. This book does not seek to entirely dismantle these two related notions. It does, however, take aim at the fact that they have, for far too long, been allowed to stand in for a proper theory of the connection between the Canada-US relationship and Canada's place in the world. Accordingly, it sets its sights on the development and testing of such a theory.

Traditional explanations of Canada's specialized international roles or of its place in the world tend to draw on variables rooted at the analytical levels of either the state or the individual decision-maker, or some loosely contrived combination of the two.[2] Conventionally, for example, the argument is routinely made that Canada's ability to be a peacekeeper or a helpful multi-lateralist in the international system stems from its tolerant and pacific political culture, its lack of an imperial past, or its democratic values, which are so highly regarded by the world.[3] Arguments are also consistently made that refer to particularly gifted or energetic Canadians, such as Lester B. Pearson[4] or Lloyd Axworthy,[5] as explanations for the country's performance of problem-solving (Suez crisis, 1956) or advocacy (the ongoing International Campaign to Ban Landmines) roles. Such arguments, like their unit-level counterparts, fail to consider Canada's position in the hierarchical continental subsystem that permits and creates the necessity for such activity in the broader international system.

To understand such an underlying causal connection requires the aid of a theory. The theory I introduce and develop in the first chapter of this work is of a general or system-level variety. In other words, what I call *structural specialization theory* (SST) has the potential to be used in explaining not just Canada-US high political relations and Canada's specialized place in the world but also analogous hierarchical inter-state relations and the patterns of behaviour followed by other subordinate states in the international system. It is thus an international relations (IR) theory with the potential to aid in explaining a specified array of hierarchical inter-state relationships and the performance of subordinate states in the international system. I make this assertion because such a mode of studying Canada-US relations and Canadian foreign policy is remarkably absent from the current body of scholarship on these separate though deeply related aspects of international affairs. There are, of course, some notable exceptions to this, but the general tendency has been to study these two subjects in a traditionalist manner, with an emphasis on providing rich detail of particular cases within the broader history.[6] As a result, to the extent that particular variables are emphasized in the explanation of these cases, they tend to be located at the analytical level of the individual or the state.

The systemic form of theorizing that I introduce here enables us to see beyond particular political outcomes to the patterns and trends they form in succession. Such a mode of explanation emphasizes variables that transcend individual political leaders or configurations of a state's regime to find the ultimate causes of a state's behaviour in the structural contexts within which it exists. While this type of theoretical explanation is common to IR scholars, it is far less common to scholars of Canada-US relations and Canadian foreign policy who have tended to pursue their craft in isolation from the theoretical and methodological trends of IR scholarship.[7]

Yet when the cases selected here for testing and analysis of SST are compared, it becomes strikingly evident that the predominant patterns in Canada-US relations and Canada's international behaviour repeat themselves despite significant variation in the individual- and state-level factors that heretofore have been credited with producing them. Looking at these cases in isolation and from the inside out, as has been the tradition, has thus provided us with interesting and rich but ultimately incomplete and proximate explanations of their outcomes. Comparing these cases through the system-level lens of SST allows for an outside-in perspective, which provides an explanation of the underlying causes of these patterns.

Beyond providing for the first time a system-level explanation of these important cases, SST provides insight into the so-called special Canada-US relationship that goes beyond its seeming uniqueness to uncover the roots of its paradoxical past. Finally, for instance, we can arrive at an explanation of Canada's partisan peacekeeper role in Vietnam, which lasted for twenty years and accomplished nothing but negatives in terms of its reputation abroad and its relations with Washington – to say nothing of the tragic results for the people of Vietnam and the stability of that region within the international system. We come to understand why Canada and the United States struggled in such an astoundingly awkward fashion to coordinate their mutual response to the Soviet installation of offensive nuclear weapons in Cuba in the Cuban Missile Crisis of October 1962. We grasp what was behind Canada's dalliances with American nuclear weapons early in the Cold War even as it fervently advocated against nuclear proliferation on the international stage and produced materials at home for the nuclear programs of other nations. We can understand why for twenty years Canada dabbled with the idea of formally participating in America's efforts to build a shield capable of defending the continent from incoming ballistic missiles, and why, despite its best efforts at persuasion for twenty years, the United States has been forced to tolerate this indecision.

The importance of this work going forward is that SST helps us understand the situation that Canada faces with its current participation in the US-led War on Terror. What ultimately caused the Chrétien government to formally denounce the invasion of Iraq while it informally contributed more to the Coalition of the Willing and its efforts than any country besides the US, Britain, and Australia is, for the first time, understood through the lens of SST. Furthermore, why it is that Canadian soldiers find themselves fighting a vicious counterinsurgency war with one hand in the south of Afghanistan, while with the other they try to play a development and diplomacy role more familiar to Canadians at home, is also explained with reference to the contrasting structural pressures illuminated by our theory.

Understanding at this theoretical level what has ultimately compelled such paradoxical behaviour in the past could help to prevent Canada's involvement in such situations in the future. It could aid in the coordination of Canadian and American efforts abroad, and it could provide insight into both the nature of America's position at the top of the international hierarchy and the relations that it must manage with the states that have become its subordinate allies. This subject is taken up in greater detail in the final chapter of this book.

At Home and Abroad

1

The Special Relationship and Canada as a Specialized Power

International systems theory provides a mentally formed image of the realm in which states operate. It should offer, to the extent that it is useful, suggestions regarding how states are likely to behave, and how they are likely to relate to one another based on assumptions about how the major driving forces in the international realm are organized at the level of structure.

Although it was heavily criticized from a variety of angles,[1] Kenneth Waltz's *Theory of International Politics* (1979)[2] formed the first mental image of the realm from which testable hypotheses about the broad patterns of state behaviour could be drawn.[3] With his work, Waltz laid the essential foundations for the social scientific discipline of International Relations. To use E.H. Carr's terms, Waltz took the discipline out of its "infancy" and set down the "beginnings of a science."[4]

Waltz constructed his *Theory of International Politics* by first conceiving the international system as being composed of a structure and interacting units. The structure of the system he defined as separate from the units themselves. Consisting of an ordering principle and a distribution of material capabilities, the structure of the system was deemed to have independent effects on the behaviour and interactions of the units. Though cognizant of the importance of nonstate actors and transnational activities, Waltz sensibly took the primary units of the international system to be states themselves.

Referring to the absence of an overarching power capable of enforcing a common body of international law, Waltz deemed "anarchy" to be the ordering principle of the international political realm. To the uninitiated, this might sound like pure contradiction, for anarchy implies chaos, not order. In this context, however, anarchy is not synonymous with a complete absence of order, nor should it be taken as suggestive of apocalypse. In the context of international relations theory, anarchy simply means that authority in the international system ultimately begins and ends with the sovereign state. There exists no higher power to preside over the states themselves.

The international system is thus ordered by the fact that each sovereign unit is ultimately responsible for its own survival.

This makes the realm of international politics – and any anarchic realm, for that matter – one of self-help or self-reliance. The self-help principle precludes what would otherwise be a third component in the structure of any political system: the functional differentiation of the units.[5] Because anarchic realms impose such high risks on cooperative behaviour leading to interdependence, units in any anarchic system, if they aspire to survive, must maintain functional similarity with their rivals. The maintenance of this functional similarity ensures that each unit retains all of the essential means to its own survival. In this way, states in the anarchic international system remain "like units."[6]

The distribution of economic and military capability structures the system in one of three possible ways: (1) if the distribution is balanced across three or more of the units, the system is multipolar; (2) if it is balanced across two of the units, it is bipolar; and (3) if one unit alone holds the monopoly of power, then the system is unipolar. Shifts from one form of distribution to another constitute a change of system. The shift from the multipolar system after the Second World War to the bipolar system of the Cold War is an example of such a structural change.

Such a state-centric view of the system ignores swaths of reality to arrive at what is basically a positional picture of the realm. While completely obscuring from view nongovernmental organizations, terrorist networks, and even international organizations, Waltz's world also intentionally ignores the unit-level attributes of states themselves. Whether a state is authoritarian or democratic, old or young, religious or secular, radical, rogue, or even fundamentalist does not matter aside from its material capabilities if we want to form expectations about the general patterns of its behaviour. Seeing the structure of the international system in this positional way provides insight into the nature and predominant pattern of international politics. It shows that states that "do not help themselves, or who do so less effectively than others, will fail to prosper, will lay themselves open to dangers, will suffer. Fear of such unwanted consequences stimulates states to behave in ways that tend toward the creation of balances of power."[7] It suggests further that the interdependence of states will be limited by the self-help nature of the system, and that states will be forced through the competitive nature of the realm to emulate those among them who have had the greatest success in accumulating the material power resources that are essential to survival.

What is useful about this theory is that it explains "the results produced by the uncoordinated actions of states."[8] In other words, by exposing at this level of abstraction the constraints and compulsions that bear down on units operating in a self-help system, the theory arrives at expectations about the predominant patterns of state behaviour that will likely obtain despite substantial variation at the unit and individual levels of analysis. In other words, regardless of a state's regime configuration or its individual leader, there are certain systemic conditions that will shape its behaviour. The development of a picture of these conditions is the purpose of systems theory. Having such a theoretical picture of these systemic conditions, however, does not constitute a *complete* explanation for a state's reactions to them. As Waltz wrote, international systems "theory explains why a certain similarity of behaviour is expected from similarly situated states."[9] It cannot fully explain any particular political outcome; for this, a theory of the state as well as a theory of the system is required. But without this knowledge of the situation within which states interact, attempts to explain their behaviour will always be incomplete. The underlying causes of state behaviour will be confused and conflated with the more proximate causes, thereby leading analysts, decision-makers, and conscientious observers astray in their attempts to explain and understand particular international political outcomes.

Waltz's 1979 work gave rise to a major research program in the field of international relations, known as structural or neorealism. Structural realists expect the underlying anarchic condition of the international system to lead to a perpetual condition of competition and conflict between sovereign states engaged in a constant struggle for survival at the very least and for total systemic domination at the very most.[10] This might be seen as a rather wide range of motivation, but survival is assumed to be the prerequisite for the attainment of a state's potential objectives, whatever they may be "other than," as Waltz points out, "the goal of promoting their own disappearance as political entities."[11] The lack of a common authority – the defining feature of an anarchic system – is thus the underlying cause of the security dilemmas that lead to the arms races,[12] alliance formations,[13] balances of power,[14] and wars[15] that form the empirical core of the structural realist research agenda.

The insight that anarchy could have such a determining effect on the play of international politics inspired other research agendas. Liberal internationalist scholars, or neoliberals, in contrast to their neorealist counterparts, took up a more optimistic position on the implications of anarchy. International regimes such as the World Trade Organization, the Organisation for Economic Co-operation and Development, and the Group of Eight are seen by adherents of this school of thinking as being capable of mitigating anarchy's effects on state behaviour (assumed to be rational and egoistic as well as competitive)[16] by creating mechanisms that allow for transparency, trust, and information sharing and iteration. Such regimes can create a more cooperative context wherein states can find ways to combine for mutual gains as opposed to being locked in constant competition for relative gain. For these scholars, anarchy remains a perpetual but potentially less pressing reality of international life, depending on the effectiveness of the institutions that states create to govern their relations and the underlying balance of power.[17]

A third perspective on the implications of anarchy has also developed largely in response to the work of structural realism. Interested in applying social theory to their understanding of world politics, social constructivists have attempted to make the case that "anarchy is what states make of it."[18] Following Alexander Wendt, they argue that the logic of "self-help" that neorealists maintain is the dominant reality of international life is, in fact, a product of social process and practice. The rules of the game of power politics are socially constructed by states through their mutual interactions, and are not actually inherent to anarchic systems at all. Under anarchy, therefore, patterns of international relations can be cooperative just as they can be conflictual, depending on the repetitive behaviours of states themselves and on the intersubjective cultures of anarchy that build up through these social encounters.[19]

Regardless of these three differing perspectives on the implications of anarchy, the case can be easily made that the recognition of anarchy as the ordering principle of the international system is the foundational insight from which modern international systems theory has derived. Indeed, this recognition amounts to the understanding that politics among nations take place within a different structural realm than politics within nations. Marking off the realm of international politics from domestic politics was a crucial early step in the establishment of the scientific discipline of International Relations.[20] Anarchy, in this way, is the touchstone of the discipline.[21] Without this basic observation, it would appear that no theoretical and thus scientific study of international politics could go forward.

Yet such important aspects of international life remain outside the explanatory scope of international systems theories, whether of a neorealist, neoliberal, or social constructivist variety, leading one to question whether the anarchy insight might require revision.[22] Chief among these aspects are the relations between great powers and the smaller states that depend on them for their economic and physical survival, and the behaviour and function of such small states in the international system. The reason these aspects of international politics have remained outside the scope of systems theory is the anarchy insight itself. This is because it implies that the structure of the system is uniformly ordered. It does not allow for the development of subsystems within the broader international anarchy that are ordered according to a different principle: hierarchy.

The recent outpouring of literature on the topic of American primacy, however, has been forced to confront the reality of hierarchy in the international system.[23] America's unipolar moment has made plain a reality that has always existed in the international political realm. Commonwealths, concerts, spheres of influence, dependencies, protectorates, hegemonies, informal empires, empires, and now unions of the European sort have been a near-constant reality of international politics since the time of the Akkadian Empire. Structural specialization theory (SST) proposes that hierarchical structures can and do form within the broader international anarchy, and that these structures have independent effects on the patterns of state behaviour. We will turn our attention to discerning hypotheses about these effects after considering the Canada-US relationship as a hierarchy within the broader international anarchy.

The Continental Hierarchy

Clearly, both Canada and the United States enjoy the status of fully independent sovereign states. Both are members of the United Nations, the Group of Eight, the Organisation for Economic Co-operation and Development, the World Trade Organization, the International Monetary Fund, the North Atlantic Treaty Organization, and many other global governance forums, organizations, treaties, and agreements. Both, in other words, have high levels of international activity across a diverse range of issue areas. Yet despite their comparable levels of participation in the international system, there exists between the two a significant asymmetry in material capabilities.

Consider, for example, that while Canada and the United States share the continent of North America more or less equally in geographical (square kilometres) terms,[24] Canada's population since the 1950s has been on average about a tenth of that of the US.[25] Likewise, the American economy rendered in terms of gross domestic product (constant 2000 US$) was in 1960 fifteen times the size of the Canadian economy. The most recent statistics suggest that the American economy is over thirteen times the size of the Canadian economy.[26] With such a large economy to trade with so close to home, the degree of asymmetrical economic interdependence that has built up between Canada and the United States is significant. The over $500 billion worth of trade that flows across the Canada-US border each year represents approximately 80 percent of Canada's exports and two-thirds of its imports. In terms of personnel in the armed forces, the American military was twenty-five times the size of the Canadian military in 1990, and this basic asymmetry has varied only minimally since then. Further evidence of this asymmetry in military capability can be seen in terms of military expenditure. Typically, the United States spends anywhere from twenty-five to thirty times what Canada spends on personnel, operations and maintenance, research and development, military construction, and military aid in any given year.[27] This asymmetry in material capability, which has been more or less constant throughout the last fifty years, has placed Canada in a position of dependency on the United States for its physical and economic security at home in North America.

Historically, this dependency was first articulated during the August 1938 Sudetenland crisis, as Europe braced for the possibility of another cataclysmic war. President Franklin D. Roosevelt, speaking at Queen's University in Kingston, Ontario, offered Canada America's protection, vowing that "the people of the United States will not stand idly by if domination of Canadian soil is threatened by any other empire."[28] Two days later, Prime Minister Mackenzie King accepted the offer and promised to do as much as could be expected of a country with limited resources of population and military equipment to keep foreign troops from launching an attack on the United States from the vast Canadian territory.[29] The exchange was an acknowledgment of the underlying imbalance in material capabilities between the two North American sovereign states. And it amounted to an exchange of confidence: in Canada, that the US would act as its protector; in the US, that Canada would do its part to keep threats to the United States from materializing north of the border. A breach of that confidence would have serious implications for Canadian sovereignty: either the United States would actively intervene on Canadian soil to "help"[30] bring Canadian defences up to American standards or, in the most extreme hypothetical situation, it would annex Canadian territory in the name of American security.

The diplomatic exchange was institutionalized exactly two years after Roosevelt's speech, in the form of the Permanent Joint Board on Defence (PJBD), which was established for the discussion of "mutual problems of defence in relation to the safety of Canada and the United States."[31] In 1946, the Military Cooperation Committee was formed to manage cooperation at the military planning level. An agreement on North American Air Defence followed in 1957-58, which integrated the Air Forces of both countries and established the North American Air Defence Command (NORAD; now known as the North American Aerospace Defence Command). NORAD headquarters were built into an American part of the Rocky Mountain range. It was agreed that the Commander-in-Chief of NORAD (CINCNORAD) would always be an American, and that the Deputy Commander-in-Chief, a Canadian, would assume decisionmaking power only when the CINCNORAD was absent.

In the 1950s, Canada collaborated with the United States in constructing the Distant Early Warning (DEW) Line across the sixty-sixth parallel to detect long-range Soviet bomber attacks. It stretched from Alaska to Baffin Island, and of the sixty-three DEW Line sites, forty-two were built on Canadian soil with predominantly American funds. By 1958, the Mid-Canada Line, also known as the McGill Fence, became operational as a second line of detection. The Mid-Canada Line ran along the fifty-fifth parallel from Alaska to the Atlantic Ocean. Below the McGill Fence, the Pinetree Line ran along the fifty-third parallel in the west and dropped down to the fiftieth parallel in the east. A second part of the Pinetree Line jutted north around Nova Scotia to Baffin Island. The Pinetree Line stations in Canada were the result of a 1951 agreement between Canada and the United States. They became fully operational in 1955.[32]

The extent of Canada-US security and defence cooperation has broadened and deepened considerably over the last fifty years, and this has been especially the case since the 9/11 terrorist attacks. Today, over 94 percent of NORAD's personnel are American, and over 84 percent of NORAD's budget is paid for with American funds. And while Canada supplies the remainder of the staff and the budget, the practical imbalance in the symbolic institution remains an obvious reflection of the hierarchy in the continental relationship. Participation in these formally equal but practically hierarchical institutions helped Canada defend itself against being formally "helped" by the Americans in protecting its territory.

Beyond being institutionalized in the combined defensive organization, the material asymmetry in the Canada-US relationship is also at the base of the construction of the identities of the two states insofar as they relate to each other. The effect this has had on the formation of the intersubjective identities of the two states can be discerned from popular characterizations of the relationship as being between partners, but nevertheless between partners of unequal size and capacity. The jacket of a book on Canadian-American relations entitled *Partners Nevertheless* shows a bold American elephant standing on its hind legs, tightening a belt with its trunk. Lashed between the belt and the elephant's massive waist is a petrified Canadian beaver.[33] Canada has been similarly characterized in the literature on its relationship to the US as *Partner to Behemoth*[34] and as an American *Powder Monkey*.[35] Perhaps the most famous ideational construction of the relationship comes from Prime Minister Pierre Elliott Trudeau, who told the Press Club in Washington during a 1969 visit that "living next to you is in some ways like sleeping with an elephant. No matter how friendly and even-tempered is the beast, if I can call it that, one is affected by every twitch and grunt."[36] William Henry Pope played on Trudeau's metaphor in the title of a book he published in 1971 on how to regain control of Canada's economy: *The Elephant and the Mouse*.[37] As further evidence of the lasting impact of Trudeau's trope on the identity formation of the two North American partners, former President George W. Bush invoked this image of the relationship in a speech he gave in Halifax, Nova Scotia, in December 2004, saying, "I realize, and many Americans realize, that it's not always easy to sleep next to the elephant."[38] Like Trudeau before him, Bush refrained from making metaphorical reference to Canada's size. Only Pope put the Canadian mouse in bed beside the American elephant to complete the mental image. Thus, materially, institutionally, and ideationally, the Canadian-US relationship appears to be structured hierarchically at home and anarchically abroad.

Implications of Hierarchy in Anarchy

The implications of hierarchical relationships forming within international anarchy in such a manner can be expected to manifest themselves primarily in six ways: (1) in relations between the subordinate and dominant states (intra-hierarchical relations); (2) in the broader foreign policy of the subordinate state; (3) in the domestic stability and bureaucratic organization of the subordinate state; (4) in the effect of the subordinate state on the dominant state's domestic stability; (5) in the foreign policy of the dominant state itself; and (6) in the stability and smooth functioning of the international system. This book focuses primarily on the first two of these implications insofar as they pertain to the Canada-US hierarchy, leaving the remainder for future inquiry.

In inquiring into the implications of specialized structures forming within the international anarchy, two related aspects of Waltz's conception of the structure of international politics become problematic. The first involves his conception of the ordering principle of the system. The second involves his elimination of functional differentiation as a component of the structure of the system. The second follows from the first. As John Ruggie explains:

> Waltz strives for a "generative" formulation of structure. He means for the three (or, internationally, two) components of structure to be thought of as successive causal depth levels. Ordering principles constitute the "deep structure" of a system, shaping its fundamental social quality. They are not visible directly, only through their hypothesized effects.[39]

For Waltz, there is one ordering principle of international politics – anarchy, and the self-reliance of states that it engenders. It is because their relations are organized in this way that states cannot become functionally differentiated, or so posits the theory. But if it is possible that alternative ordering principles might constitute the deep structure of subsystems within the international anarchy, then functional differentiation among the units becomes a possibility. How would we know if this were the case? As Ruggie describes above, such an alternative ordering principle would be discernible only through empirical evidence of its hypothesized effects on the patterns of affected state behaviour. In other words, structure is not something that can be measured directly. Its effects can be ascertained only through the logical deduction of the patterns of behaviour it can be expected to produce across space and time.

The formation of hierarchical structures in more restricted domains or subsystems within the international system does not necessarily eliminate the structural effects of anarchy on the states involved. Rather, there will be specific situations where both structural contexts – hierarchy and anarchy – overlap to bear down simultaneously on the affected states. There will also be instances where hierarchical pressures are primary and anarchic pressures more or less drop out of the equation. The specification of these situations hinges on the distinction between *high* and *low* politics. High politics always unfold in the international anarchic context. This is a result of their far-reaching, or system-wide, implications. Accordingly, in high political situations in which both superordinate and subordinate states find themselves, the pressures of their hierarchical relationship and the broader international anarchy will simultaneously affect their interactions. Low politics, on the other hand, can be defined as interactions between states that have implications that are circumscribed within the dyadic relationship. In these situations, the structural pressures of hierarchy predominate, while anarchic pressures are minimized.

The Pattern of Paradox

To arrive at our first hypothesis about the patterns of behaviour likely to be produced by the contrasting structural pressures of hierarchy and anarchy requires us to first develop separate expectations about their effects in isolation. Under anarchy alone, states can be expected to guard their sovereign independence jealously as a means of preserving their survival. Accordingly, they can be expected to refrain from intruding on the independence of others for fear of retribution or retaliation from that state or others fearing for their own independence.[40] Decisionmaking processes and policy outcomes should follow a logical trajectory, tending towards the pursuit of self-interest. Under hierarchy alone, the superordinate state can be expected to exert its will over its subordinate, and expect that will to be followed. Likewise, the subordinate state should be expected to follow that will. Decisionmaking processes and policy outcomes should follow a logical pattern of leadership and followership, tending towards the pursuit of mutual self-interest.

Under the dual structural influence of hierarchy and anarchy, we cannot expect the pattern of interaction between the superordinate and the subordinate state to be either logical or linear, since each actor is pushed and pulled simultaneously in opposing directions towards opposing objectives or obligations.[41] For example, the pressures of hierarchy incline the subordinate state towards succumbing to the will of the superordinate state, while the pressures of anarchy incline it towards the opposite assertion of its sovereign autonomy. These contrasting pressures push and pull the subordinate state in opposing directions within a bounded range. The unwanted implication of this is that subordinate states will follow an oscillatory pattern of behaviour, countering moves of subordination with moves of self-assertion. Similarly, in the case of the superordinate state, moves of domination conditioned by the hierarchy will be countered by moves of respect for the subordinate state's sovereignty conditioned by the international anarchy.

Such oscillations can be expected to leave a contradictory imprint on the policy outcomes of both states.

Subordinate states can be expected to assert their autonomy when (1) their *survival* (defined in terms of sovereign legitimacy at home) is threatened by *internal* forces of irredentism or illegitimacy, and (2) when the leadership of the superordinate state conflicts with the subordinate state's perceived place in the international system (defined in terms of its array of specialized roles therein) and therefore threatens to undermine the basis of its *external* survival (defined in terms of sovereign legitimacy abroad). Under such circumstances, subordinate states can be expected to act autonomously from the superordinate state, and indeed must do so in order to ensure their survival. Such insubordination, however, will provoke a response from the superordinate state. Attempts to compensate for the insubordination will also be recognizable in the actions or policy decisions of the subordinate state.

Similarly, the superordinate state, influenced by its own position in the hierarchy, will be inclined to assert its will over the subordinate state by privately commanding the latter's compliance or publicly interfering in its domestic politics to gain that compliance. This temptation to forcefully exert its will over the subordinate state will be countered by the strictures of the international anarchy, which compel respect for state sovereignty. Without such restraint, the superordinate state's position in the hierarchy will shift in one of two predictable directions. The superordinate state could forcefully establish an imperial relationship in which the subordinate state ceases to be formally sovereign and becomes the superordinate state's vassal. Alternatively, the subordinate state could potentially revert to a warfare state model in a desire to throw off the yoke of the superordinate state. More frequent and more volatile moves of self-assertion without corresponding moves of subordination would be observable in response to moves of unchecked domination by the superordinate state. Subordinate states could also, or in combination with reversion to a warfare state model, seek to balance against the power of the superordinate state in their geographical region by forming alliances with powers outside the region.

Formal empire is, however, a costly and revolutionary grand strategy to pursue in a universal system of sovereign states. Acting in their own self-interest, then, superordinate states in the modern international system are unlikely to formalize their position in their hierarchical inter-state relations. Instead, superordinate states will demonstrate a tendency towards what leading international relations theorist Stephen Walt has described as "self-restraint"[42] in an effort to keep in abeyance the tendency of the rest of the world to balance against its power. Superordinate states do not have an interest in inciting competitive and conflictual behaviour among their subordinates. On the contrary, they are better off focusing their competitive and conflictual energies on real power rivals. In their dealings with their subordinates, therefore, superordinate states will also follow a nonlinear policy course leading to contradictory policy outcomes, as moves of domination are countered by moves of respect for subordinate state sovereignty. This pattern, as with that of the subordinate state, will be observable in reverse also, with moves of respect for subordinate state sovereignty being countered by moves of domination should it be perceived that the subordinate state is getting a "free ride," or is not complying or "pulling its weight."

The time leads and lags on such sequences of interaction are unpredictable within any meaningful degree of certainty. But whether such paradoxical patterns unfold in rapid succession, within hours, or over a more drawn-out period of a day or a week or a month, is of minimal importance to the verification of the theoretical insight in question here. What is important is whether the pattern is discernible at all. Each specific situation will have its own constraints and pressures, but if the predicted pattern is observable across specific situations, it can be recognized as being general and thus ultimately produced by deep structural causes as opposed to unit-level or individual-level causes. This predicted paradoxical interaction pattern leading to contradictory policy outcomes for both states is the first hypothesized implication of structural specialization.

The Pattern of Specialization

The second implication of hierarchy in anarchy is that the subordinate state must take on a new mantra. In anarchic settings, the mantra of those who wish to survive is, as Waltz says, "Take care of yourself!" In hierarchical subsystems, however, the self-help imperative does not obtain for the subordinate state in the dyad. In choosing to partner with a state of significantly greater material capabilities in this fashion, the subordinate state must take on a new mantra if it wishes to maintain its sovereignty and survive. "Specialize" becomes the mantra of subordinate states operating within the broader international system. The function of such states becomes to perform the system-ameliorating tasks unsuited to great powers.

Hierarchy is the permissive or generative cause of specialization. Just as the individual in domestic society must specialize in some trade or vocation in order to make himself or herself necessary to that society and thereby ensure his or her survival and well-being, so a subordinate state in the international system must find a way to make itself necessary to the superordinate state and to the broader international society in order to ensure its survival and well-being. This necessity provides the impulse for the subordinate state to specialize, playing particular roles in the international system that are different from those most suited to great powers.

Interestingly, the Canadian delegates to the San Francisco Conference articulated this tendency towards specialization in the spring of 1945. Tasked with the monumental responsibility of drafting a charter for the United

Nations from the proposals generated by the great power authors of the Dumbarton Oaks proposals, and struggling to find a role for Canada in the emergent world order, Prime Minister Mackenzie King and key members of the Department of External Affairs maintained that responsibility for the establishment and preservation of stability in the system should not be left entirely to the great powers themselves. An emergent class of middle powers (to which Canada belonged) should be involved in aspects of systemic maintenance in which they could be expected to make important contributions. Moreover, they should be represented in the decisions leading to such involvement. The charter and the organization to which it would give birth must create this space for non-great power involvement in the major movements of international affairs, or risk isolating the middle powers entirely. Isolation of the middle powers would create a top-heavy and unstable postwar order, prone to toppling back into systemic chaos.

What came to be known as the principle of functional representation was eventually embedded in the United Nations charter in number of ways.[43] The principle was not solely a way of creating space for the involvement of non-great powers in the play of international politics, however. Contained within the logic of the principle was a clear sense of what aspects of international politics were outside the ambit of middle powers. In particular, the Canadian delegation had no objection to the permanent place of the great powers on the Security Council, or their individual wielding of veto power over the decisions of the Security Council. Matters of high security were predominantly the domain of the great powers.[44] It was in the other, more specialized aspects of international affairs that middle powers could have an influence.

The principle of functional representation, in other words, contained within its logic a strategy for Canada's future involvement international politics. To separate at a conceptual level the strategy from the principle, we might label the strategy dimension "specialization." The driving forces behind the strategy are not altogether separate from the realities that inspired the invention of the principle, but they do require separate analysis, as they can be recognized only from a deeper level of abstraction.

Specialization in the international system is related to the internal functional differentiation allowed to the subordinate state by virtue of its position within the hierarchy in the international anarchy. To clarify: when, by virtue of its dependency on another sovereign state for its physical and economic security, a state is enabled to become less of a typical Westphalian warfare state (and to channel more of its resources into education or health care or infrastructure) – in other words, when a subordinate state becomes *internally* functionally differentiated – it takes on the characteristics that enable it to become *externally* functionally differentiated.

A direct and immediate connection might exist between a subordinate state's internal functional differentiation and its external functional differentiation; for example, state emphasis on health care might provide the domestic background expertise and material capability for structural specialization in preventing and combating the transnational spread of infectious disease. Canadian expertise and interest in food, aviation, and population in the early postwar era, for example, were used to justify its involvement in the UN's Food and Agriculture Organization (FAO), the International Civil Aviation Organization (ICAO), and the UN Relief and Rehabilitation Administration (UNRRA).[45] More generally, however, it is the movement away from warfare that both allows and compels the movement towards structural specialization. A state's movement away from maintaining an independent warfare capability negates the threat it poses to other states, thus creating the internal preconditions for that state to take on a benign, as opposed to potentially malignant, external posture. This gives the subordinate state a comparative advantage in the performance of roles unsuited to great powers that maintain an independent war-fighting capacity and thus the power to impose their will on other states through coercive force.

The internal functional differentiation of subordinate states recommends structural specialization as a means of survival in the anarchic international system. Compelled to work towards ensuring their survival through means other than the accumulation of material power and power balancing – the strategies recommended by the otherwise anarchic structure of the international system – subordinate states can be expected to exploit their comparative advantage in the performance of roles in the international system not suited to their superordinate partners. The performance of these roles will contribute to the preservation of their external and internal sovereignty through the construction of a distinct international identity. The development of a distinct identity (reinforced and reimagined through the continued performance of these roles) in the world will help preserve the state's legitimacy and its authority over its society.

A subordinate state's performance of a given specialized role is determined by three constraints imposed by the dual structural pressures of hierarchy and anarchy.

First, since the subordinate state comes to derive a portion of its internal cohesion from its external functions, internal constraints arising from its domestic society will play a role in determining its specialized behaviour in the international system. The dominant ideas about the state's place in world politics formed within its society as a result of its pre-existing patterns of behaviour in the international system will set the parameters of possible (legitimate) state action in this realm. These parameters of legitimate behaviour act as both constraining and compelling internal or domestic structural pressures on the state. On the one hand, they limit what the state can and cannot do in the external sphere with the broad-based support of its population. On the other hand, they suggest what the state ought to do when presented with certain opportunities – and perceived obligations – to engage in world affairs.

Second, since the ability of the subordinate state to specialize in the international system is a result of its position in the inter-state hierarchy, the requirements and needs of the superordinate state will be a factor determining the specialized behaviour of the subordinate state in the international system. In the performance of roles in which it has a comparative advantage over its superordinate partner, the subordinate state will be expected to carry its share of the burden of system management. The interests of the superordinate state will always, therefore, be a structuring influence on the particular modes of behaviour pursued by the subordinate state in the international system.

Finally, the specialized behaviour of the subordinate state must be of some utility to the functioning of the status quo international system. Subordinate state specialization is thus generated in part by the demand for non-great power intervention in a complex international system that requires more to remain functional and stable than great power leadership and direction alone. States with specialized capabilities carry out functions unsuited to great powers in an effort to ameliorate potential systemic ruptures and to serve as a buffer between those states that benefit and those states that struggle under the status quo world political and economic system.

Subordinate states can be expected to fill one of these functions, or what in the literature on Canadian foreign policy has been described as "niches,"[46] when at least two of the structural imperatives to do so coincide with an opportunity. If only one of the structural pressures is present, the subordinate state can be expected to reject the opportunity to pursue a specialized role in the international system. The following roles conform to the triad of structural pressures that influence subordinate state specialization in the international system:

- In the aftermath of inter-state warfare or civil war, states with neither the capacity for nor the inclination towards imperialism are necessary to separate combatants and prisoners of war, establish stability, help implement peace treaties, and withdraw. The term often associated with this mode of behaviour is peacekeeping. We will label it *mediation/supervision*. Great powers, of course, have the military and diplomatic capability to carry out mediation and supervision. Their subordinate partners have a comparative advantage in this regard, however, due to their internal functional differentiation, which gives them an unthreatening external posture particularly suited to mediation/supervision roles.

- In situations where communication breaks down between states in conflict or where conflict is imminent, it becomes necessary for a third party to play an interlocutor or intermediary role. Great powers, either because they are often on one side or the other of these situations, or because they have a perceived myopic self-interest in the outcome, are especially un-suited to the performance of such a *messenger* role. Subordinate states, due again to their internal functional differentiation and their broader inher-ent interest in peace and stability in the international system, have a comparative advantage in carrying out this intermediary function.

- Raising awareness of a collective action problem, generating inter-state cooperation for its resolution, and/or defending a particular position (e.g., West versus East) on an issue are *advocacy* roles that often fall to subordin-ate states. The conventional political term used to describe this type of behaviour is *multilateralism*. Because of their superior material capabilities, great powers are strongly inclined towards unilateralism. This inclination can be countered by the work of profound political leaders and statesmen; nevertheless, it is a tendency associated with great power. Yet there remains the need for collective action to resolve otherwise intractable international problems. A comparative advantage in performing such an advocacy role thus exists for subordinate states that, without the ability to "go it alone," have a genuine interest in generating multilateral action towards collective measures in order to resolve problems in an interdependent, anarchic system of sovereign states.

- International crises create opportunities for a state to display ingenuity and initiative in working towards their resolution. Such "helpful fixing" is particularly suited to subordinate states because they are, for the most part, "outside the box" of great power politics. They are thus more able to see the modes of conflict resolution, methods of crisis prevention, and courses of action towards the resolution of problems that have eluded the great powers themselves. We will label this mode of specialization *problem-solving*.

- Uncertainty and misperception are constant and potentially deadly factors in international politics. Occasions repeatedly arise when nonprincipal powers will be granted access to crucial information that the principals are not privy to. The accurate gathering and communication of such in-formation is thus a specialization suited to subordinate states.

Case Selection and Method

The method used to test this theory will be structured, focused comparative case study.[47] The first three cases will focus on the Cold War era, while the next three will focus on the post-Cold War era. The *Vietnam War* and *War on Terror* cases represent the war and armed conflict subclass of the broader phenomenon of high political interactions. The *Nuclear Weapons* and *Missile*

Defence cases represent the security subclass of high political interactions. The *Cuban Missile Crisis* case represents both the war and armed conflict subclass and the security subclass, with the added element of a crisis situation.[48]

The sixth case, *Continental Security after 9/11,* has been selected to control for the international anarchy variable. Instead of following a paradoxical pattern, these interactions and outcomes between the superordinate state and the subordinate state on matters of transnational security will predictably follow a pattern wherein the superordinate state exerts its will on the subordinate state, and the subordinate state conforms to that will with little resistance. Neither state should be influenced by the logic of the international anarchy enough to produce the paradoxical patterns and outcomes hypothesized above, because transnational security relations between two states immediately involve just the two states – they are, in other words, purely bilateral relations. While they might raise some interest or draw attention in the broader international community, the primary structural determining force will remain the continental system.

Part 1
Cold War Case Studies

2
The Vietnam War, 1954-73

Conventional wisdom on Canada's involvement in the Vietnam conflict is divided. On the one hand, there are those who view Canada's involvement as being primarily shaped by and in service to the United States. Canada was more an accomplice than an agent for peace throughout a conflict that ended so badly for the United States and the people of Vietnam. On the other hand, there are those who are of the opinion that the Canadian engagement was primarily shaped by and in service to the broader peace interest of the international system. In agreeing to work on the commissions charged with bringing peace and stability to Indochina, Canada was responsibly carrying out a necessary role, with the ideals of systemic stability and peace as its primary motivations.

Through the lens of structural specialization theory, this chapter arrives at a more balanced interpretation of the evidence. It suggests that what each of these two opposing schools of thought has taken as evidence in support of its position is representative of but one side of the paradoxical interaction patterns that led Canada and the United States towards contradictory policy outcomes throughout their mutual engagement in Vietnam.

It should be stated from the outset that this chapter is not a complete history of the twenty years that Canadian diplomats and soldiers spent in Indochina. Instead, it examines key features of this drawn-out engagement in an attempt to discern their common elements and to arrive at a common explanation for why Canada and the United States failed from the start to coordinate their mutual involvement and interest in Vietnam; and why Canada, despite repeated failures in its role as mediator/supervisor of the settlement, prolonged and compounded its commitment with interlocution, intelligence gathering, and advocacy roles, and even agreed to recommit itself to this seemingly lost cause when a new commission was established to help implement a ceasefire that was finally brokered during negotiations in Paris in 1972.

Taking on Roles

Southeast Asia was the staging ground for the hot proxy wars that constituted the early rounds of the long Cold War. From 1950 to 1953, the US and its allies struggled to keep Korea from falling under communist control, while the French battled to do the same in Indochina. In the spring of 1954, a major conference was convened at Geneva to negotiate a peace settlement for Korea. The Battle of Dien Bien Phu, which ended the war between the French and the Vietnamese revolutionary forces with a crushing defeat of the French forces, prompted the powers to also discuss peace for Indochina at the Geneva Conference.

Canada was directly involved in the negotiations over Korea. It had been a significant combatant in Korea, and had thus been invited to participate by the Big Four (the United States, the United Kingdom, the USSR, and France) plus China. Canada was not, however, directly involved with the Indochina side of the conference. That said, since both negotiations were going on simultaneously as the world watched in nervous anticipation of their crucial and interdependent outcomes, the Canadian diplomats were well aware of what was happening in the Indochina negotiations.[1]

Although a permanent peace failed to evolve from the Korean negotiations, precarious settlements were reached for Vietnam, Cambodia, and Laos on 20 July 1954. The International Commission for Supervision and Control (ICSC) was established to help implement the accords concerning the settlement of Indochina.[2] These accords set down the protocols and deadlines for making sure that the French and Vietnamese troops withdrew from the region north of the seventeenth parallel, and the Viet Minh from the region to the south; that prisoners-of-war were released; that refugees were treated with respect; and that no outside powers interfered in the region.[3] Unexpectedly, in the final stages of the Geneva Conference, Chou En-lai, China's foreign minister, nominated Canada to serve on the ICSC with India and Poland.

Canada proved an acceptable nomination to the Big Four, in large part because it had already demonstrated an interest and ability in mediation/supervision with its efforts to bring about the armistice in Korea. Moreover, Canada had already acquired a reputation for objectivity among the NATO countries.[4] As a Western nation, Canada was nevertheless expected to play a balancing role against Poland,[5] which would inevitably hold fast to the communist cause within the ICSC troika. As a self-consciously nonaligned state, India was expected to cast the swing vote on the commission. The politics of the Cold War were thus built into the construction of the ICSC. A degree of fairness and "judicial" impartiality was nevertheless expected of the states serving on the commission.[6]

None of the nine states that took part in the conference that gave birth to the Geneva Accords actually signed on to them officially. The basis for the ICSC's authority was therefore never clearly defined; nor was it ever clearly defined to whom the ICSC ought to report. Canada's involvement with the commission – which was not in any way connected with the United Nations – was therefore bound to be complicated from the start. Of this the Department of External Affairs had "no illusions."[7] Nevertheless, instead of staying out of what was from the start a precarious high political situation, Canada opted for involvement out of what its ambassador to the United States, in conversation with the US deputy undersecretary of state, described as being "a matter of stern international duty."[8] Ottawa felt compelled to fulfill the role the situation in Indochina had created for specialized power intervention in the international system.

The US delegation at Geneva made it clear, however, that it preferred Belgium for the role, and was nonplussed by the nomination of Canada. Ottawa sought to offset this displeasure with Canadian participation by communicating to Washington that it would have no problem acting as America's intelligence gatherer on the ground through its work on the commission. Canada's nomination for service on the ICSC was thereafter considered by the US to be beneficial to its cause, although the agreement to serve as Washington's intelligence gatherer was to remain unpublicized. Information on Indochina would flow in both directions between the two North American states throughout the Vietnam War. The US provided intelligence to the Canadian ICSC delegation on the Soviet supply of the Democratic Republic of Vietnam with new weaponry in violation of the Geneva Accords. Presumably, this information was designed to help Canada advocate the Western case from within the ICSC, thus revealing a third dimension to Canada's involvement.

Canada's primary role in Vietnam was mediation/supervision of the settlement established by the Geneva Accords. There was an obvious systemic need for Canada's specialized services in this capacity. The US, although initially unconvinced of Canada's suitability to the task, quickly warmed to the suggestion once it became clear that Canada would be willing to combine its mediation/supervision role with intelligence gathering and advocacy roles. Such a conflicted Canadian involvement in Vietnam would ultimately serve neither Canadian, nor American, nor international systemic interests. It would set the stage for a long series of paradoxical interactions between Canada and the US that would culminate in contradictory policy outcomes for both states after nearly twenty years.

Refugees and Reports

Although the ICSC had teams working in Vietnam, Laos, and Cambodia, this analysis focuses on its involvement in Vietnam. Each national delegation to the ICSC Vietnam was led by an ambassador, who would be advised politically, militarily, legally, and administratively by separate committees of representatives of the national delegations. The ICSC teams working on the ground in Vietnam consisted of members of the armed forces of India, Canada, and Poland.

The ICSC teams were given the authority to investigate, mediate, and observe the peace settlement between the two new political entities, North and South Vietnam, which had come into being after the Geneva Accords divided the country provisionally into two separate zones along the seventeenth parallel. The communists, led by Ho Chi Minh's Democratic Republic of Vietnam (DRV) regime, were to withdraw to the north, while the noncommunists, led initially by Bao Dai, were to settle in the south. Bao Dai was replaced at the suggestion of the Americans by Ngo Dinh Diem, who was elected president of the new Republic of Vietnam (RVN) in 1955 with an overwhelming and obviously tainted 98.5 percent of the popular vote.

One of the primary tasks of the commission was to observe the peace process and to publish written recommendations for how any disputes or difficulties along the way could be resolved. The commission itself, however, had neither the capacity nor the authority to enforce these recommendations, which it made on the basis of majority vote on routine matters and on the basis of unanimity on key violations of the Geneva Accords. The reports themselves, therefore, were of the utmost importance as political outputs of the ICSC. Ultimately, the ICSC was supposed to preside over free general elections by secret ballot throughout Vietnam in 1956. It was hoped that the elections would reunite the country just two years after its division, and bring to an end the ICSC's involvement in Vietnam.

During the first 300 days of its mandate, the commission supervised the separation of the former belligerents almost without incident. It encountered difficulties, however, with the exchange of prisoners and particularly with refugees, and divided politically over these issues for the first time along predictable Cold War lines. Here we take up the refugee issue.

Hundreds of thousands of Vietnamese Catholics who had long lived under the protection of the French were attempting to escape religious persecution by the communist regime by heading to the southern zones of Vietnam. The flow of refugees was going overwhelmingly in one direction, with over 800,000 fleeing for the south. According to Article 14(d) of the Geneva Agreement on Vietnam, there was to be nothing preventing the people of Vietnam from living in whatever zone of the country they wished, provided they moved within 300 days of 11 August 1954.

Fearing the loss of its captive electoral majority in the north, Ho Chi Minh's regime resisted this migratory flow, using severe methods against even the most helpless women, children, and elderly. The tactics of Ho's regime "shocked" the Canadian ICSC delegates[9] and strengthened their beliefs about of the evils of communism. It was at this point that the US State Department began to pressure the Canadian government to take a firmer approach to its ICSC commitments, and to intervene more forcefully on behalf of potential refugees fleeing from the north. Pressure on the home front was also starting be felt on this issue, as the Canadian public in general, and Christian Canadians in particular, began to question whether their government was doing all it could to enforce the terms of the Geneva Accords. Problematically, if Canada were to demand that all violations of the freedom of movement clause of the Geneva Accords be investigated and documented, it ran the risk of putting the ICSC out of business and the settlement in jeopardy; on the other hand, neglecting to take such an approach to a human security issue would be to compromise its role as advocate of Western principles on the ICSC, while betraying hundreds of thousands of people suffering for their faith.

In Ottawa, Secretary of External Affairs Lester B. Pearson spoke out publicly against the DRV's actions on three occasions between 24 March and 26 May 1955. In general, he made sure to point out the "frustration and disappointment and irritation" that he and Sherwood Lett, Canada's ICSC Vietnam Commissioner, felt over the DRV's interference with the free flow of refugees; to emphasize the difficult position both Canada and the ICSC were in; and to reinforce the fact that despite the DRV's unsatisfactory record, thousands of refugees from the north did get clear of the DRV and were now free in the south due to the ICSC's work.[10]

Meanwhile, Lett was working hard to get an extension of the 300-day freedom of movement window against opposition from the Polish member of the commission. A 60-day extension was agreed to, but as the new deadline approached with little progress being made on the ground, Lett began to wonder whether it was not time to temper criticism of the DRV to create a more favourable negotiating climate for the pending election consultations. After all, it was difficult to push too far in criticizing the DRV for its violations of Article 14(d) when under Ngo Dinh Diem the RVN was proving to be more and more in violation of 14(c), which required each party to undertake to refrain from any reprisals or discrimination against persons or organizations on account of their activities during the hostilities and to guarantee their democratic liberties.[11] Moreover, Diem's regime was having difficulty coping with the large numbers – somewhere in the area of 700,000 – of refugees that had already arrived. Pearson agreed with Lett, noting that public demand for action on the refugee issue had subsided somewhat since the extension was won. Significantly, the Canadian delegation included only a note of dissatisfaction with the DRV's record of compliance with Article 14(d) with its support of the unanimous Third Interim Report of the ICSC. It did not issue a separate minority report on the issue.

When Diem officially came to power in South Vietnam in the summer of 1955 with the help of the US government, he declared that the Geneva Accords would not bind him. Citing the fact that the totalitarian regime to the north would not hold free and fair elections, Diem cancelled the elections in the south that were aimed at uniting Vietnam. As his regime was expected to prevail, Ho Chi Minh condemned Diem's action, as did the Polish and Indian delegates on the ICSC. Canada tellingly refrained from such a condemnation in the commission's Fourth Interim Report. Instead, it issued a five-page minority report that sought to document comprehensively the failures of the Viet Minh on the freedom of movement issue. The Department of External Affairs actively promoted the report to its audiences in Washington and New York, as well as at home in Canada.[12]

Thereafter, the People's Liberation Armed Forces – known more popularly as the Viet Cong – stepped up its guerrilla attacks in South Vietnam. American buttressing of Diem's regime increased in response. The Eisenhower administration decided to actively attempt to make Diem's regime a viable alternative to Ho Chi Minh's, and began to view the ICSC Vietnam as a means to that end.[13] As the commission subsequently became more and more intractable, Canada found itself facing damaging accusations from members of the international community that it was acting as America's instrument in its capacity as a member of the ICSC.

The refugee issue highlights the triad of pressures felt by the Canadian state when it engages abroad in a specialized capacity. On the home front, the state felt compelled to take a firm stand through its position on the ICSC in condemnation of Ho Chi Minh's treatment of the Catholic refugees attempting to cross into the south of Vietnam. This pressure was compounded by the desire of the US to paint the communist regime in the north in as negative a light as possible. Conflicting with these impulses was the apparent need to maintain the functionality of the ICSC in its service to the people of Vietnam and to the broader international system, which would suffer in the event of further war and instability in the Southeast Asian subsystem. Canada's conflicted reaction to these pressures was thus predictable. In an effort to do its part for the international community and try to keep the commission functional, Canada attached to the Third Interim Report only a note of discomfort with the DRV's lack of compliance on the refugee issue. In the Fourth Interim Report, however, Canada broke with the Indians and the Poles to issue a minority position that attempted to justify Diem's blanket declaration of noncompliance with the Geneva Accords by documenting the DRV's failure to comply with the freedom of movement clause. In the Third report, the interests of peace won out over the interests of the Cold War, but in the Fourth report the tables turned. Canada was compelled by the pressures of the continental hierarchy to counter the move it had made on the Third report with a subordinate move on the Fourth report. The ICSC was essentially debilitated after these two reports were issued, but it remained in service for another eighteen years.

Missions to Hanoi

By the end of 1963, American military support of the South Vietnamese government in Saigon and the conflict across the north/south partition had escalated considerably. At home in North America, Pearson's Liberal minority government had taken control of the House of Commons, President John F. Kennedy had been assassinated, and Lyndon B. Johnson had assumed the presidency of the United States. Ngo Dinh Diem had also been assassinated, and South Vietnam was consequently in a considerable state of uncertainty.

Prime Minister Pearson and Secretary of External Affairs Paul Martin were understandably worried about the situation in Vietnam, but they trusted the American leadership enough in 1964 to agree to use Canada's position on the ICSC to open a secret channel of communication between Washington and Hanoi. According to the man who would become that secret channel (an operation codenamed "Bacon"), Blair Seaborn, "Canada hoped that the use of this channel might open a dialogue between Hanoi and Washington in the interests of peace."[14]

Some members of the Johnson administration, however, had other things in mind. The United States wanted to send a message to the DRV that it would stand firm against any efforts to exploit the instability in the South that had followed in the wake of Diem's assassination. They wanted to communicate clearly that the South still had the support of the US government, and they wanted the DRV to understand that the future course of events in Southeast Asia rested squarely on its shoulders: if peace were to come about, Ho Chi Minh's regime would have to cease interference in the South. Economic benefits would follow from peaceful coexistence with the Western world. Otherwise, only the gravest of consequences could be foreseen. This was known as the "carrot and stick approach" in Johnson's Democratic administration.[15] Canada would play a significant role in its communication, and in so doing add a fourth dimension to its involvement in Vietnam. Along with acting as mediator/supervisor of the broader situation, it would also collect intelligence on behalf of the United States, advocate the Western position within the ICSC, and perform interlocution (messaging) services between Washington and Hanoi.

While in Ottawa in the spring of 1964, US Secretary of State Dean Rusk suggested in conversation with Paul Martin and Lester Pearson that Canada's incoming commissioner on the ICSC be placed in this "interlocutor" role.[16] In preparation for Blair Seaborn's first communication with Hanoi, Henry Cabot Lodge, the US ambassador in Saigon, wrote Secretary of State Dean Rusk: "It is not rpt not at all necessary that the Canadians either agree or disagree. What is important is that the Canadian transmit the message and be willing to do that and report back accurately what is said."[17] This cable suggests that at least Lodge, if not the rest of Johnson's men, expected complete Canadian compliance with their will on this matter.

Along with reporting back accurately the DRV's response to the American message, the Americans had more elaborate instructions for Seaborn. "By listening to the arguments and observing the attitudes of the North Vietnamese," Seaborn was also to "form an evaluation of their mental outlook. He should be particularly alert to (a) differences with respect to the Sino-Soviet split, (b) frustration of war weariness, (c) indications of North Vietnamese desire for contacts with the West, (d) evidence of cliques or factions in the Party or Government, and (e) evidence of differences between the political and military."[18] This list of intelligence-gathering points was sent to the Canadian embassy in Washington as part of a lengthy communication detailing Seaborn's duties in Hanoi.

The logic of Seaborn's role in the coming escalation of the war was set out in a frank message from Henry Cabot Lodge to President Johnson dated 15 May 1964:

> If prior to the Canadian's trip to Hanoi there has been a terroristic act of the proper magnitude, then I suggest a specific target in North Viet Nam be considered as a prelude to his arrival. The Vietnamese Air Force must be made capable of doing this, and they should undertake this type of action. I much prefer a selective use of Vietnamese Air power to an overt U.S. effort perhaps involving the total annihilation of all that has been built in North Viet Nam since 1954, because this would surely bring in the Chinese Communists, and might well bring in the Russians. Moreover, if you lay the whole country to waste, it is quite likely you will induce a mood of fatalism in the Viet Cong. Also, there will be nobody left in North Viet Nam on whom to put pressure. Furthermore, South Viet Nam's infrastructure might well be destroyed. What we are interested in here is not destroying Ho Chi Minh (as his successor would probably be worse than he is), but getting him to change his behavior.[19]

There was thus a scenario planned for escalating American involvement in the war, and Seaborn was a crucial element. But no "terroristic attack" of sufficient significance to justify American retaliation had taken place by the time Seaborn was first dispatched to Hanoi, although the Joint Chiefs of Staff had been instructed to make detailed plans for air strikes against North Vietnam should one occur. Pearson was informed of these plans by Johnson during a brief meeting between the two at the Hilton New Yorker Hotel on 28 May 1964.[20]

Seaborn's first visit to Hanoi as interlocutor took place less than three weeks later. On 18 June, he met privately with Prime Minister Pham Van Dong and conveyed to him the warning, "drafted by U.S. officials and coordinated with the Canadians, that 'U.S. public and official patience with North Vietnamese aggression is growing extremely thin,' and that if the conflict should escalate, 'the greatest devastation would of course result for the DRV itself.'"[21] Seaborn reported home that Pham Van Dong did not betray any fears of American escalation, and had nothing specific to convey back to Washington other than his position that "a just solution" to the conflict would depend on American withdrawal and a negotiated settlement between Saigon and Hanoi. He also reported that morale seemed high in the North; resolve to persevere over external involvement in the country seemed strong; there were no apparent political divisions or rivalries within the DRV; the people were healthy; and, most importantly, the DRV did not believe that the US was willing to risk escalating its involvement to the point of a third world war, and even if it were, it would ultimately fail in its objectives.[22]

By late July 1964, just prior to Seaborn's second trip to Hanoi, the American and South Vietnamese navies engaged in a series of provocative manoeuvres in the Gulf of Tonkin (in or extremely close to North Vietnamese coastal waters), which ultimately resulted in an attack on an American destroyer, USS *Maddox,* by three North Vietnamese patrol boats on 2 August. *Maddox* countered with a crippling attack on one of the North Vietnamese boats. This initial incident, however, was deemed too minor by the Johnson administration to merit significant retaliation. Instead, the decision was made to send another destroyer, USS *Turner Joy,* into the Gulf of Tonkin to assist with the patrols that had provoked the first attack. Johnson also ordered combat air protection for the destroyers, and altered their rules of engagement to allow them not only to repel any attacks but also to sink any attackers.[23] A further implication of this attack on *Maddox* was that it set in motion the political forces necessary to generate a Congressional resolution giving President Johnson a mandate to intensify the effort in Vietnam.

Within three days of the 2 August attack, Captain John J. Herrick, commodore of the two-destroyer flotilla, sent word to the Pentagon that *Maddox* and *Turner Joy* were under "continuous torpedo attack" in the Gulf of Tonkin.[24] Messages conveying the highlights of the battle continued to flow into the Pentagon for a full two hours on 4 August, during which time plans were set in motion for retaliatory air strikes against North Vietnam. Then, one hour after his last message, Herrick reported that the entire encounter may not have actually happened. Hypersensitive sonar men may have misinterpreted the sound of their own sonar beams bouncing off the rudders of their own ship, and since the entire affair took place in total darkness, nothing of the event could be confirmed one way or the other.[25] The retaliatory air strikes followed, nevertheless, and Congress pushed through what became known as the Gulf of Tonkin Resolution, which gave the president carte blanche to wage war against North Vietnam. This resolution would pave the way for large numbers of American ground troops to be sent to Vietnam, fundamentally altering the nature of the conflict and indicating that the war now had as much to do with the freedom of South Vietnam as it did with the American effort to contain the spread of Communism in the region. This brought with it the increased possibility of direct conflict of a potentially nuclear variety with China or the USSR, or both simultaneously.

Seaborn was sent back to Hanoi shortly after the second Gulf of Tonkin incident on 10 August. The message he was to convey to Pham Van Dong was, according to Daniel Ellsberg, who assisted with its drafting, "one of the most closely held secrets in the administration." "It was a very dubious role," Ellsberg recounts, "for an ICC [ICSC] Commissioner to be conveying U.S. threats to Hanoi. (An intermediary was necessary because the United States had no formal representation or contact with the Hanoi regime.) That role could not be known to the other members of the ICC, Poland and India, or to the Canadian public, which would not be as quick to accept it as Canadian Prime Minister Lester Pearson."[26] Here Ellsberg outlines the triad of pressures that would have been brought to bear on this particular instance of Canadian specialization in the international system had it not been conducted in secret. Canada's role on the ICSC would have been jeopardized, as well as the legitimacy of Pearson's minority government. Accordingly, structural specialization theory would expect Canada to have turned down this opportunity to act as an interlocutor on behalf of the superordinate state were this role to have been played openly.

Seaborn's instructions for this second meeting with Pham Van Dong were to convey again the threat of intensified US involvement in Vietnam, this time with the examples of the air strikes that followed the Gulf of Tonkin incident and the Congressional resolution that had passed with near unanimity, supporting the president's prerogative to do so, as evidence of the threat's validity. This time, Dong was less receptive to having Seaborn as interlocutor. This was likely because it was no longer possible for him to view Seaborn as a "dispassionate intermediary" – as Lyndon Johnson would describe him in his memoirs.[27] Rather, he must have seen Seaborn as a willing pawn in the American escalation strategy, for he must have calculated that the Canadians, by that point, were well aware of American plans for an intensified bombing campaign on the north, and were thus willingly sacrificing the integrity of their position on the ICSC for the benefit of the United States.

Seaborn was sent back to Hanoi in December and then again in March 1965, but the DRV had ceased to take him seriously as the US Air Force carried out Operation Rolling Thunder over its territory. Pearson, Martin, and Seaborn wanted to perform a functional service for the international community in the interest of peace in opening up the Canadian channel, but in agreeing to do so, they found themselves, however unwillingly, in the service of war. The United States wanted intelligence on Ho Chi Minh's regime – its state of mind, its morale. Paradoxically, when Seaborn reported from his first mission to Hanoi that Ho's regime was confident it could withstand the worst that American military muscle could deliver, that crucial piece of intelligence was ignored in Washington.

Once the Seaborn missions to Hanoi ceased, the ICSC became further mired in the Cold War's tensions. Paul Martin immediately began looking for another way to involve Canada in a solution to the Vietnam conflict. This was partly a bid for a Nobel Peace Prize, partly a way to "demonstrate to the Canadian people that Canada had not just been a U.S. satellite but had done what it could to bring about a solution,"[28] but mainly a way to maintain a specialized role for Canada in the conflict. "Public opinion in Canada would welcome an initiative which would be presented as a contribution to the search for peace in Vietnam," Martin assured Pearson.[29]

Martin decided on a semi-independent Canadian approach. He would send Chester Ronning, a retired Canadian diplomat with a good reputation in Asia and a poor one in Washington, on a peace initiative to meet with the North Vietnamese and the Chinese. According to Greg Donaghy, Martin argued "that Ronning would fulfill an American need for a mediator and add to Canada's standing in Washington."[30] Although the Chinese refused to see him out of anger at Canada's support for the US Vietnam policy, Pham Van Dong told Ronning that talks with the Americans were a possibility if they were to unconditionally cease their bombardment of the North. The American response to this offer was delayed, largely due to their disdain for the Canadian initiative. Variations on this type of mission had been repeated over and over without results by international political heavyweights from Pope Paul VI to Charles de Gaulle throughout the course of the conflict. The Americans were planning an escalation in their bombing of the North. It would involve targeting petroleum, oil, and lubricant (POL) factories. They were anxious to carry it out but the Canadian peace initiative was getting in the way. This was the likely cause of their irritation at the news of the Ronning mission.

The so-called POL strikes were postponed while Ronning carried the American message back to Hanoi during his visit of 14-17 June 1966. The message indicated that the US was open to talks but not on the condition of a unilateral halt to its bombing of the North. Nguyen Duy Trinh, the DRV's foreign minister, "declared that the Canadians were helping the Americans by contributing to a diplomatic 'peace offensive' when there were no new offers to be discussed and the US was 'escalating' the bombing."[31] Indeed, Washington fully expected the offer they sent with Ronning to be rejected by Hanoi. The first waves of POL were launched shortly after Ronning returned to North America empty-handed 29 June.

Evidently, Pearson, Martin, and Ronning remained in the dark about the planned POL strikes until they were launched. The Americans did not mention the escalation plan in their consultations with the Canadians about the peace initiative. On the contrary, Ronning would later reveal to the *Globe and Mail* that presidential adviser William Bundy had assured him that the US would not resume bombing.[32] Paradoxically, the Americans could not tell the Canadians to stop meddling, or that their initiative was coming at an inopportune time, since they had previously utilized just such a Canadian channel themselves with the Seaborn missions. Out of respect for Canadian sovereignty, the Johnson administration "naturally had to say [upon the announcement of the Canadian peace initiative] we would have no objection to such a visit and indeed could only welcome any constructive initiative."[33] The unintended consequence of this was that Ronning's missions to Hanoi appeared as deceptive efforts by the US to justify an escalation of the American bombing campaign on the North, just as Seaborn's missions to Hanoi had between 1964 and 1965. Clearly, neither the US nor Canada nor the broader international community benefited from this outcome.

The Sermon at Temple

Between the two Canadian missions to Hanoi, the ICSC issued a report on Operation Rolling Thunder. Poland and India denounced the bombing campaign as a violation of the Geneva Accords. The Canadian minority statement argued, however, that the majority view was "an oversimplified and misleading impression of the root causes of the dangerous instability in Vietnam."[34] The Canadians made an effort to excuse the bombings as responses to Communist attacks on South Vietnam. This was the last significant act of the ICSC in Vietnam. It remained intact symbolically, but its teams were reduced considerably in size and were removed altogether from the North.[35]

Five days before the 1965 ICSC report was published, Prime Minister Pearson outlined the logic of the Canadian diplomatic approach to the United States in what was proving a troubling time, as an American military advisers' base had been raided by the Viet Minh just 200 miles from Saigon, at Pleiku, and retaliatory bombs rained on North Vietnam. In a speech to the Canadian Club in Toronto, Pearson made this argument:

> We must protect and advance our national interests, but we should never forget that the greatest of these is peace and security. The achievement of this aim – it is chastening to realize – does not depend on our policies so much as it does on those of our neighbour. This will mean, in practice, that our official doubts about certain U.S. foreign policies often should be expressed in private, through the channels of diplomacy, rather than publicly by speeches to Canadian Clubs ... Pulling the eagle's tail feathers is an easy,

but a dangerous, way to get a certain temporary popularity, as well as a feeling of self-satisfaction at having annoyed the big bird. It's a form of indulgence that we should keep strictly under control – for national and international reasons.[36]

In this address, Pearson described the doctrine of *quiet diplomacy,* which had been set out in the controversial Merchant-Heeney report of 1964. With its paradoxical logic of publicly supporting US ends while privately criticizing US means, such an approach to the Canada-US relationship and to the broader aspects of Canadian foreign policy is not blind to this country's position in the continental hierarchy. Approaching the "big bird" quietly and cautiously, being careful not to ruffle his feathers, is a diplomatic course of subordination, which stems entirely from the realistic and, in Pearson's words, "chastening" recognition that Canada's security depends on America's policy, and not on its own. The compulsion to approach the "big bird" in the first place stems, however, from Canada's sovereign status in the international system, which suggests that it has the right to speak its piece about such matters.

Despite Pearson's recognition of the inherent logic of quiet diplomacy, it was not long before structural pressures conspired to make him disregard his own advice. In the midst of Operation Rolling Thunder, the growing unpopularity of the war in both the US and Canada, the concern that China and Russia could soon become involved, and the fear that nuclear weapons might be employed, Pearson, who was regarded by many as a champion of peace after his efforts to resolve the Suez crisis in 1956, but who was also in a minority government situation with an election looming and a dovish Quebec watching,[37] was pressured by the Toronto *Globe and Mail,* by his son Geoffrey, by the Washington journalist Marquis Childs, and by prominent others,[38] to exercise his right as the leader of a sovereign state to suggest moderation at a time when it was feared the hawks of the Johnson administration were gearing up for an ill-conceived escalation of the Vietnam War.

On the occasion of his acceptance of another peace prize, Pearson gave a speech at Temple University in Philadelphia that was balanced, to say the least. Although it was far from a diatribe condemning the war, however, evidence suggests that Pearson knew it would cause a "blow-up" in Canada-US relations.[39] For one thing, as Kim Richard Nossal points out, "the prime minister had chosen to ignore the ethos of diplomacy, which dictates that government leaders do not criticize the policies of other governments while on their soil."[40] Indeed, Paul Martin, on reading the speech in draft form, "took violent issue with it at once." He threatened to resign over the speech, after storming into the prime minister's office saying, "If you publicly criticize the United States like this, you're going to discount our influence in Washington and your own forever. And you must not do that."[41] Canadian

Ambassador to the United States Charles Ritchie suggested that Pearson at least supply the White House with an advance copy of the speech.[42] Pearson eventually ignored the advice and went ahead with the speech, regardless of the fact that it appeared to challenge the trajectory of American policy.[43]

He began by citing the "honourable" motives of the US, and the great sacrifices it had made for its intervention on behalf of the South Vietnamese. He accused the North Vietnamese of "wanton" murder of US civilians trying to do peaceful work in Vietnam, and generally attempted to portray them as the aggressors. But he also suggested that at some point the US might consider the possibility that the message it was trying to send with its air bombing campaign had gotten through to Ho Chi Minh. A limited pause in the bombing might, "at the right time," go some length towards the resolution of the war by giving North Vietnam an opportunity to "to inject some flexibility into their policy without appearing to do so as a result of military pressure."[44]

The message did not go over well with President Johnson, who had just won re-election by a significant margin. (The Democratic Party in general had also won a substantial victory, adding thirty-seven seats to its majority in the House of Representatives.) After his speech, Pearson was asked to join the president for lunch at Camp David. The prime minister and his aides arrived to a cool reception. After lunch, Johnson moved Pearson out onto the terrace alone. In the eyes of the Texan, Pearson had "pissed" on his "rug"[45] – the ultimate act of insubordination. According to John English, Johnson felt that "the Canadians had no right to complain."[46] Nevertheless, when asked about Pearson's speech by the press, Johnson was sobered by structural pressure to respect Canadian sovereignty. Johnson's line to the press was the following: "It is not a matter for me to pass judgment on what other governments do. It is his expression. He has expressed it very well."[47]

While out on the terrace, Pearson attempted to explain to LBJ the domestic politics behind his remarks.[48] Public opinion on Vietnam was souring in Canada, especially in Quebec. Questions were being raised about the Seaborn missions and the Canadian government's complicity in the increasingly unpopular American actions in Vietnam. In a minority government situation, Pearson feared appearing too much as an American "echo," and thus felt the need to make a suggestion, however minor, for how peace might be achieved in Southeast Asia.[49] His rationale fell on deaf ears at Camp David.

Pearson would also explain himself to his foreign minister, Paul Martin. He told Martin that the speech was a "political act" designed to "shape the public record" of the government on the issue of its concern for the civilians of North Vietnam.[50] To Martin this must have seemed self-evident, as the speech contradicted both his own and Pearson's previous positions, which had been fully supportive of the American Vietnam policy. Only the indelible structural pressures stemming from the international system to maintain the integrity of Canadian sovereignty could have caused the prime minister to act in a way that was so clearly bound to cause a disruption in Canada's continental relations. Pearson's ill-fated attempt to reconcile the division of his loyalties to the US and to the Canadian public effectively ended whatever quiet diplomatic influence on American Vietnam policy Canada may have had, and led to a rocky period in the relationship between the two North American states.

Consequences of Contradiction

Meanwhile, the Canadian public grew increasingly dissatisfied with America's handling of the Vietnam war and their own government's role in the conflict.[51] The country's clergy and professors joined ranks with its youth in opposition to Canadian complicity in the US Vietnam policy. Antiwar demonstrations and teach-ins from Vancouver to Halifax became more and more part of Canada's political landscape. With the country's centennial fast approaching, Canadian nationalism was on the rise. Prominent nationalists such as Abraham Rotstein, Melville Watkins, and Walter Gordon began to speak out publicly against Canada's roles in the Vietnam War.

Televised accounts of the savagery of the war fuelled anti-American sentiment. For the first time in history, the horrors of war were transmitted into the kitchens and living rooms of ordinary Canadians. They did not like what they saw, especially in Quebec. At Expo 67 in Montreal, Johnson endured chants of "Hey, hey, LBJ, how many kids did you kill today?"[52] The rabidly anti-American Front de libération du Québec (FLQ) – the province's revolutionary terrorist organization bent on the cause of Quebec separatism – even threatened to assassinate the person who unfurled the Stars and Stripes at the American pavilion at the world fair, which the federal government had bid on and won in order to commemorate Canada's centennial.[53] In its first notice to the Canadian public (9 March 1963), which followed in the wake of its firing of Molotov cocktails at three Canadian military establishments in Montreal, the FLQ stated boldly that it would also "attack all American cultural and commercial interests, natural allies of English colonialism."[54] By 1970, the FLQ leadership was moved to declare: "There is no difference between the struggle here and the liberation movement of Palestine, of Vietnam, of Black Power."[55]

News that, under the Defence Production Sharing Agreement, Canadian corporations were actually supplying the American military with cartridges, guided missiles, ammunition, aircraft engines, aircraft launch equipment, sonar equipment, personal armour, Bata boots, and green berets, not to mention napalm and Agent Orange to be used against the North Vietnamese, and that they were profiting greatly from the sales of these items to the US, reached Canadians. That Canada was supplying the equipment that was aiding so much in the destruction of their country convinced the North

Vietnamese that Canada's position on the ICSC might not have been solely in the interests of peace.[56] In a speech at Victoria College, University of Toronto, on 10 March 1967, Pearson responded by citing the imperatives of the continental hierarchy. Any move to stem the flow of Canadian-made military equipment to the United States would have "far reaching consequences which no Canadian government could contemplate with equanimity ... it would be interpreted as a notice of withdrawal on our part from continental defence and even from the collective agreements of the Atlantic Alliance."[57]

Officially, Canada was supposed to be acting for the cause of peace through its position on the ICSC. The country's place in the continental hierarchy, however, had it acting in the service of war, producing arms for the effort ($1.3 billion worth between 1959 and 1966) and even turning its ICSC role into an instrument for intelligence gathering and escalation.

Faced with a potential legitimacy crisis, the Liberals responded first in the House of Commons, in April 1967, with a so-called four-point peace concept to end the war in Vietnam. Championed by Martin, the plan called for (1) reciprocal disengagement, (2) an agreed ceiling on military activity, (3) an eventual end to hostilities, and (4) a return to the ceasefire provisions of the Geneva Accords. But Pham Van Dong, who maintained that there would be no peace until the US unconditionally ceased its bombardment of his country, rejected the plan. Also in that month, Pearson advocated extended bombing pauses to an audience at the University of California at Santa Barbara. Walter Gordon, president of the Privy Council, went further the next month, arguing in a speech in Toronto that the US had made a horrible mistake in intervening in Vietnam, one that could potentially lead to the most devastating of consequences: Soviet-American nuclear confrontation. Professors from the Department of Political Economy at the University of Toronto had helped significantly to shape his views. Martin would make one final public effort to bring about peace in a speech to the UN General Assembly, in which he called on the United States to unilaterally and unconditionally stop bombing North Vietnam as the first step towards resolution of the deepening crisis. The Canadian government never publicly deplored the US assault on Vietnam, however.

Complicit all along in the American war effort, willingly or unwillingly, knowingly or unknowingly, the Canadian government nevertheless kept trying to find a solution to the conflict in an effort to avoid legitimacy problems at home and a tarnished reputation abroad. The eventual end to the crisis, however, would have nothing to do with Canada's efforts. The two warring parties held negotiations in Paris in 1968. Five years later, the signing of the Paris Agreement on Vietnam led to the withdrawal of American troops from that country.

During the Paris negotiations, iron bombs continued to rain down on Hanoi, while bombs of a political nature detonated in the United States. In 1971, seven years after Seaborn's secret diplomatic missions to Hanoi, the Pentagon Papers became front-page news in both Canada and the United States, but for different reasons in each country. In response to their contents, Minister of Foreign Affairs Mitchell Sharp had to rise in the House of Commons on 17 June 1971 to deny that the previous Liberal government was made aware of the Johnson administration's intention to escalate the war.[58] There had been outrage among the Opposition in the House of Commons when the Pentagon Papers were published.[59] Sharp's attempt to explain them away provoked calls of "hypocrisy" from the Opposition for the government's previous condemnations of India and Poland for their lack of neutrality in the ICSC.[60] From R. Gordon L. Fairweather, Member of Parliament for Fundy-Royal, came this criticism of Canada's specialized role:

[I] say with great respect that Canada has found her membership on the ICC to be of great comfort and convenience over the years. Whenever prime ministers or foreign ministers were questioned about this or that example of extended bombing or search and destroy operations or any other aspect of the war they were able to hide behind the cloak of neutrality and our membership on the International Control Commission. They were able to trot out little homilies about neutrality preventing our making any attempt to protest. The record is loaded with these references. If we cannot and do not intend to bring neutrality to our membership, how do we justify our continuing to be a member of the ICC? The reason for our involvement with the ICC was to promote peace; it was not to be an errand boy bearing threats of expanded war.[61]

This particular reaction in the House of Commons to the secret history of Canada's involvement in the Vietnam War might be seen as evidence of how the contrasting pressures of the continental and international systems forced the government to pursue a contradictory policy, which in the end led it down the path of deception and hypocrisy. After the publication of the Pentagon Papers, Canada might have been expected to bow out of its Vietnam commitments. Structural pressures combined again, however, to compel the government to take on a similar role in the coming peace.

Vietnam Redux

In October 1972, with the Paris talks on the verge of finally producing a ceasefire, it was announced that an international commission – this time with representatives from Canada, Hungary, Poland, and Indonesia – would supervise the implementation of the agreement. Canada had been hinting since 1969 that it would be hesitant to take on another ICSC-style commitment. In 1970, Pierre Trudeau's Liberal majority government published its review of Canadian foreign policy, which indicated that such forays into "helpful fixing" (problem-solving) would be rejected in favour of an approach to international affairs conditioned more by considerations of the "national interest."[62] Nevertheless, the section on Canada's relations with the Asia-Pacific states indicated that the country would be willing to make a peace-keeping contribution to Vietnam under certain conditions, the most important of which was that there had to be a time limit to the commitment. Washington failed to take this condition into consideration when it announced Canada as a prospective member of the commission in 1972.

Regardless, rejection of the specialized role would have made relations with the United States intensely difficult for Canada. Too much money and far too many lives had been expended in Vietnam, and any Canadian decision that negatively affected the ability of the United States to bring its involvement in that country to an end would have poisoned Canada-US relations for decades. Moreover, it would inevitably mean the replacement of Canada and all of its mediation/supervision expertise with another, more willing nation. There was also an obvious systemic need for Canada to play the part. Further instability in the Southeast Asian subsystem could easily have had broader implications, and the possibility of a nuclear confrontation's turning the Cold War hot was the ultimate reason for Canada to do its part in system amelioration.

Accordingly, the Liberal government agreed to take up the position after receiving the terms of the Paris Agreement just three days before they were to be formalized on 24 January 1973. This move of compliance countered the government's previous move of insubordination, when on 4 January 1973 it had passed a motion condemning the continued bombing of Hanoi by the Nixon administration, which in turn led to a freeze in Canada-US diplomatic relations.[63] The freeze thawed when Canada agreed to serve on the new International Commission of Control and Supervision (ICCS), initially for a trial period of sixty days.

During these sixty days, Canada carried out what it called its "open mouth policy." Michel Gauvin, Canada's acerbic ambassador to Greece and a fervent anticommunist, was chosen to head the delegation precisely because he had what Mitchell Sharp considered "the right qualifications to carry out the 'open mouth' technique."[64] Gauvin was instructed to speak out whenever the ICCS ran into difficulties. He was to be as clear as possible in arguing that the ICCS was no more effective than the ICSC. This would suggest that there was no reason for Canada to spend an extended period of time in service to the ICCS, and essentially provide Canada with an exit strategy. Ottawa had to justify its decision to leave to only "two readily identifiable parties": its domestic public and the United States. This was made clear in a telegram sent to Gauvin by the government in May 1973.[65] Once the Americans withdrew from Vietnam, the Canadians too would have a way out of the conflict.

Gauvin carried out his duties with intensity, working long hours seven days a week to demonstrate that the ICCS's efforts were futile. Daniel Molgat recalls that Gauvin regularly appeared on the "world's television screens (but, as time went on, chiefly on Canada's screens) saying what was going on."[66] As the sixty-day period wound down, he recommended that Canada remain on the commission for no longer than another ninety days. Concerned over the effects an early withdrawal might have on Canada-US relations, Canada's ambassador in Washington, Marcel Cadieux, had been pushing for a nine-month extension.[67] In the end, Sharp decided on a sixty-day extension, to be followed by a thirty-day grace period to aid in finding a replacement for Canada if things failed to take a turn for the better in the commission's work. The next day, the last American troops were flown out of Da Nang and Saigon aboard their so-called freedom birds, and the last sixty-seven American prisoners-of-war made their way out of Hanoi via Gia Lam airport.[68]

It would have been bad diplomatic form had the 270 Canadian ICCS delegates left Vietnam in the American tailwind. During the short extension of Canada's ICCS service, however, things only got worse. A clearly marked ICCS helicopter was shot down and Canadian Captain C.E. Laviolette was killed in the crash. This was all Sharp could handle. He wanted to announce the end of Canada's participation in what he termed the "charade" at the end of June 1973,[69] but Nixon's National Security Adviser, Henry Kissinger, convinced him to remain an extra thirty days. Beaten to the punch, Sharp announced Canada's withdrawal from the ICCS as of 31 July,[70] an hour after Kissinger announced to a Washington press conference that he was not happy with the Canadian decision but understood that "strong domestic opposition" was behind it. "You can say we regret it but understand it,"[71] Kissinger concluded.

Trudeau later recounted that Nixon was angered at the Canadian decision and called him "some nasty names" in response.[72] But this was in the midst of the Watergate scandal, and Nixon no doubt had other things, such as his impending resignation, on his mind. In the end, Canada slipped out the backdoor of its ICCS commitment just after it had accomplished the task Mitchell Sharp had quietly envisioned: "To help the United States extricate itself from Vietnam."[73] Ironically, however, this was not appreciated by the United States. The broader international community certainly did not appreciate it either, as Iran replaced Canada on the ICCS and the commission later slipped into the diplomatic equivalent of oblivion.

Once the North American states had withdrawn from Vietnam in what Nixon dubbed an honourable peace, fighting between the two Vietnamese states continued. Saigon fell in 1975 and became Ho Chi Minh City.

Throughout the long engagement in Vietnam, Canada-US relations followed the predicted pattern of paradoxical interaction leading to contradictory political outcomes for both states involved. Despite their mutual interest in cooperation and coordination of their very different roles in Vietnam, neither Ottawa nor Washington succeeded in overcoming the contrasting structural pressures of hierarchy in anarchy. Both succumbed consistently to these pressures throughout the conflict regardless of political leadership or regime configuration. The notion, then, that individual- or unit-level variables are sufficient to explain particular aspects of this case is faulty. Systemic factors were at work throughout, impelling Canada-US relations in Vietnam on their paradoxical course and compelling Canada to take on an array of specialized roles in the conflict. In the following chapter, we will see these patterns repeated as we examine the effects of hierarchy in anarchy under much tighter time constraints, in the case of the Cuban Missile Crisis.

3
The Cuban Missile Crisis, 1961-62

The end of the Cold War did not bring about the end of the nuclear threat to North America. Accordingly, this case study is relevant to the analysis and practice of Canada-US security cooperation. The fact that President John F. Kennedy estimated the probability of a nuclear catastrophe resulting from the Cuban Missile Crisis as "between 1 out of 3 and even" provides a chilling perspective on how close things came to an apocalyptic end in the fall of 1962, and makes all the more troubling the paradoxical patterns of behaviour followed by the two North American states in their handling of the crisis.

The operationalization of offensive Soviet nuclear weapons in Cuba that sparked the crisis began in the summer of 1962, and considerably altered North America's security situation. In and of itself, the Soviet nuclear threat was not new, but the proximity of operational warheads represented a radical change, with the stark implication that most continental American cities and every Canadian city east of Regina could have been annihilated within a few minutes of an initial launch from Cuba. Moreover, the clandestine manner in which the offensive build-up took place in Cuba suggested the possibility of a Soviet attempt to launch a surprise attack on America's nuclear arsenal, potentially triggering all-out nuclear combat.

In terms of how this development was treated within the Canadian-American relationship, the US discovery of the Soviet build-up in Cuba could have led to either of two predictable courses of action on Washington's part. If NORAD mattered, as liberal internationalists (neoliberals) believe it should have in this situation, the Kennedy administration would have immediately informed the Canadian government of the developments (i.e., on 14 October, when the initial U-2 reconnaissance plane intelligence that revealed the Soviet nuclear installations was delivered to the president), and begun consultations with the Canadian government shortly thereafter. The regime that had been designed to foster joint Canadian-American defence of the continent would have been employed for just that purpose. Alternatively, the Kennedy administration could have reasoned that the US alone had the capability to deal with the Soviet plot, as neorealists would have expected, and NORAD would have been either commandeered by the US or cut entirely out of any role in the crisis. This would have exposed the myth of the regime that masks the vast asymmetry in security capabilities between the two states in the continental hierarchy, with serious repercussions for the tenor of the Canada-US relationship. Washington's chosen course of action combined elements of both options. This suggests that it was reacting to the structural imperatives created by the international anarchy and the continental hierarchy.

From the perspective of the Diefenbaker government, the Cuban Missile Crisis confronted Canada with a clear and present existential threat. Placing its armed forces at the service of a plan designed exclusively in Washington was the only real option Ottawa had for dealing with the threat. Diefenbaker's reluctance to follow this course was influenced by a desire to maintain the integrity of Canadian sovereignty. Contradictory as this was, the fact that he sought a specialized role for Canada in resolving the crisis as a means of accomplishing this aim is not surprising, given the pressures of the international anarchy. Despite his reluctance to follow the American lead, the fact that he ended up doing so after deciding three times in three days that he would not was influenced by the reality of the continental hierarchy. The long period of divergence in his position on raising the alert during which the Canada-US relationship deteriorated and continental security was potentially further threatened can be explained by the contrasting structural pressures of hierarchy in anarchy felt by both Washington and Ottawa throughout the crisis.

Conventional wisdom in this case emphasizes the indecisiveness of Prime Minister John Diefenbaker, his dislike of President Kennedy, and Kennedy's own dislike of Diefenbaker as crucial variables in explaining what went so obviously wrong during this critical moment in the Cold War, when seamless cooperation between the asymmetrical allies would have been expected.[1] These variables were proximate causes of the events reviewed in this chapter. They were, not, however, the ultimate cause of the paradoxical pattern followed during the crisis, nor were they the ultimate cause of its contradictory conclusion.

Build-up

Fidel Castro's revolutionary movement swept the Batista dictatorship from power in Cuba in January 1959, to such great international acclaim that the US and Canada instantly granted diplomatic recognition to his new regime. Within a year, however, Castro's regime became affiliated with the communist cause, nationalizing sectors of the economy and forcing foreign (mainly American) businessmen to return home empty-handed after their property had been expropriated. In May 1960, Soviet Premier Nikita Khrushchev announced that the Soviet Union would support Cuba in the event of American aggression, making the island a crucial Cold War site. By October, Washington had unilaterally announced a complete trade embargo on Cuba, further amplifying the island nation's role in the struggle between East and West.

Despite these developments, Ottawa maintained full diplomatic contact with Havana, and objected to the American embargo on the grounds that, as a trading nation, Canada was always looking for markets (communist or capitalist) to sell its goods. According to the Canadian embassy in Havana at that time, "the Cuban government was publicizing every Canadian statement or action that could be interpreted as a policy of non-intervention in Cuba."[2] The Cuban press also devoted considerable attention to Canada, "slanting reports to convey the impression that virulent Canadian nationalism was resisting United States political and economic pressures."[3] Canada even welcomed a Cuban delegate to its Export Trade Promotion Conference that fall, a move that drew criticism from Washington and subjected the Canadian embassy in that capital to picketing by anti-Castro demonstrators. All of this seems to have been tolerated at the official level in Washington because of the great utility of the intelligence-gathering role that Canada was playing on behalf of the US from its diplomatic outpost in Havana.[4]

In April 1961, the Central Intelligence Agency supported a counter-revolutionary exile force's attempt to storm the Cuban beaches and overthrow Castro's regime. The mission had been authorized just three months into Kennedy's presidency. It ended in debacle. Across Canada and the world, the "Bay of Pigs" disaster was viewed as a tragic blunder by a young and inexperienced president. It reinvigorated the floundering Castro regime and pushed it irreversibly into the orbit of the Soviet Union. Diefenbaker, however, refrained from open criticism of the incident in preparation for Kennedy's visit to Ottawa, which would follow in a month's time. In a speech to the House of Commons, he suppressed the urge to condemn the irresponsibility of the CIA and Kennedy, and contradicted his own government's policy position, saying that Cuba was "a bridgehead of international communism threatening the Hemisphere, a danger to which Canada could not be indifferent."[5] Diefenbaker made these remarks against the advice of External Affairs Minister Howard Green, and at considerable political risk, given the general perception among the Canadian public that American policy towards Cuba was misguided. His words were well received in Washington.

Green's self-assertive suggestion that Canada might play a mediation role in the conflict between Cuba and the US was received with considerably less appreciation. Three days before Kennedy was to make his first trip to Canada, Green, while in Geneva attending disarmament negotiations, suggested that "the more Cuba is pushed the greater becomes her reliance on the Soviet Bloc. Of course Canada is further away from Cuba than the United States and so it's easier for us to seem more dispassionate. But we would hope to solve this problem when the situation slows down and eases a bit."[6]

After Washington made it clear that it was not impressed with the suggestion, Green denied having ever made it.[7] Diefenbaker furthered the subordination by telling Kennedy as soon as he arrived that Canada had "no intention of acting as a mediator," and that "there was no foundation for the press report that such an offer had been put forward."[8]

Despite these early acts of deference, the relationship between Diefenbaker and Kennedy took an acrimonious turn. During the president's visit to Ottawa, a working paper entitled "What we want from the Ottawa trip," which had been drafted by Assistant Secretary of State Walt Rostow, was mistakenly left behind on a table in the Cabinet room. Diefenbaker found the document and learned from it that Kennedy had a list of things to push for during his official visit.[9] These included getting Canada to join the Organization of American States (OAS); to make a larger foreign aid contribution, particularly to India; and to provide "active support at Geneva and beyond for a more effective monitoring of the borders of Laos and Vietnam."[10] The list outraged Diefenbaker, but instead of publicizing it or returning it to the Americans, as he arguably should have (it was, after all, their property), he did nothing with it other than use it to fuel a growing dislike of Kennedy and his administration.

Despite the working paper's revelation that Kennedy intended to push Canada on a number of issues, American officials recognized that Canada would probably "not comply with a US request to impose a total embargo on Canadian goods [destined for Cuba]," being, as it was, so "extremely sensitive to US public display of our right to control subsidiaries."[11] This, however, did not stop Kennedy and his team from pushing, nor did it stop the American press covering the trip from accusing Canada of trying to make a profit off the American embargo.

Following Kennedy's visit, the two leaders traded insults through diplomatic gossip channels, and both came to dislike each other to the point where they were no longer communicating at the time Kennedy learned of the Soviet build-up in Cuba. This personal tension was a proximate cause of the paradoxical approach Canada and the US took to their relations during the crisis, but it cannot be deemed the ultimate cause. The acrimonious relations between the two leaders were symptomatic of the contrasting structural environments within which they were interacting.

The Cuba issue dropped beneath the radar in Canada from the spring of 1961 until mid-October 1962. Canadians, along with most NATO countries, tended to see the American concern over Cuba as exaggerated.[12] Most of the Western capitals expected the next hot flash in the Cold War to be over Berlin.[13] In the US, however, the Cuba issue remained prominent throughout this period. Indeed, the Republican Senatorial and Congressional Campaign

Committee announced in the months leading up to the crisis that Cuba would be "the dominant issue of the 1962 campaign."[14] Throughout August and September 1962, Kennedy made a number of statements on America's Cuba policy designed to combat Republican claims that his administration was doing nothing about the shipments of Soviet arms and personnel that had begun arriving in Cuba during the second half of July. Calls for a full-scale invasion of the island were made by prominent voices in Washington. On 13 September, Kennedy announced that his administration would take action if presented with evidence that the Soviet Union, in collaboration with Castro, had attempted to install offensive weapons in Cuba. To that point, the photographic reconnaissance supported the Soviet contention that the arms build-up in Cuba was strictly of a defensive nature.

On 15 October, however, an American U-2 reconnaissance plane on a flight over Cuba photographed the installation of three battalions of medium-range ballistic missiles (MRBMs), with a range of up to 1,000 miles.[15] Later flights would spot two battalions of intermediate-range ballistic missiles (IRBMs), with a range of up to 2,000 miles. Two days before the photos were taken, Soviet Ambassador to the United States Anatoly Dobrynin denied that his government had any intention of putting offensive weapons in Cuba.[16] Khrushchev himself had assured Kennedy through "the most direct and personal channels that he was aware of the president's domestic political problem and that nothing would be done to exacerbate this problem."[17] The U-2 reconnaissance photographs exposed these lies. Khrushchev, in collaboration with Castro, had taken a significant step towards disrupting the Cold War balance.

Crisis

Having made such strong public pronouncements, President Kennedy could not politically tolerate the presence of offensive nuclear missiles in Cuba. He immediately called a top-secret meeting of fifteen of his highest-level advisers, a group that would be known as ExComm (short for Executive Committee), to discuss possible courses of action. Between 14 and 21 October, six possible tracks were secretly researched and debated by the group. From least aggressive to most aggressive, the options were: (1) doing nothing at all, (2) putting pressure on Khrushchev through diplomatic channels provided by either the OAS and/or the United Nations, (3) giving Castro the option of splitting from Soviet protection or facing annihilation, (4) blockading Cuba, (5) using air strikes against the missile installations, and (6) invasion of the island.[18]

Secretary of State Dean Rusk suggested that the Canadian ambassador in Havana be used to carry out the third option in secret. On 16 October, at the first ExComm meeting, Rusk was asked by Kennedy to take the first crack at assessing the six options. After he ran through the list, Rusk concluded:

I think also that we ought to consider getting some word to Castro, perhaps through the Canadian ambassador in Havana or through his representative at the UN. I think perhaps the Canadian ambassador would be best, the better channel to get Castro privately and tell him that this is no longer support for Cuba, that Cuba is being victimized here, and that the Soviets are preparing Cuba for destruction or betrayal. You saw the [New York] Times article yesterday that high Soviet officials were saying "We'll trade Cuba for Berlin." This ought to be brought to Castro's attention.[19]

Even before Blair Seaborn had assumed his role as messenger in the Vietnam conflict, Washington had considered the strategic option of using Canada in such a specialized role. This is suggestive of the structural origins of subordinate state specialization in the international system.

Elaborate precautions were taken to prevent disclosure of American awareness of the offensive missiles in Cuba. None of the NATO allies was made aware of the intelligence before an initial decision by ExComm had been taken. Kennedy even went so far as to endure a two-hour meeting on 18 October with Soviet Foreign Minister Andrei Gromyko and Ambassador Dobrynin, during which the former repeatedly lied to the president, assuring him that the weapons in Cuba were strictly of a defensive nature.

Two days after this meeting, Kennedy opted to impose a blockade on Cuba. The administration's next task was to inform its allies of the proposed course of action, and to generate diplomatic support for the quarantine recommendation. A whirlwind of diplomatic exchanges resulted in French President Charles de Gaulle, British Prime Minister Harold Macmillan, West German Chancellor Konrad Adenauer, and the entire Organization of American States giving their full support to the decision. The OAS charter subsequently provided the legal basis for the quarantine, which Kennedy proclaimed effective at 10:00 a.m. on 24 October.

Canada was caught up in this whirlwind. Just two hours before Kennedy's momentous television address on 22 October, Diefenbaker, Green, and Minister of National Defence Douglas Harkness received Livingston Merchant, the former American ambassador to their country, on a special assignment from Kennedy. With the U-2 photographs in hand as hard evidence, Merchant briefed the Canadians on developments thus far, and delivered a personal message from President Kennedy to Prime Minister Diefenbaker. In the message, Kennedy explained to Diefenbaker that he planned to present a resolution at the UN demanding the withdrawal of the missiles, and instructed him to have his "representative in New York work actively with us and speak forthrightly in support of the above program in the United Nations."[20] Here, Kennedy was calling on Canada's specialization as an advocate to generate multilateral support for his administration's handling of the crisis.

Merchant then read to the Canadians the speech that Kennedy was scheduled to deliver that evening. At one point, Diefenbaker interrupted to express his discomfort with the way the Soviet foreign minister had been characterized. The phrase that painted Gromyko in a negative light was removed from the speech despite considerable time constraints, a move that seemed a respectful gesture towards the Canadian government (considering Gromyko's attempt to deceive Kennedy in the days leading up to the speech), perhaps designed to counter the dominant moves that had preceded it, with Canada being left essentially in the dark about a matter of vital importance to continental security and invited to perform in a particular way at the UN. Merchant left the meeting under the misimpression that he had Ottawa's full support for Kennedy's initiative. What he did not know was that Diefenbaker had caught wind of the impending crisis twenty-four hours earlier. Rather than being blown away with surprise, Diefenbaker was likely stewing over the fact that what Merchant was presenting to him was a situation report. It was not a consultation, as it should have been in Diefenbaker's opinion, as stipulated by the NORAD agreement and three subsequent agreements entered into by the Canadian and US governments between 1958 and 1960.[21]

Two hours later, Kennedy informed his country and the world of the events that had brought the planet to the brink of nuclear war. He argued:

> This secret, swift, extraordinary buildup of Communist missiles – in an area well known to have a special and historical relationship to the United States and the nations of the Western Hemisphere, in violation of Soviet assurances, and in defiance of American and hemispheric policy – this sudden, clandestine decision to station strategic weapons for the first time outside of Soviet soil – is a deliberately provocative and unjustified change in the status quo which cannot be accepted by this country, if our courage and our commitments are ever to be trusted again by either friend or foe.[22]

Kennedy announced the quarantine of Cuba and the increased surveillance of the island, threatened further action if the build-up continued, demanded the removal of the missiles, and warned that their use against any country in the Western Hemisphere would be regarded as an attack against the United States, "requiring full retaliatory response upon the Soviet Union."[23]

After Kennedy's speech aired, Lester B. Pearson, the leader of the Liberal opposition, called Diefenbaker and requested his presence at an evening session of Parliament to discuss the dire situation. The prime minister acquiesced, despite his prior agreement with the Americans to hold off on commenting on the situation until the next day. In his address to the House of Commons that night, Diefenbaker urged calm in the face of crisis. Making no mention of Livingston Merchant's visit to Ottawa that day, and giving no indication of the U-2 reconnaissance photographs of the missile launch sites in Cuba that he had been shown, the prime minister proceeded to suggest that a group of nations be convened under the auspices of the UN (perhaps the eight neutral nations that had met on the UN Disarmament Committee) to do an inspection of the facts as they were on the ground in Cuba.[24]

> This is the only suggestion I have at this moment [said Diefenbaker]; but it would provide an objective answer to what is going on in Cuba. As late as a week ago, the U.S.S.R. contended that its activities in Cuba were entirely of a defensive nature, and that the hundreds, if not thousands, of citizens of the U.S.S.R., mechanics, technicians and the like, were simply in Cuba for defensive purposes. As to the presence of these offensive weapons, the only sure way that the world can secure the facts would be through an independent inspection.[25]

Diefenbaker did not endorse Kennedy's plan of action; nor did Pearson, who expressed support for Diefenbaker's position, saying, "I think it is important, as the Prime Minister has indicated, that these international organizations should be used for the purpose of verifying what is going on."[26] The Social Credit Party from the right and the New Democratic Party from the left were also pleased at the UN suggestion. From Vancouver, the leader of the NDP, who had just won a seat in the House of Commons in a by-election that day, argued that it ought to be remembered "that for fifteen years the Western powers have been ringing the Soviet Union with missile and air bases," and that "we have only the statements of the Americans" to confirm that the Soviets have responded in kind.[27] Thus it did not matter, as John J. Kirton points out, that it happened to be Diefenbaker in the prime minister's chair at that moment: all four party leaders initially chose the United Nations over the United States.[28] This suggests that all four party leaders felt the same pressures stemming from the anarchic nature of the international system to assert through whatever means available their country's sovereign right to have a say in its own political destiny.

Diefenbaker's comments in the House of Commons "dumbfounded" President Kennedy, however. His brother Robert told political organizer Dalton Camp that the president could not believe that "of all the nations in the world, the only one that gave him any trouble was Canada."[29] Why did Diefenbaker fail to make the same decision as De Gaulle, Macmillan, and Adenauer in backing Kennedy's response immediately? Why did he propose an alternative response to the crisis and suggest Canadian involvement? Why did he agree, in the first place, to make the statement in the House of Commons that evening?

Conventional wisdom suggests that the answers to these questions can be traced to Diefenbaker himself. Representative of this wisdom, Peter Haydon argues, for example, that "because Diefenbaker disliked the American President and consistently resisted US overtures to bring the foreign policies of the two countries closer together, taking an independent stand was completely consistent with his personal views."[30] Diefenbaker's personal aversion to Kennedy is clearly insufficient to explain his speech in the House of Commons that night. Based on their support of his speech, it is reasonable to expect that each of the other federal party leaders would have made similar points had he been the prime minister. Moreover, three short days later, Diefenbaker was singing a much different tune in the House, while "posturing as a strong, faithful ally of the United States."[31]

Diefenbaker's address to the House of Commons came only hours after Canadians learned from President Kennedy that they might not survive the night, and all he could offer them was a suggestion that the UN get involved in the hopes that Canada could play a specialized role in resolving the crisis. He could not say that he had been consulted by Kennedy, only informed. He could not say that he had been involved in the decision to quarantine Cuba, only told that it was going to happen. He could not say that he expected to have any direct influence whatsoever on the outcome of the crisis. The fate of his sovereign state was in the hands of another sovereign state. And in those moments when he was addressing his colleagues and country, the reality of Canadian sovereignty, more than any personal dislike of Kennedy, more than any personal affinity for the UN, more than any pressure from his minority Parliament, compelled a speech that undermined the superordinate state even as it attempted to aggrandize the potential role of the subordinate state in resolving the crisis. The speech was a move of self-assertion to counter the American dominance that had preceded it; paradoxically, it ensured that Canada would be entirely left out of any resolution to the crisis. On Thursday, the reality of Canada's position in the continental hierarchy would cause the prime minister to go back on those words.

Meanwhile, the build-up in Cuba proceeded. Reconnaissance photographs from 22 October indicated that IRBMs with nuclear payloads had been installed on new launch pads, thereby operationalizing the possibility of a quick nuclear attack on many North American cities. In terms of continental defence at this point in the crisis, there were reports that the United States had requested Canada's permission to arm its interceptor squadrons at Harmon Field and Goose Bay with nuclear warheads brought into Canada from Bangor, Maine.[32] Jon McLin reports further speculation that the US had sought permission to disperse its atomic interceptors to other Canadian airfields, and that it had expected that permission to be granted "as a matter of course."[33] And Henry M. Pachter reports that Diefenbaker "denied the use of Canadian airports to SAC [Strategic Air Command] nuclear bombers – a slight for which Kennedy was to take revenge not long afterward."[34] The Canadian government has never denied or commented on these reports, suggesting that the American moves of domination under crisis conditions were countered by moves of Canadian self-assertion to the potential detriment of both countries.

Delay and Deception

After Kennedy's televised speech, and after the House of Commons had adjourned for the evening, the government learned that the US had raised its NORAD units to DEFCON 3 alert status. The US command at NORAD asked the Royal Canadian Air Force (RCAF) to assume a similar state of readiness. Defence Minister Harkness and his senior advisers were almost certain that immediate compliance with this request would be approved, but they were unsure whether they had the authority to approve it themselves. According to the old Canadian War Books, the prime minister had the authority, but according to the new books that had yet to be approved by Cabinet, the defence minister had the authority. Harkness then sought prime ministerial approval, but Diefenbaker chose to decline, insisting that the decision be delayed until the Cabinet meeting on Tuesday morning.[35] External Affairs Minister Green did announce that night, however, that Canada had withdrawn permission for Russian planes to fly over its airspace or to land at Canadian bases on their way to Cuba. (As evidence of its cooperation with the Americans throughout the crisis, the Diefenbaker government would later cite this seemingly obvious precautionary measure.)

At the Cabinet meeting the next morning, most ministers favoured raising the alert and expected this to be done with little debate. Diefenbaker and Green prevailed, however, and the meeting ended with a decision to delay. Kennedy telephoned Diefenbaker that afternoon to personally request (1) Canadian support at the United Nations for the quarantine, (2) more cooperation on continental defence, and (3) formal authorization for the Canadian forces to raise the alert status of the Canadian NORAD component to the equivalent of the American DEFCON 3. Not happy with these requests, which to him must have seemed more like demands, Diefenbaker derided the lack of consultation he had received and rejected Kennedy.

During his visit the day before, Livingston Merchant had not informed the Canadians that such requests would be issued. Under the terms of the NORAD agreement, this was a problem. In 1957, the Diefenbaker government had entered into the NORAD joint defensive command to better defend the continent against sudden or surprise Soviet attacks through the combination and coordination of Canadian and American defensive and warning capabilities. In the event of an alert, it was informally agreed that the president and the prime minister would consult one another about the action to be taken. In dispatching Merchant to Ottawa with the intelligence briefing and the instructions on how to proceed, Kennedy had informed the Canadians but he had not consulted them. It was about this lack of consultation that Diefenbaker chose to demonstrate his frustration. Kennedy had taken Canada for granted, according to Gordon Churchill, who was close to Diefenbaker, and "that's not right, never right."[36] The fact that Kennedy had done so in the midst of an extraordinary crisis did not seem to matter to the prime minister: the integrity of an international agreement and the sovereignty of Canada had been slighted. Kennedy and his ExComm crowd had not followed the requirements of NORAD, and as leader of a sovereign state, Diefenbaker did not like the idea of automatically assenting to an American demand.

Harkness knew that none of the prime minister's concerns were of consequence. He authorized the alert on his own after Diefenbaker had refused to grant him permission on Monday night. As John J. Kirton points out, this raises "profound questions about civil control of the military in Canada, and about whether the Canadian defence establishment was following the political authority of its own government or that of the United States."[37] Indeed, the action did amount to a "failure in the civil control of the Canadian military," according to one retired Canadian naval commander.[38]

All the requirements for the alert were met by the Royal Canadian Navy (RCN), aside from a few minor details (such as the recalling of men on leave, which would have alerted the general public, not to mention the prime minister). In league with US naval authorities, the RCN established a "surface, submarine, and air sea barrier extending well to the southeast of Argentia, Newfoundland, and cooperated in the administration of this barrier as though both our countries were at war stations," according to Vice Chief of the Naval Staff Jeffrey V. Brock.[39] The Atlantic fleet, consisting of twenty-five surface ships, deployed under cover of darkness to play a significant role in the quarantine. Their efforts to secure a 1,000-by-250-mile region of the North Atlantic south of Newfoundland from penetration by Russian submarines and the Russian fishing fleet enabled the US Navy to concentrate its efforts further south, in the heart of the blockade zone closer to Cuba.[40] The possibility exists that the RCN covertly accepted American nuclear weapons at the height of the crisis, despite the government's policy that it would not do so.[41] Regardless, the Atlantic fleet did record over 130 Soviet submarine contacts in the three-week period that marked the height of the crisis.[42]

The RCAF was also placed on alert at this time, and there are also rumours concerning whether its Argus and Neptune aircraft were uploaded with nuclear depth charges.[43] As a result of these actions, Canada was the only American ally (nuclear-armed or not) to participate militarily in the blockade.

Paradoxically, all of this took place while Diefenbaker debated with his Cabinet whether to formally raise the alert.

During the two days the Cabinet spent debating the alert question, Harkness was placed in the difficult position of having to respond to questions from the Official Opposition regarding the actions the government had taken in response to the crisis. When asked whether the navy had any role in the blockade, Harkness answered in the negative. (Technically, the Atlantic fleet was running a "NATO training exercise.") When asked whether Canada had gone on alert in a fashion similar to that of the Americans, Harkness again answered in the negative. When asked, then, whether the government had not just effectively defaulted on its NORAD obligations, Harkness could truthfully answer again in the negative. A question was also put to Minister of Trade and Commerce George Hees: Would trade continue with Cuba? The policy remained the same, according to Hees. The minister of national defence had seemed to find a middle path between the constraints of anarchy and the constraints of hierarchy. Canada had gone on alert without officially going on alert; it had participated in the blockade without officially participating in the blockade; it had practically supported its NORAD partner without symbolically doing so, in an attempt to preserve its sovereign dignity and reassure the Soviets. To cut this fine middle path, however, a degree of deception was involved on the part of Harkness. Strangely enough, this deception and his disregard for Diefenbaker's authority did not get Harkness fired or charged criminally. It did, however, create a rift in Cabinet that would later see Harkness resign over a separate but related issue – Canada's acquisition of nuclear weapons and the end of the Diefenbaker government.

External Affairs Minister Howard Green was also very busy during these two days. His efforts were directed towards trying to manipulate the optics of his government's response to and role in the crisis. During a televised interview conducted by Charles Lynch, head of Southam News Service, and Norman Depoe, the Canadian Broadcasting Corporation's parliamentary correspondent, Green responded to questions for thirty minutes. In that time he never once came out in full support of the US quarantine.[44] Instead, he emphasized an independent approach to the situation and a desire to see the UN get involved. Asked whether the crisis had anything to do with Canada's NORAD obligations, Green responded, "Not at the moment."[45] He must have thought that there was something to be gained politically by refraining from placing his government's full support behind the Americans in a time of obvious crisis, but he was wrong. The Young Conservatives called the government's response "wishy-washy" in a telegram they sent to the prime minister after watching the CBC interview.[46] They demanded support for President Kennedy. According to Patrick Nicholson, "Gordon Churchill later remarked that Green's appearance on television that evening was one of the most damaging events in the Diefenbaker years."[47]

While Green was downplaying the crisis on the CBC, the quarantine had gone into effect and US General Thomas Power had raised the Strategic Air Command alert level to DEFCON 2, indicating full readiness for war. The crisis was reaching its boiling point. Khrushchev was threatening to sink naval vessels enforcing the quarantine (presumably, Canadian ships could have been targeted since by this time they were unofficially involved in the quarantine), and was declaring that the US would have to get used to having Soviet missiles in Cuba.[48] Those strong words uttered, Soviet ships encountered the American quarantine and turned back. The immediate success of the quarantine only served to prevent any further offensive build-up in Cuba, however. It did nothing to remove the offensive weapons. It was on the questions of how to remove those weapons and at what cost that the crisis now hinged. That said, 24 October 1962 was the turning point in the crisis, the day the Soviets and Americans were "eyeball to eyeball," and the Soviet side blinked. It was a triumphant moment for the West.

On the afternoon of Thursday, 25 October, Diefenbaker finally announced to the House that Canada was officially raising its alert status. Significantly, it was only after it was "determined that there was no essential role for Canada in finding a United Nations solution to the Cuban crisis," according to Diefenbaker, that "we then authorized that our air defence squadrons be placed at the same alert level as their United States counterparts."[49] This revelation serves as evidence of how the impulse on the part of subordinate states to serve in a structurally specialized capacity can exacerbate intra-hierarchical tensions. In actuality, of course, Harkness had issued the alert on Monday night, and Diefenbaker himself (redundantly) had given Harkness the prime ministerial go-ahead to raise the alert on Wednesday. But Diefenbaker avoided disclosing this in the House that day when asked point-blank by NDP MP Douglas Fisher: "What is the degree of civil defence preparedness at this particular critical moment?"[50]

In his speech to the House on Thursday, which has been quoted at length above, Diefenbaker rejected arguments about the illegality of the quarantine, calling them "sterile and irrelevant," finally condemned the Soviets for having gone so far to disturb the "world balance," and expressed his government's intent to "support the United States and our other allies in this situation."[51] Significantly, this was the first Canadian government endorsement of the American action since Kennedy's speech on 22 October. The endorsement was half-hearted at best. In the 1,200-word address, President Kennedy was mentioned only twice, and in passing. By contrast, the British prime minister mentioned Kennedy and his administration twelve times, and with admiration, throughout the course of his speech to the British parliament that same day.[52] Instead of showing strong allied solidarity, Diefenbaker chose to celebrate U Thant, the acting UN secretary-general, for "the speed with which he has acted to discharge the heavy responsibility he bears as the executive head of the UN. His proposal for a standstill is designed to gain the time that is so urgently needed while the search goes forward for some formula which will provide an acceptable solution."[53]

The previous afternoon, U Thant had sent private appeals to both Kennedy and Khrushchev to avoid risking general war through any unnecessary confrontations. He called on Kennedy to voluntarily suspend the quarantine for two to three weeks, and on Khrushchev to voluntarily cease arms shipments to Cuba. Khrushchev, having little to lose, accepted U Thant's recommendation, but Kennedy rejected it, probably on the grounds that since the Soviet shipments of offensive weapons and nuclear warheads had been done in a clandestine fashion in the first place, Khrushchev could not be trusted to keep his word, and while the quarantine was lifted, more and more of the weapons systems that had already been shipped to Cuba would become operational.

Only after the crisis appeared to have turned in favour of the US did Diefenbaker announce that he would finally comply with the American request to raise Canada's alert status and to take all of the practical defence precautions that this entailed. He condemned Khrushchev for dangerously destabilizing the Cold War balance, but refused to join Kennedy in demanding the removal of the missiles from Cuba, instead advocating a UN plan that would have allowed more of the weapons systems to become operational. The next morning, his speech was praised in a *Globe and Mail* editorial entitled "Prudent Precautions." Further commendations for Diefenbaker's handling of the crisis would be few and far between. The paradoxical path he followed to this contradictory policy outcome would eventually bring his government down.

End Game

On Friday morning, a letter from Khrushchev was delivered to the US embassy in Moscow. It proposed to withdraw Soviet missiles from Cuba in exchange for a pledge from the United States not to invade Cuba. On Saturday morning, however, Khrushchev appeared to backtrack. In a message broadcast on Moscow radio and heard the world over, he vowed to remove the Soviet missiles from Cuba only if Kennedy removed the American missiles from Turkey (the missiles had been there long enough to have become obsolete). That same morning, Soviet surface-to-air missiles shot down an American U-2 plane over eastern Cuba, killing its pilot, Major Rudolf Anderson Jr. Tension continued to mount that evening as Kennedy refused to remove the missiles from Turkey but offered a non-invasion pledge contingent on UN inspections confirming the removal of Soviet missiles from Cuba.[54]

That night, Howard Green went to sleep thinking he would not see morning. Three months later, he confessed to the House of Commons that

"I believed ... that before morning Ottawa might be demolished, as well as Montreal, Toronto and my home city of Vancouver."[55] Green expected a nuclear holocaust that night, commencing with a full-scale strike on North America. Yet he had joined Diefenbaker days earlier in insisting that Canadian forces should not be placed on alert to protect the country,[56] and had made a CBC television appearance during which he indicated his desire "to keep the Canadian people from getting all excited about this business, and from panicking."[57]

By Sunday morning, Khrushchev and Kennedy had cut a deal. Kennedy agreed publicly not to invade Cuba and secretly to pull America's Jupiter missiles from Turkey. In return, Khrushchev agreed to crate up the weapons he had assembled in Cuba and ship them back to the Soviet Union.

In the immediate aftermath, Diefenbaker bragged to reporters about how Canada had played its "full part" in the cooperation among the Western allies that led to the successful end of the crisis.[58] A week later, he continued to rewrite the past, stating to a Toronto audience that "there was never any question as to where Canada stood on the Cuban situation and the establishment of missile bases by the USSR. We supported the United States clearly and unequivocally."[59] At a NATO meeting in December, Green "praised U.S. policy and affirmed that Canada had supported Washington throughout the crisis."[60] These statements were meant to heal the wound in national morale that Diefenbaker's handling of the Cuban crisis had caused. In Canada, as in the rest of the Western world, Kennedy had emerged the hero of a generation. Diefenbaker's performance throughout the crisis paled in comparison.

By January 1963, however, after trying to argue that Canada had actually done its full part as a US ally throughout the crisis, Diefenbaker explained his hesitation to raise the alert with reference to the "short notice" and "insufficient information" he had received from Washington.[61] A year later, Green went so far as to assert that Canada had played a moderating role in the crisis, by being careful not to raise its alert prematurely.[62] Thus, even a year after the crisis had ended, the contrasting structural pressures of hierarchy in anarchy continued to push and pull Diefenbaker and Green in different directions, compelling them to make further contradictory statements about Canada's performance throughout those notorious thirteen days. This no doubt contributed to the tensions of an already tense Canada-US relationship under the leadership of Diefenbaker and Kennedy.

American military officials were "furious" over Canada's "sluggish reaction" to the crisis.[63] The Atlantic fleet, however, due to Harkness' disloyalty to Diefenbaker, actually began implementing the blockade at the same time as the US Navy. True, the Canadian government itself was slow to react officially to the crisis, but for all practical purposes, Canada fulfilled its obligations in this instance as the subordinate member of the continental hierarchy.

Unofficially, Canada raised the alert in tandem with the United States. Officially, it remained idle, fractured, and insubordinate until the crisis was essentially over. The Kennedy administration might have recognized this but did not, or chose not to, which led in turn to a souring of the Canada-US relationship after a crisis that arguably ought to have brought the two states closer together in Cold War solidarity.

The paradoxical pattern of behaviour that led to this contradictory outcome had a negative impact on the Canada-US relationship, for which Diefenbaker bore the brunt of the blame. This analysis suggests, however, that the contrasting structural pressures of the international and continental systems were ultimately behind the paradoxical interactions of the two North American neighbours throughout the Cuban Missile Crisis. In Kennedy's long delay in informing the Diefenbaker government through Livingston Merchant of the threat, and in his administration's agreement to amend his televised speech of 22 October at Canada's request; in Diefenbaker's self-assertive sermon after Kennedy's speech that night, and in Harkness' act of subordination to the dominant state and insubordination to his own; in the Kennedy phone call to Diefenbaker and in Diefenbaker's initial defiance but subsequent subordination; and in the fallout in the Canada-US relationship that followed, the discrete contrasting structural pressures of hierarchy in anarchy were at work. Each of these four related intra-hierarchical high political interactions built towards one contradictory policy outcome for both states.

Canada also sought a specialized role for itself in the prelude to the crisis as well as in the midst of the crisis itself. Moreover, the US found an intelligence-gathering role for Canada in Havana in the prelude, as well as an interlocutory role for that country in the midst of the crisis. The Canadian emphasis on a UN-based fact-finding mission to Cuba was predicated on the assumption, later revealed by Diefenbaker in his memoirs, that "the situation might prove analogous to that at the time of Suez in 1956, when international action to contain and put an end to the fighting was instituted almost simultaneously with the national action taken by France and Britain to protect their vital interests."[64] Of course, Canada had played a sizable role in the resolution of the Suez crisis. Lester Pearson had been awarded a Nobel Peace Prize for his efforts, and Canada subsequently gained a specialized reputation as a mediator/supervisor in the international system.[65] Kennedy, however, disapproved of the suggestion of an onsite inspection. He had, after all, gone to the trouble of sending his reconnaissance photographs up to Ottawa with Merchant as evidence of the Soviet nuclear build-up. The Diefenbaker suggestion therefore enraged Kennedy and contributed further to intra-hierarchical tension throughout the crisis and beyond.

Before long, Diefenbaker would be defeated in a federal election and Kennedy would be assassinated. The repercussions of the Cuban crisis would therefore not linger long in the upper echelons of the Canada-US relationship. Beneath the pinnacle of power, however, significant changes in continental defence would follow. After having been officially "open at the top" during the missile crisis, Canada, as we will explore in the following chapter, would equip a number of the weapons systems it had been provided with by the US with American nuclear warheads, and a major reorganization of the defence ministry would result in the integration of the Canadian Navy, Air Force, and Army into the Canadian Forces to strengthen civilian control. Even after the Cuban crisis, however, which could have been expected to demonstrate to both Ottawa and Washington the need for closer cooperation and policy coordination in defence of North America, both states would be pushed and pulled in contrasting directions by the structural forces of the continental hierarchy and the international anarchy in the coming years as they attempted (unsuccessfully) to negotiate agreements on nuclear weapons for Canada and Canadian participation in the establishment and functioning of a ballistic missile shield. In the next two chapters, we will explore the paradoxical dynamics of these cases, respectively, as well as the constant efforts of Canada to find specialized roles in international politics.

4
Nuclear Weapons, 1945-2009

In the late 1950s, Canada committed its armed forces to taking on nuclear roles under the auspices of both NATO and NORAD. The Diefenbaker government invested considerable sums in an effort to fulfill these commitments, only to backpedal in the early 1960s once the scare of the successful Russian Sputnik satellite launch in the autumn of 1957 had worn off, and after coming to the belief that the Diefenbaker government might keep Canada from playing a significant role in the multilateral nonproliferation negotiations. After the Cuban Missile Crisis, and under the leadership of Lester B. Pearson's Liberal minority government, Canada decided that it *would* arm a variety of its weapons systems stationed at home and abroad with American nuclear warheads. Within two decades, however, the country had completed the task of expunging those warheads from its arsenal and returning them to the United States.

The US spent billions of dollars trying to supply Canada with nuclear warheads and the necessary weapons systems for their deployment. At the height of the Cold War, the US even agreed to rearrange its security plans in an effort to meet Canadian needs. More remarkably, it agreed to continue investing in the production and supply of a weapons system it knew to be suboptimal in an effort to facilitate the supply of nuclear weapons to its subordinate in the continental system. As Canadian leaders delayed their decision to accept the nuclear weapons systems, the US was forced to concede the existence of a yawning hole in North American defence.

Throughout this entire period, Canada's advocacy of nuclear disarmament never wavered,[1] but neither did Canada ever cease to pay its membership dues in NATO, an alliance that to this day retains its right to employ nuclear arms, and to do so in a "first-use" mode even long after its victory in the Cold War. Throughout this period, moreover, Canada remained secure under the American nuclear umbrella and continued to produce materials for use in the nuclear weapons programs of other states.

Conventional wisdom on this subject has tended to focus on the proximate causes of particular episodes within the greater history of Canada's involvement with nuclear weapons.[2] It tends to pass over the underlying *ultimate* (structural) causes of the patterns of behaviour in question here. Despite leadership changes in both countries, despite changes in the configuration of each country's regime, and despite the major systemic change from a bipolar to a unipolar structure following the end of the Cold War, these patterns are shown here to have persisted across a half-century timeframe.

Independent Nuclear Nation?

The history of Canada, the United States, and nuclear weapons begins in the advent of the nuclear era. The two countries' governments, their national industries, and their most prominent scientists were all involved in the fateful Manhattan Project to transform the energy locked inside the atom into the ultimate destructive force.[3] Canada's role in the Manhattan Project, its store of rare uranium, and the considerable increase in its relative capability in the postwar world left it in a position in which neorealists would have expected it to develop an independent nuclear capacity as a means of significantly increasing its material capability and thus the means to ensure its own survival. On the basis of recently declassified defence documents from the 1940s, 1950s, and 1960s, however, Brian Buckley argues in *Canada's Early Nuclear Policy* that the country never seriously considered the option of becoming a nuclear-armed state.[4]

The popular *political cultural* explanation for this suggests that Canadians, as a pre-eminently peaceful people, have an inherent abhorrence of such weapons and never would have been comfortable with a nuclear arsenal of their own. The fact that public opinion in the early 1960s swung in favour of Canada's becoming a nuclear weapons state after the shock of Sputnik seems to confound this line of reasoning, as does the fact that the country was a dependent (American) nuclear weapons state from 1963 to 1984, and the fact that Canada continued throughout the Cold War to profit extensively from the export of uranium mined in Port Hope, Ontario, and plutonium produced just outside Ottawa for use in other countries' nuclear weapons programs.[5]

A second school of thought emphasizes Canada's place in the international system at the time, and is thus closer to a structural analysis of the issue. John Holmes argued that instinctively the British, who were in a worse position economically than the Canadians at the time, knew that they would have to bear the cost of developing an independent nuclear arsenal. "It was taken for granted that a country of Britain's assumed stature in the world would have [the bomb]," Holmes reasoned. "The Canadian situation was the reverse. At no time was serious consideration given to producing Canada's own bomb."[6] Holmes chalks this up to a matter of standing in the international system. As a recently self-styled middle power, Canada had no ambition to take on the "responsibilities of great-power status."[7] The plausibility of Holmes's analysis aside, becoming a nuclear weapons state would have virtually guaranteed Canadian security against any foreseeable conventional, state-based threat. Had the country gone independently nuclear at an early stage, it would have guaranteed Canada a vastly more prominent position in both the continental and international systems. Further explanation is therefore required.

A second structural factor was behind Canada's decision not to pursue an independent nuclear arsenal. If Canada instinctively grasped the constraints of its position in the broader international system, it also instinctively grasped its position in the continental system. By virtue of its subordinate but sovereign status in North America, Canada was already protected from any potential nuclear threat – however far off in the future – by the dominant power of the United States, which would unquestionably attain a nuclear arsenal to rival that of any other. Any independent nuclear capacity for Canada would therefore be a redundancy, not worth the investment.[8] The logic of the continental hierarchy was also at work on this decision to refrain from becoming an independent nuclear weapons state.

Dependent Nuclear Nation?

Although Canada decided not to become an independent nuclear weapons state, the question of whether it would become dependently nuclear by taking on American nuclear warheads as part of its contribution to fighting the Cold War remained. Louis St. Laurent, who had been prime minister for nearly a decade before Diefenbaker replaced him on 22 April 1957, left this question, along with two other critical defence-related policy decisions to his successor. Diefenbaker would have to determine whether Canada would (1) join the North American Air Defence Command (NORAD), (2) proceed with the increasingly expensive Avro Arrow project, (3) and acquire nuclear weapons from the United States.

The first of these decisions was made with great efficiency compared with the others, perhaps because it dealt, at least initially, with a matter fundamentally influenced by the structural hierarchy in Canada-US relations: combined defence of the continent. Within two months, Diefenbaker had reinforced his country's end of the Canada-US confidence bargain and integrated operational control of the Royal Canadian Air Force with the US Air Force. The chairman of the Canadian Chiefs of Staff, General Charles Foulkes, was "astounded that the decision had been made with so little discussion,"[9] though he himself admitted to having "stampeded" the new government with the urgency of approving the agreement.[10] The agreement was publicly announced on 1 August 1957, and legitimated by a formal exchange of diplomatic notes between the two governments in May 1958, after some public controversy in Canada over the rapidity of its initial approval. NORAD itself, however, stood up nine months earlier, on 12 September 1957.[11] It institutionalized the Canada-US security hierarchy that had first been formally articulated by Prime Minister Mackenzie King and President Franklin D. Roosevelt in 1940 at Ogdensburg, New York, and was largely a product of the strategy of containment and deterrence that America was following in its pursuit of an eventual Cold War victory over the Soviet Union.[12]

The decision to cancel the Avro Arrow project took more effort and time, perhaps because Diefenbaker was influenced to some extent by the structural logics of both the continental and international systems. The Arrow project to produce an advanced supersonic, twin-engine, all-weather interceptor jet was intended to be a significant Canadian contribution to continental defence, as well as a symbol of Canadian leadership in the international aeronautics field. The Arrow was to be the most advanced aircraft of its kind. The decision to cancel it due to actual financial and potential strategic reasons,[13] which was finally made on 20 February 1959, was a hard pill for Canadians to swallow. Significantly, it marked the last time Canada would engage in an attempt to produce weapons systems on its own.

Canada's move towards becoming a dependent nuclear weapons state began in the winter of 1957 (post-Sputnik), when Diefenbaker met with the other NATO leaders in Paris. It was agreed that the alliance would establish nuclear stockpiles for its forces in Europe as a first line of defence against the Soviet threat. Canada had troops stationed in Europe at the time, and was a contributing member of the alliance. Diefenbaker's endorsement of this agreement therefore implied his acceptance of American nuclear weapons for Canadian air and land forces in Europe. At least it did for General Foulkes, who said that at the meeting in Paris, "the Diefenbaker government agreed, without reservation, to adopt a nuclear strategy for the NATO forces in Europe." Defence Minister George Pearkes concurred, stating that "we accepted the nuclear role in NATO."[14]

In the summer of 1959, the Canadian government firmly agreed to have eight squadrons of the Lockheed F-104C Starfighter ready for strike-reconnaissance against specified targets in East Germany within ten months. The Starfighters were rigged to carry nuclear warheads. In addition to the Starfighters, Ottawa decided to equip its brigade group in Europe with a battery of Honest John rockets – short-range tactical artillery missiles that could take either conventional or nuclear payloads. The Canadian Honest John contingent was trained at home and then sent to Europe late in 1961, where it remained for two years without nuclear tips for its weapons.

On the continental front, the Arrow decision led to immediate pressures on the Diefenbaker government to contribute in another way to the defence of North America.[15] Without the Arrow to contribute to continental security, Canada was left with little choice but to take a more subordinate path, accepting American nuclear weapons as a way to do its part to augment the deterrent threat against the Soviet Union. Pressures from the international system amplified this imperative. As a sovereign nation geopolitically locked between two nuclear-charged superpowers embroiled in an ideological struggle for systemic dominance, the Canadian state was compelled to take some kind of action to ensure its own security. The Canadian economy, however, was running into balance-of-payments problems during this period, making significant defence expenditures difficult.

At the time, the Americans were planning to set up around 30 Bomarc missile bases in the northern part of the US to protect the main industrial centres there against the threat of Soviet bombers. This would have meant that in the event of a Soviet attack, the thermonuclear engagement would occur directly over Toronto and Montreal. Diefenbaker's government negotiated with the Pentagon to have two of the Bomarc bases moved north to avoid such a possibility. One was to be located in North Bay, Ontario, the other in La Macaza, Quebec. Each base would be equipped with twenty-eight missiles, each with a range of 400 miles. The Americans agreed to pay for the missiles. Canada would have to cover only the support costs, which amounted to some $14 million.[16]

The Bomarcs were "oversold" to the Canadian public by an overexcited government spokesman who mistakenly suggested that the missiles would be more effective than the Arrows would have been in defending against a Soviet intercontinental ballistic missile (ICBM) attack.[17] The fact of the matter was that, like the Arrows, the Bomarcs were strictly an anti-bomber defence and provided no protection from incoming ICBMs. That the government had been misleading the public on the Bomarc issue became even more evident after the missile system failed its first seven tests. Even Lester Pearson, however, who would be compelled to flip-flop repeatedly on this issue going forward, agreed at the time with Diefenbaker's decision to accept nuclear warheads for the Bomarc IM-99B (Bomarc B) missiles.

Canada's agreement to accept such a significant defence handout was a subordinate move determined by the country's inability to effectively defend itself from the threat of a nuclear war developing in its airspace.[18] This subordinate move was countered on 4 July 1960, when Diefenbaker announced that if Canada were in fact to obtain the nuclear warheads necessary to arm the Bomarcs, the weapons would be under the control of the Canadian government alone. Designed to protect the integrity of Canadian sovereignty, such a declaration explicitly called for an exemption to Section 92 of the United States Atomic Energy Act, which forbids the transfer of American nuclear warheads from American custody. Were Canada to accept American nuclear warheads on its own soil or among its brigades stationed in Europe, it would also have to accept the American troops that would be sent to safeguard the warheads.

As it turned out, however, the Americans realized after test failures that the Bomarc B missiles were not as effective as anticipated, and were quite costly besides. They contemplated terminating the program altogether,[19] but the Canadians campaigned vigorously to keep it alive – so much so that the US Secretary of Defense reportedly told President Eisenhower that "if we were to go out of the Bomarc business [I don't] think we could live with the Canadians."[20] In a respectful gesture to his sovereign subordinate, Eisenhower gave his word to Diefenbaker that he would do what he could to save the Bomarc and to provide the Canadians with a replacement for the Arrows. The project was salvaged, and by February 1962 the Bomarc base in North Bay had been completed. Remarkably, the Americans agreed to pay to provide Canada with a weapons system they did not believe would be effective.[21] Even after this contradictory gesture of goodwill, however, Diefenbaker – in a move of self-assertion that stood in stark contrast to his previous lobbying for the Bomarcs – refused to allow the American soldiers carrying the nuclear warheads for the missiles into the country.

After the Brink
By the time of the Cuban Missile Crisis, Canada had invested $685 million on systems intended for use with nuclear weapons, but had yet to actually acquire the necessary payloads from the US. After the missile crisis was defused, the nuclear weapons controversy between the US and Canada escalated considerably. Ottawa's performance throughout the crisis had given Washington the impression that Canada was wavering in its commitments to continental defence. Thereafter, Washington exerted greater pressure for Ottawa to pay its dues by agreeing to arm with nuclear warheads the weapons systems that the US had provided.

As early as two months before the crisis, however, President Kennedy had sent a forceful private letter to Diefenbaker reminding him of his promise to arm. Kennedy feared entering a nuclear confrontation with Khrushchev with the entire northeastern United States exposed because of Diefenbaker's disinclination to accept nuclear warheads for the Bomarcs. The letter, which had been marked secret, spurred Diefenbaker towards finalizing the deal; he even told the president so in his reply. Somehow, though, the secret Kennedy communication found its way into the hands of the North American press. Headlines such as "JFK Presses Canada on Nuclear Warheads" in the *Montreal Star* portrayed the country in too subordinate a light for its prime minister's liking. Almost instantly, Diefenbaker again began to vacillate on the issue of taking on a nuclear role for his country.

The prime minister, in a minority government situation, was willing to follow the American will as long as it was not publicized. As soon as it was, concerns for his country's sovereignty conditioned by the imperatives of an international system came into conflict with the structural pressures of the continental system, and impaired his ability to proceed coherently on the acquisition of nuclear weapons. Although the inaction may have been deliberate, it still resulted in the contradictory outcome of Canada's arming itself for the Cold War with hundreds of millions of dollars worth of useless weapons systems.

The Cuban crisis might not have done much to change the prime minister's mind, but it seemed to change Canadian public opinion on the question of acquisition of nuclear weapons. Influential segments of the press reversed their previously held positions, came out in favour of acquisition, and proceeded to condemn the government for flip-flopping on the issue. Gallup and other polls taken in the postcrisis environment suggested that the electorate had also swung around in support of nuclear weapons for Canada.[22] Piles of letters poured into Diefenbaker's office, however, condemning the idea. This led the prime minister to suspect that the grassroots would not support him were he to make good on his commitment to the Americans.

With the nuclear issue now number one on the Cabinet's agenda, deep divisions soon arose. Secretary of State for External Affairs Howard Green was firmly against Canadian acquisition because he had been extremely active at the Geneva conference on disarmament held in March 1962. Indeed, Green was at the time among the most ardent anti-nuclear crusaders on the international political scene.[23] He felt that Canada was "as much a leader as any other nation in this field, and we had very good support from the Americans too because they were very much interested in winding down the arms race."[24] In the days leading up to the 1962 federal election, he propounded: "No country has a greater opportunity [than Canada] of giving wise leadership in the field of disarmament negotiations and it is in that field that we may achieve our destiny."[25] Canadians enthusiastically embraced this advocacy role and the identity it created for their nation on the international stage. An editorial in the *Toronto Star* boasted: "There is something that Canada can be proud of in the persistent undeflatable [sic], industrious optimism of External Affairs Minister Howard Green on the subject of a nuclear test ban treaty."[26] Others in the Canadian press expressed their praise with equal exuberance.[27] With a special role in the international system embraced by the country as a source of pride, and apparently supported by the US and other states in the system, Green reasoned that Canada's acquisition of the very weapons he was crusading against would significantly undermine his efforts to fulfill the Canadian "destiny" to work in the interest of international systemic stability.

Minister of National Defence Douglas Harkness took the opposite position. For over two years, he had been making public statements regarding Canadian defence policy both at home and abroad, all of which been based on the assumption that Canada would equip the weapons systems it had spent, in his estimate, "some $700 to $800 million to acquire," with nuclear warheads. In Harkness' words, "we had trained our personnel in the use of these weapon systems, and it was an indefensible position as far as I was concerned then not to conclude the agreement with the United States for the joint custody of the warheads and to put the warheads on the weapons."[28]

With respect to the rest of the Cabinet, Jocelyn Ghent-Mallet tellingly explains that "if some members of cabinet leaned towards Green's point of view because they were worried about questions of sovereignty and control, others supported Harkness because they were concerned with the possibility of American economic redress, and the fate of defence production-sharing."[29] The contrasting logics of the international and continental systems were at work in unravelling both Diefenbaker's Cabinet and Diefenbaker himself.

Despite the chasm that had opened across the Conservative front benches, negotiations with the Americans were being conducted with a new sense of urgency. The Canadians were inventing all manner of innovative designs to avoid being pulled apart by the contrasting structural pressures bearing on them. The Americans were very tolerant of the Canadian situation, which was also their own.[30] One scheme was to have the warheads parked at the border, to be delivered and fitted to the Canadian weapons systems should a crisis arise. Another involved the Americans' retaining a critical component of the weapons system, again near the border, which could be brought in to complete the circuit more rapidly and cost-effectively than bringing in the actual nuclear warheads themselves. Such schemes were seriously presented and seriously considered by the respective governments. In retrospect, they seem absurd, but through the lens of structural specialization theory, they begin to be understood in seriousness as the contradictory results of contrasting structural pressures.

The negotiations dragged on through 1962 while the US tried new and more domineering tactics to compel Canadian consent. NORAD commander General Laurence Kuter and his deputy, Air Marshal Roy Slemon, made a number of speeches on Canadian soil in an effort to shape public opinion in favour of acquisition. A charismatic and influential RCAF officer named Bill Lee "lobbied reporters and editors to plant stories designed to demonstrate the lunacy of Diefenbaker's nuclear policy."[31] Livingston Merchant gave backgrounders over beer and spaghetti to Parliament Hill reporters in the basement of one of the US embassy's workers. These were thinly veiled attempts to instruct the Canadian press on how to criticize Diefenbaker's indecision. They were also thinly veiled moves of domination.

The most notorious interference in Canadian domestic politics occurred on 3 January 1963, when NATO's newly retired Supreme Allied Commander in Europe, General Lauris Norstad (an American), paid a visit to Canada as part of his farewell tour. At a press conference, Norstad voiced his views on the Canadian nuclear weapons dilemma, saying that he felt the country would not be fulfilling its obligations to NATO if it refused to take on a nuclear role. Diefenbaker and Green interpreted this to be a direct and flagrant public interference on the part of the United States in Canadian domestic politics. The Canadian press only amplified these sentiments, making a scandal of the visit and placing Diefenbaker and his Cabinet in a very difficult political situation. The Conservative government was now caught between its obligations to NATO and the United States and its desire to uphold the integrity of Canadian sovereignty.

After Norstad's visit, the leader of the Official Opposition, Lester B. Pearson, stepped up the pressure on Diefenbaker's government. Pearson and his Liberal party had been officially opposed to Canadian nuclear weapons but had reversed course on the issue after the defence critic, Paul Hellyer, had taken a tour of the Canadian Forces bases in Europe and reported low levels of morale among the troops who were stationed there without atomic ammunition. Moreover, Hellyer reported to Pearson that officials at NATO headquarters had indicated that if Canada did not decide to take on a nuclear role soon, it would be pressured to withdraw from the alliance.[32]

On 12 January 1963, Pearson announced his change of heart on nuclear weapons during a speech in Scarborough, Ontario. This intensified Diefenbaker's dilemma. He was convinced that Pearson and Kennedy – who were close friends – were conspiring to oust him from power. Accordingly, the prime minister felt obliged to oppose Pearson's position, and decided to further delay the nuclear decision. Within a week, his Cabinet reached a critical level of disarray. Harkness was threatening to resign, and a rebellion against the prime minister was being plotted by key members of his party. On 25 January, with his back against the wall, Diefenbaker gave a major defence policy address to the House of Commons. The speech was, by at least two accounts, next to incomprehensible.[33]

The press interpreted the speech in one way, Harkness interpreted it in another, and the Americans interpreted it as a fraud. The press read the speech as saying that Canada would attempt to continue straddling the fence on the issue of nuclear weapons. Harkness, in response to this interpretation, took the unprecedented step of issuing a clarification of the speech, suggesting that the government had finally come out in favour of acquiring a nuclear capability. The US State Department issued a press release that corrected a number of points made in the speech. First, Diefenbaker had indicated that NATO was considering a return to an emphasis on more conventional forms of weaponry. This, he suggested, had been the result of the meetings between Kennedy and British Prime Minister Harold Macmillan at Nassau. Diefenbaker had used this apparent fact as a way of justifying further delay on Canada's acquisition of nuclear arms. The State Department stated firmly in response to this that conventional forces were not viewed by the United States as an alternative to nuclear weaponry, and that the Nassau agreement had been published and had indicated no question of the appropriateness of nuclear weapons. Finally, the State Department derided Diefenbaker's claim that negotiations had been going on between the two governments to arm weapons systems stationed in Canada with nuclear warheads, saying that the discussions were merely exploratory in nature and that the Canadian government had not yet proposed an arrangement "sufficiently practical to contribute to North American defence."[34]

The State Department had called Diefenbaker a liar, and taken a bold step of interfering publicly in Canadian affairs. In response, the prime minister recalled Charles Ritchie, Canada's ambassador to Washington, an equally bold step of self-assertion in the face of such domination. Harkness resigned. The Liberal opposition pounced on the evidence that Diefenbaker had lost control of his Cabinet and moved for a vote of no confidence that dissolved Parliament and sent the country into an election. Pearson's party won the election with the help of an American public relations firm previously employed by Kennedy.

On 16 August 1963, Pearson's minority government announced that it had reached an agreement with the US to arm the Bomarc, Voodoo, Starfighter, and Honest John weapons systems with American nuclear warheads. The warheads, which were stationed at Canadian bases in Canada and in Europe, remained officially in the custody of US troops. Indeed, John Clearwater characterizes these installations as "little more than extensions of U.S. military deployments and strategy."[35] And it is a matter of considerable ambiguity as to whether Canada would have had any say whatsoever over the use the nuclear devices.[36]

The Americans had also insisted on creating storage facilities in Canada for some of its nuclear arsenal, and wanted Canadian consent on this at the same time as its consent on arming its weapons systems. The Pearson government – in a move of self-assertion – refused, at least initially. It would later reverse this refusal and agree on 9 October 1963 to permit the storage of American stockpiles of nuclear weapons on Canadian soil.

Pearson tabled neither of these agreements on the grounds that they were executive understandings. Making them public would be a breach of national security. Pearson nevertheless assured the House of Commons that Canada's sovereignty had been protected.

In and Out

From 1963 to 1984, US nuclear warheads were stationed at Canadian bases, both at home and in Europe. They were removed on the initiative of Pearson's successor to the Liberal leadership, Pierre Trudeau. Trudeau, who was from the province of Quebec, had been opposed to the Canadian acquisition of American nuclear warheads from the start,[37] as had the majority of Quebecers. Perhaps fearing further fuel for the sovereignty movement in his home province, which would threaten Canadian internal survival, Trudeau initiated the removal of the nuclear weapons from Canadian bases in 1968. This process of purging the American-supplied Canadian nuclear arsenal was not completed for sixteen years, however.

During this time, Trudeau was actively engaged in Canada's specialized advocacy of disarmament. Making a virtue out of paradox and contradiction, in 1978, he cited Canada as an example to the UN General Assembly: "Not only the first country in the world with the capacity to produce nuclear weapons that chose not to do so, we are also the first nuclear armed country to have chosen to divest itself of nuclear weapons."[38] That same year, he articulated his strategy of nuclear suffocation, which called for a multilateral agreement to end the further development of technology used for destructive purposes. Later, he would make a foray into high politics with a three-continent tour intended to defuse the escalation of the Cold War caused by the Korean Air Lines incident of 1 September 1983.[39] Secure under the American nuclear umbrella, with nuclear weapons still in the two countries' joint possession, and with nuclear reactors still being produced by Canada for sale to questionable customers,[40] Trudeau nevertheless articulated a view that Canada should be seen as a leader in the quest to rid the world of the most destructive force humankind had ever harnessed.

Moreover, Trudeau even agreed to allow the US to test its new cruise missile over Canadian territory.[41] The decision contradicted his proposed policy of nuclear suffocation, a harsh reality that was even publicly admitted by the prime minister. It also generated a considerable degree of controversy in Canada.[42] A Gallup poll taken in 1983 revealed that over half of Canadians opposed cruise missile testing over their northern landscape.[43] And yet their elected officials voted nearly unanimously against opposing the tests. Prime Minister Trudeau offered a frank explanation for this when he said that "it is hardly fair to rely on the Americans to protect the West, but to refuse to lend them a hand when the going gets rough."[44]

On 6 March 1984, the first cruise missile test took place over northwestern Canada. Although officials in Ottawa had known about the test scheduled for that day, they gave Canadians only two days' notice, significantly reducing the possibility of public protests. Fifteen further tests of the original cruise missile followed. During this time, the Department of National Defence announced that a new North Warning System to replace the old Distant

Early Warning Line would be required in response to the anticipated development of the Soviet answer to the American cruise missile. Howard Langille argues that "rather than help to suffocate the flight-testing of a new strategic vehicle, Canada had facilitated another round of the action-reaction process propelling the arms race."[45] Testing would continue under the Conservative government of Brian Mulroney, this time with the AGM-129 Advanced Cruise Missile.

During the period of Conservative government that followed the 1984 cruise missile test, Canada further agreed to allow about fifteen US nuclear submarines per year to travel under the surface of the Dixon Entrance, a disputed Pacific Coast strait, on the way to an acoustic testing site along the Alaska Panhandle. The snap decision was made by Cabinet order without environmental review or public hearings. It generated accusations of illegality from NDP MP Jim Fulton, and court challenges from a collection of concerned groups, including British Columbia Aboriginal people, the nuclear disarmament group Greenpeace, and BC fishermen's unions.[46]

The Advocate

While American cruise missiles were being tested over Canadian soil, and American nuclear-powered submarines were being tested under Canadian waters, Canada continued to be active in its advocacy of nuclear nonproliferation and disarmament at the multilateral level. With the nuclear standoff of the Cold War fading into memory and the new era of globalization coming into focus, the time seemed right in 1996 for Minister of Foreign Affairs Lloyd Axworthy to request that the House of Commons Standing Committee on Foreign Affairs and International Trade review Canada's nuclear policy.

At the time, it seemed that the world was poised to move towards a moral condemnation of nuclear weapons that would culminate in their eradication from the planet. There were hopes among many in the international community that the contradiction in the Nuclear Non-Proliferation Treaty – that some states could have nuclear arsenals while others could not – would be righted, and that the nuclear weapons states would finally move towards the disarmament promised by that treaty. A number of significant reports sponsored by Western nations added to this "abolitionist upsurge," including the *Canberra Commission on the Elimination of Nuclear Weapons,* the *Tokyo Forum Report,* and Canada's own *Canada and the Nuclear Challenge: Reducing the Political Value of Nuclear Weapons for the Twenty-First Century* in 1998.[47]

The Standing Committee's 1998 report was the product of two years of extensive research, public hearings, and expert testimonies. In the end, fifteen significant recommendations were presented to guide Canada's policy towards nuclear weapons in the post-Cold War world. First and most prominent was that Canada would "work consistently to reduce the political legitimacy and value of nuclear weapons in order to contribute to the goal of their progressive reduction and eventual elimination."[48] The report recommended that in order to advance this objective, the government could employ the tactics of the so-called Ottawa Process – an alternative method of operating in the international diplomatic sphere, employing non-governmental organizations and public shaming to generate momentum towards international agreements such as the 1997 Mine Ban Treaty.[49] Finally, the report recommended that the government argue "forcefully within NATO that the present re-examination and update as necessary of the Alliance Strategic Concept should include its nuclear component."[50] Once such a report is produced, the government must respond to it within ninety days, providing its own policy position. The opposition parties must also respond.

It might seem that the committee was setting the government up to take a hardline disarmament position that would be difficult to sustain on the world stage, given the pressures of the continental system. As Axworthy notes, however, the report could have been much more adamantly anti-nuclear than it was in its final form:

> The American Embassy and the British High Commission were in a perpetual state of agitation over the work of the committee. What had them exercised was the possibility that we would issue a "no first use policy" ... The fear was that such a policy would be contagious and would be taken up by other NATO countries. To offset this possibility, American and British diplomats engaged in a variety of persuasive techniques, especially with Liberal members of the committee, including private briefing, dinners and not so veiled warnings of consequences, not unlike those issued by Ambassador Cellucci that our non-participation in the Iraq war could affect border issues ... If I had ever believed that policy-making in Canada is a simple exercise, or that solely domestic forces dictate the result, this experience dispelled such notions. The scrutiny and pressure from outside and the full court press being executed by the nuclear states, especially the Americans, had an effect. You could call it an advancing case of cold feet; several of my colleagues, to say nothing of certain officials in DFAIT and DND, were discovering serious reservations to the nuclear review strategy.[51]

In the end, the committee backed down from calling for the removal of US nuclear weapons from Europe, and from recommending that NATO adopt a policy of no first use.

Three weeks before the report was published, a crucial nuclear disarmament resolution was voted on at the United Nations. Axworthy's preferred position was clear: he wanted to vote in favour of the resolution, which called for a new disarmament agenda, one that would have put pressure on

NATO to purge its nuclear weapons and to do away with its first-use policy.[52] Canadians were overwhelmingly with him on this – 92 percent of those polled by Angus Reid that year had said they wanted their country to play a lead role in global negotiations to eliminate nuclear weapons[53] – and in doing so he would have been following the spirit of the Standing Committee's pending report. He could not find another NATO member to vote with him on the issue, however. They had all gotten "cold feet," in Axworthy's words. Furthermore, the US government – in a move of domination – intervened, telling him to oppose the resolution.[54] So on 13 November 1998, Canada, along with thirty-two other states, abstained from voting on the resolution that called on nuclear weapons states to demonstrate unequivocal commitment to the elimination of nuclear weapons through negotiations and practical steps. Ninety-seven countries voted in favour of the resolution, and just nineteen opposed it.

After the report had been published and the government had given its response endorsing the recommendation to continue stressing the necessity of devaluing "the political significance of these weapons,"[55] Canada again abstained from voting on an important nuclear disarmament resolution that was before the UN. Ireland, Sweden, Mexico, South Africa, and a number of other countries sponsored the resolution. It called on nuclear weapons states to move decisively towards disarmament. A month prior to this abstention, Axworthy boldly told two separate audiences in Boston that the United States was going backward on a series of nuclear issues.[56]

Despite his inability to vote firmly against the NATO line at the UN, Axworthy continued to push his agenda within the alliance. At NATO's fiftieth-anniversary summit, Axworthy and his German and Dutch counterparts managed to gain a commitment from the alliance to "consider options for confidence and security building measures, verification, non-proliferation and arms control and disarmament."[57] Towards the end of 1999, the NATO foreign ministers met and discussed the possibility of undertaking a review of NATO's nuclear options, but there was no further progress towards this end. Despite making an initial conciliatory move, the US decided against any changes to the alliance's nuclear strategy. After the second Bush administration took power in Washington in 2001, and after the 11 September suicide attacks by Osama bin Laden's al-Qaeda network, this position seemed immovable.

On this issue of nuclear weapons, three Canadian prime ministers and three American presidents, irrespective of their particular personalities or relationships, and irrespective of their regime configurations, all found themselves pushed and pulled in the expected ways by the contrasting structural forces of the continental and international systems. It was these structural forces that *ultimately* gave the relationship its paradoxical dynamics on this issue throughout the period in question. The particular leaders and their regime configurations were *proximate* causal factors in the continuation of a pattern that has been seen within the continental hierarchy for fifty years. This paradoxical pattern, and the concurrent pattern of specialized behaviour followed by Canada in its external relations, is examined again in the next chapter, on the ongoing missile defence controversy.

Part 2
Post-Cold War Case Studies

5
Missile Defence, 1983-2009

Accompanied by controversy from the start, progress towards realizing the American dream to build a defence against ballistic missile strikes began a little over a quarter of a century ago. In 1985, President Ronald Reagan requested Canadian participation in the research for this dream, which came to be known as the Strategic Defense Initiative (SDI). Prime Minister Brian Mulroney politely declined the invitation, but made sure to point out that Canadian firms should feel free to compete for any contracts stemming from it. Throughout the late 1990s, President Bill Clinton put pressure on Canada to reverse its position on what was then still the prospect of a missile defence capability, on the grounds that it had taken a much less ambitious form since Reagan had first envisioned it over a decade earlier, and rogue states had replaced the Soviet Union as the chief threat to continental security. Prime Minister Jean Chrétien agreed to enter negotiations on possible Canadian participation in the project, but retired before making a final decision after debating the possibility for over two years. Under the direction of President George W. Bush, the project was taken up with renewed enthusiasm. Canada's participation was again requested, and again, after much deliberation, declined – this time by Prime Minister Paul Martin – but not before the NORAD agreement had been amended to make sure that information gathered by that organization would be made available to US commands operating ballistic missile defences.

Reagan, Clinton, and Bush; Mulroney, Chrétien, and Martin – all found themselves and their governments subject to the contrasting influences of hierarchy in anarchy. None, therefore, can be entirely credited with producing the paradoxical dynamics and contradictory outcomes reviewed in this chapter. At most, these individuals and their particular regime configurations played *proximate* causal roles. This chapter also demonstrates that in response to the American plans to build a missile shield, Canada repeatedly advocated system stability and thus opposed each incarnation of the potentially destabilizing US initiative at the international level.

"Star Wars"

In March 1983, as the United States was ramping up defence spending after the long period of détente, President Reagan asked the following of his fellow Americans:

> Up until now we have increasingly based our strategy of deterrence upon the threat of retaliation. But what if free people could live secure in the knowledge that their security did not rest on the threat of instant US retaliation to deter a Soviet attack; that we could intercept and destroy strategic ballistic missiles before they reached our soil or that of our allies[?] I know this is a formidable task ... But is it not worth every investment necessary to free the world from the threat of nuclear war?[1]

Reagan was questioning deterrence and considering the possibility of defence in an offence-dominated world. In doing so, he was reviving an idea the US had been grappling with since the dawn of the atomic age.[2] No president had ever been fully comfortable relying on the deterrence of others to ensure the security of Americans. Nevertheless, the notion of *assured survival* at a time when *assured destruction* was the fulcrum of Cold War stability held ominous possibilities for the nuclear balance of terror. That Reagan's vague proposal to make ballistic missiles "impotent and obsolete" was taken perhaps less seriously than it might have been by the American media at that time was understandable, given that it was only a vision for a research program – a call to arms for the scientific community. The press dubbed his proposal "Star Wars," on account of both its seemingly science fiction-based inspiration and the fact that he had previously referred to the Soviet Union as the "Evil Empire" in what the press had aptly termed the "Darth Vader speech."[3]

The introduction of nuclear weapons and ballistic missiles into the international security environment had instantly rendered strategic defences impotent. From the TNT blockbusters of the Second World War to the "Super" H-bomb of 1951, the explosive capacity of warheads had intensified "a million times."[4] When intercontinental ballistic missiles (ICBMs) and submarine-launched ballistic missiles (SLBMs) entered the arsenals of the United States and the Soviet Union in the 1960s and 1970s, the speed and distance of offensive strikes were similarly revolutionized.[5] In such a technological era, the strategic offence was at a distinct advantage over the strategic defence – so much so that the US abandoned efforts to develop defences against such attacks, and instead channelled all of its efforts into creating a retaliatory capacity of such catastrophic lethality that the Soviet Union would be deterred from attacking. It was on the doctrines of massive retaliation (1954), graduated deterrence (1959), and mutual assured destruction (MAD, 1964), that America based its homeland defence strategy. These doctrines assumed that the Soviet Union would rationally assess the implications of a first strike and regard the American retaliatory threat as credible.

After the period of détente effectively came to a close with the Soviet invasion of Afghanistan in 1979, the renewed interest in building up a strategic defence against a Soviet nuclear strike thus ran contrary to the concept that had ensured Cold War stability to that point. MAD was enshrined as the legal linchpin of the Cold War order in the 1972 Anti-Ballistic Missile (ABM) Treaty.[6] Initiating research on the technology that could assure survival was disruptive to the balance of terror[7] in an offence-dominated world, and represented a considerable escalation in the arms race.[8] All states, therefore, had a stake in SDI, including, and especially, Canada. On the one hand, as a beneficiary of the security provided by the American deterrent threat, as a member of NORAD and NATO, and as a sovereign state geostrategically locked between the two nuclear superpowers, Canada could only gain from an American initiative to delink continental security from the MAD doctrine. On the other hand, as a structurally specialized state with vested interests in multilateralism and a concern for stability at the broader international level, Canada was compelled to view Reagan's initiative as destabilizing.

Following Reagan's announcement, the issue was discussed in the Canadian House of Commons. Pierre Trudeau's Liberal government passed a unanimous motion to condemn SDI on the grounds that it was a new and potentially disastrous escalation in the arms race.[9] Trudeau and his government said a firm no to SDI after saying a reluctant "okay, fine" to cruise missile testing on Canadian soil, before the prime minister headed off on his peace initiative to reduce Cold War tensions.

In September 1984, with Brian Mulroney's newly elected Conservatives in power with a majority government, Minister of Foreign Affairs Joe Clark, speaking to the United Nations, encouraged middle-sized powers together with Canada to work towards encouraging "the superpowers to ban weapons in outer space."[10] Canada's Ambassador for Disarmament, Douglas Roche, made a similar statement to the UN, urging efforts towards preventing an arms race in space. Canada was pursuing its usual specialization as advocate of peace and stability, but this time in direct opposition to the initiative that Reagan had outlined in his "Star Wars" speech.

Clark expressed further concern at a NATO meeting in Brussels in December. As he did so, he indicated that divisions over "Star Wars" were forming within the Canadian Cabinet between himself and Minister of National Defence Robert Coates. From his position as the minister of a department deeply integrated with the American military and defence industry, Coates saw the initiative as a potential source of revenue for Canadian aerospace firms, and as a chance to put the Canadian Forces on the cutting edge of space technology. Clark stated that the defence minister was "more enthusiastic" than he was about the "Star Wars" initiative. Clark viewed the situation from the perspective of Canada's reputation for working towards stability and peace through multilateral advocacy. Supporting a unilateral American initiative that could potentially lead to instability and war would significantly undermine that reputation. The prime minister, feeling the structural pressures of this developing issue from both its continental and international sides, commented that he was "less than enthusiastic" about "the militarization of space."[11]

After these initial disclaimers, and as the issue gained prominence in Canada and the broader international community, Clark announced to the House of Commons on 21 January 1985 that although "Star Wars" was still "highly hypothetical," nonetheless, "in the light of significant Soviet advances in ballistic missile defence research in recent years and deployment of an actual ballistic missile defence system, it is only prudent that the West keep abreast of the feasibility of such projects."[12] Following Clark's comments, Mulroney stated that the "Star Wars" proposal "merits the approval of an ally."[13] This begged the question: Did Canada intend, then, to participate in "Star Wars"? In response, Clark said, "No ... there is no plan, current, pending, or anticipated, that would have the government of Canada involved in any way."[14]

Less than two weeks later, the 2 February front-page headline of the *Globe and Mail* read "PM Support of Star Wars Pleases U.S."[15] The article detailed a press conference during which Mulroney "stoutly backed Star Wars research and admitted that Canada had best get its act together on acid rain before demanding action on the part of the United States."[16] These comments were "immediately interpreted by U.S. embassy officials as important conciliatory gestures" in preparation for Reagan's visit north in March.[17] Responding to a reporter's comment, Mulroney said in effect that Canada was not the only NATO ally to back "Star Wars," that Margaret Thatcher of Great Britain had also backed Reagan's initiative.[18] From these statements, it seemed as though Canada *had* agreed to support "Star Wars" for US, if not for its own, interests. Indeed, as Stephen Clarkson wrote, "using language as hawkish as Margaret Thatcher and showing no apparent concern for the destabilizing consequences of the militarization of space for East-West relations, Mulroney executed an about-face from Trudeau's peace initiative, which he had endorsed during the 1984 election campaign."[19]

Later in February, opposition MPs discovered that a clause had been quietly deleted from the NORAD agreement during the 1980-81 review and renewal. The sentence specified that NORAD would not involve Canada in any commitment to participate in an active ballistic missile defence. With this clause now conspicuously absent from the agreement, there was no longer a legal barrier to Canadian participation in "Star Wars." The opposition then began to ask whether Canada-US defence integration through the new North Warning System (NWS; formerly the Distant Early Warning Line) and NORAD did not already mean that Canada would be practically involved in "Star Wars" regardless of whatever symbolic decision the government decided to take. The Conservatives responded again in the negative, asserting that the North Warning System was not capable of detecting ballistic missiles (only cruise missiles and long-range bombers), that SDI was just a research program, and that the Canadian government was holding strong in its support of the ABM Treaty.[20]

Opposition concern, coming most forcefully from the New Democratic Party, intensified when Paul Nitze arrived in Ottawa as part of a diplomatic offensive designed to generate support for Reagan's initiative. Nitze told the press corps that whether the North Warning System would be used as a component of "Star Wars" remained to be seen. As Joseph Jockel wrote, this inevitably led some Canadians "to imagine scores of BMD [ballistic missile defence] installations located across their northland, operated by Americans and put there with or without Canadian endorsement."[21] The next day, Washington responded officially with a more respectful gesture towards Canadian sovereignty, characterizing Nitze's remarks as misleading while paying due homage to Canadian autonomy.

All this said, it was not until 7 March 1985, when Reagan officially launched the Strategic Defence Initiative, that it became a global issue of primary importance.[22] That day, Reagan spoke to Congress about his vision of a large-scale defensive system with thousands of sensors and interceptors based on land, in the sea, in the sky, and in space, and requested the extraordinary sum of $26 billion to fund it over the next five years.[23] Understandably, the missile defence debate began in earnest thereafter in the US, in Canada, and throughout the international community.[24] "Star Wars" had to be taken seriously.

"Shamrock Summit"

Ten days later, President Reagan flew to Quebec City aboard Air Force One for the "Shamrock Summit" with Prime Minister Mulroney. After the symbolic shows of a new era of repaired continental relations guided by two leaders of common Irish ancestry had finished on St. Patrick's Day, US Defense Secretary Caspar Weinberger opened day two of the visit by informing CTV's *Canada AM* that missile launchers to intercept Soviet cruise missiles could be positioned on Canadian soil at some point in the future. Weinberger's remarks generated the same concerns about Canadian sovereignty as Nitze's had in February. Again, both Canadian and American officials tried to defuse the issue with assurances that Canadian sovereignty would be respected with regard to any developments flowing from SDI. Without Canadian permission, no American weapons systems would ever be deployed in Canada, they said.

Within hours, however, Reagan was asserting the American will in a luncheon speech in Quebec City. After severely denouncing communism and the Soviet Union, and referring to the nuclear allergy suffered by New Zealand earlier in the year, when it had banned nuclear-powered ships and submarines from entering its ports, Reagan informally extended an invitation to the Mulroney government to participate in SDI research. In the lead-up to Reagan's visit, the peace movement in Canada had taken up the SDI issue with considerable enthusiasm. The Toronto Disarmament Network, the peace and disarmament committees of the Ontario Federation of Labour and the Metro Toronto Labour Council, the United Auto Workers, a large number of Canadian scientists and engineers from the country's universities, as well as the *Globe and Mail* and the *Vancouver Sun* all came out against Canadian participation in SDI.[25] For Reagan to come to Canada, then, and take a position on where Ottawa should end up on SDI was a serious intervention in Canadian domestic politics – a move of domination, in other words, on the part of the superordinate state. Indeed, it must have felt like arm-twisting to the Mulroney government, which was still, the prime minister's comments to the contrary, hedging on a final decision. To the opposition, the Weinberger and Reagan comments were suggestive of a secret plan to bring Canada into SDI through the back door of NORAD and the NWS.

Further suspicion and confusion ensued when Defence Minister Erik Nielsen returned from a NATO meeting in Luxembourg in early April with a formal invitation to participate in SDI. Nielsen had encouraged the US to move ahead with SDI, but instead of coming clean in the House of Commons about what had transpired in Luxembourg, Nielsen allowed Clark to declare in the House that no such invitation had been issued by the United States. Clark even went so far as to "scold an American government official in Washington for being 'wrong' in suggesting that an invitation had already been extended."[26] Clark walked right by Nielsen on his way to his seat in the government front benches that day.

After a show of excitement about the work SDI might give Canadians and the profits that Canadian companies might reap from the weaponization of space, Mulroney remarked, on a visit to his riding in Quebec, that it was one thing to offer support for the research but "it is quite another – quite another – to be invited to participate actively in a project where you are not the big player, where you don't set the thrust and where you have no control over the parameters."[27] This led Jean Chrétien, the Liberal foreign affairs critic, to challenge the Conservatives to take a stand one way or the other on SDI. "You are in or you are out," he said in the House. "You can't be half virgin and half pregnant."[28]

The Conservative government then assembled an all-party parliamentary committee to study the issue. Over the course of five weeks during the summer of 1985, the committee toured seven cities, soliciting the public's view on SDI. Many Canadians believed Canada should be in no way involved in "Star Wars." "We believe that an enormous tragedy is waiting to happen," the national chairman of Veterans for Multilateral Nuclear Disarmament told the committee. "What sense is there in making money out of preparing your own destruction?" he asked.[29] Others favoured Canadian participation. Joel Sokolsky, then a professor at Dalhousie University, told the committee that Canadian businesses should not be held back from participating in "Star Wars." "In the long run, we are going to be involved. The challenge for Canada is to manage that involvement," he said.[30] After the parliamentary committee study had been completed, eight of the committee members (those from the opposition parties) wanted Canada to decline the American offer of participation in SDI research. The other nine (the Progressive Conservative members) felt that the country should further delay a decision until the government had obtained more information about the initiative.

Despite the efforts of the committee, Mulroney seemed to rely more heavily on the advice of Arthur Kroeger, whom he had dispatched on a fact-finding mission to Washington, DC, before the parliamentary committee had even been assembled. Kroeger returned from the US skeptical about the economic benefits of supporting SDI but convinced of its importance in terms of Reagan's own perception of his political legacy. Canada, therefore, could not afford to reject SDI as an affront to peace and stability in the international system. This analysis was subsequently supported by a study undertaken by the Canadian Centre for Arms Control and Disarmament.

Mulroney announced his decision in September: Canada's "own policies and priorities do not warrant a government-to-government effort in support of SDI research," but Canadian industries and institutions would not be prohibited from participation in the initiative.[31] As Jim Manly of the NDP said in the House of Commons afterwards, the decision reminded him of the old song "Your lips tell me no, no, but there is yes, yes in your eyes."[32] Mulroney wanted to have it both ways on SDI, and it appeared (at least to himself) as though he had achieved that aim. Afterwards, he gloated about pulling the rug out from under his critics with his "polite no" to government participation.[33]

Mulroney's path towards this contradictory outcome had consequences of its own, however. His "polite no" to SDI did not discredit the nature of the initiative. No condemnation of the destabilizing effect that the weaponization of space would have on the Cold War order was made, despite the specialized efforts of Clark and Roche at the United Nations to generate a middle-power movement against SDI. Mulroney said that it would be fine for Canadian firms to profit from the very initiative that Clark and Roche[34] were opposing. Thus, in pulling the rug out from under his critics, Mulroney also pulled the rug out from under his own country's specialized role in the disarmament and nonproliferation effort of the broader international community. How could Canada be taken seriously in this capacity if its government valued jobs and profits over the survival of the human race? Moreover, Defence Minister Nielsen's job could not have been made any easier with respect to his relations with his NATO and American counterparts by this decision.

Washington was reportedly "not even upset" by Ottawa's SDI decision. Reagan even thanked Mulroney for the opportunity to work with Canadian firms.[35] At first blush, this is surprising, given the intensive lobbying Reagan and his staff had done in Ottawa to bring Canada on board with SDI. When one considers Mulroney's position further, however, and from the perspective of its nullification of Canada's potential role in opposing SDI at the international level, the reason for Washington's lack of open disappointment becomes somewhat clearer. Canada had combined its assertion of autonomy with a subordinate move that eliminated it from effectively participating in any international campaign to oppose SDI. If Washington's moves of domination could not win outright Canadian support for SDI, at least it could keep Canada from playing a role in the international advocacy campaign against it. This is the reason for Reagan's polite thank you to Mulroney. It did not mean, however, that Canadian defence firms would see a share of the profits from SDI research. Almost immediately, according to University of Manitoba political scientist James Fergusson, Canada found itself "cut out of crucial contacts with the Pentagon."[36]

The prominence of SDI in terms of the Canada-US relationship faded as a result of subsequent events, not the least of which was the end of the Cold War. Beyond this monumental transformation in the international system, initial ambitions for "Star Wars" were reduced due to technological limitations. It became clear that a roof in space capable of defending against an all-out nuclear attack was not possible. The advanced technologies that would have been required for such a project ("x-ray lasers and directed energy weapons")[37] were too costly and farfetched for Congress to fund. The Soviets were likely aware of the inherent technological difficulties with Reagan's vision of SDI, and could have predicted that subsequent Congresses would have been likely to reduce funding. Accordingly, their professed outrage at the prospect of SDI might then have been taken at less than face value.[38] The potentially destabilizing effects of the initiative at this time might therefore have been overstated. Nevertheless, Mulroney's decision tightened "up the flow of information" between the United States and Canada on evolving continental defence policy.[39]

Mulroney's firm but "polite no" to SDI had the unintended consequence of making continued Canada-US defence cooperation on the issue difficult to coordinate. Because of the structure of the countries' defence relations,

Canada cannot pick and choose which aspects of continental defence it wants to be part of as decisively as the policy debates over SDI suggested.

Episode II

SDI research took on a more conventional focus in the years following Ronald Reagan's presidency. Its scope was reduced to trying to provide defence against a limited or small-scale nuclear attack from terrorists or rogue states. The first Bush administration (1989-93) supported continued efforts towards the development of a National Missile Defense (NMD) system, as did – although reluctantly – the Clinton administration (1993-2001). In 1998, the Rumsfeld Commission reported that the missile threat from rogue states was much greater than previously conceived.[40] Shortly thereafter, North Korea tested a Taepodong-1 missile over Japan. This came as a surprise to most American analysts,[41] and generated the political pressure necessary for President Clinton to sign the National Missile Defense Act into law in 1999. Pressure was then exerted on American allies to support the project. Canada might have been expected to have been one of the first to come on board, given that the 1994 Defence White Paper had reversed Prime Minister Mulroney's 1985 "polite no" by reopening the possibility of official government participation in missile defence.[42]

Predictably, however, Ottawa hesitated and expressed reservations. At the summit level, this did not lead to any serious tensions in the relationship. By 1999, President Clinton and Prime Minister Chrétien had developed a friendly rapport. The Democrat and the Liberal had bonded golfing. Clinton even seemed content to allow Canada's foreign minister to pursue pulpit-style diplomacy fuelled by Canada's specialized international reputation.[43] Canada's waffling on missile defence, however, was not as easily overlooked by Vice Admiral Herbert Brown, the number two at the US Space Command, who openly questioned why the United States would bother to protect Canada from incoming ballistic missiles if it refused to participate in NMD.

Brown said he was "tired of asking" "if Canada can participate," and implied on 3 May 2000 that Canada should either be coerced into cooperation or cut off from protection. The next day, the US government tried to backtrack from Brown's comments. Richard Boucher, a spokesman for the US State Department, disavowed Brown's remarks, saying that they did not reflect the official policy of the government.[44] From the vice admiral's position at the Space Command, Canada was the beneficiary of American protection, and therefore did not have the right to decide whether it would or would not go along on matters the US deemed vital to continental security. Its consent was expected. Boucher's comment, however, suggested that the US had to demonstrate a degree of respect for Canadian sovereignty.

From his position at the State Department, unless the US wanted to take on a more formally imperial role in the continental system, Canada had to be given the option to consent to the American will. In response to Brown's remarks, Canadian Minister of National Defence Art Eggleton noted that he would not be "blackmailed" by American threats.[45]

The Pentagon was involved at this time in another arm-twisting campaign to get Canada on board with the American plan. US Deputy Secretary of Defense John Hamre was sent to Canada for public speaking engagements designed to generate support for NMD. Hamre warned Canadians that President Clinton might request them to "provide forward radar stations to warn of incoming missiles even if it means the scuppering of the 1972 ABM pact," and said that the "pivot point" of Canada-US relations was missile defence.[46] He told an audience in Calgary that he believed Canada needed to take the lead in "helping to communicate with the rest of the world why it is important to amend the ABM Treaty."[47] "If you want to defend the treaty, you help us modify it," said Hamre[48] in an effort to pressure Canada into performing a specialized role in service to the superordinate state.

Russia also attempted to create an opportunity for Canada to mediate the negotiations over the abrogation of the ABM Treaty. On a visit to Ottawa late in 2000, Russian leader Vladimir Putin stated that he was under the impression that "Canada believes it would be able to play the role of mediator between Russia and the United States."[49] Washington reacted with disbelief to the suggestion, and with that Chrétien's government immediately backed away from the possibility of any mediatory involvement in the abrogation of the treaty. This was a move of subordination reminiscent of Howard Green's retraction of his suggestion that Canada could play a mediating role in discussions between Havana and Washington in 1960.

Clinton left office in January 2001 after deciding not to deploy NMD due to a lack of confidence in the technology behind it. Nevertheless, the intense pressure that he had placed on Canada to support the missile shield helped cause a division in the Chrétien Cabinet, with the defence ministry openly endorsing Canadian participation and the foreign affairs ministry raising serious concerns about the potential fallout from tearing up the 1972 ABM Treaty. This division in Chrétien's Cabinet mirrored that of Mulroney's Cabinet during the negotiations regarding Canada's participation in Reagan's SDI. Arguably, this might be a reflection of organizational culture within the Canadian bureaucracy. Moving up a level to systems analysis, however, enables us to recognize why such contrasting organizational cultures build up within the subordinate state's bureaucracy. The ultimate concern of Canada's defence ministry is to maintain its end of the confidence bargain with the United States concerning continental security. The ultimate concern of Canada's foreign affairs ministry is to maintain Canada's specialized reputation in the broader international system. These structurally compelled imperatives are embedded in the organizational cultures of the bureaucratic departments responsible for meeting them.

The New American Century

Missile defence became a top priority again in January 2001, when the Republican administration of President George W. Bush took control of the White House. Officials during President Bush's first term consisted of a number of prominent members of the neoconservative movement in the United States who were "concerned with the decline in the strength of America's defenses, and in the problems this would create for the exercise of American leadership around the globe and, ultimately for the preservation of peace."[50] Developing and deploying global missile defences to protect the American homeland and act as a "secure basis for U.S. power projection around the world"[51] factored prominently in the neoconservative plan to rebuild America's defences for the "new American century."

Within a few months, the new president was publicly calling for Canadian participation in the missile shield project. In response, a senior member of the Chrétien government told the *National Post* that Canada would ultimately support the plan of the Bush administration, arguing that "the advantages of supporting the proposed NMD system far outweigh the disadvantages of opposing the United States. Opposing NMD would cost Canada jobs and hundreds of millions of dollars of high-technology contracts." "If we don't support NMD, it's the end of NORAD. NMD is the son of NORAD," the official said. "So we will play a role to try to safeguard the [1972] Anti-Ballistic Missile Treaty and work with our European allies on that, but, in the end, Canada will support the United States."[52] The official's statement was based on the familiar "defence against help"[53] logic, which assumes that if Canada is to maintain its symbolic sovereignty, it has to go along with major decisions that the US deemed critical to continental security. It was thus a sound speculation.

Prime Minister Chrétien also projected a supportive stance by praising the cuts the Bush administration pledged to make to its nuclear weapons programs as part of the plan to build the missile defence system. Along the same line, Minister of National Defence Eggleton appeared to lend support for the official American rationale for the system:

What I think has to be recognized is there is a proliferation of weapons of mass destruction in this world, and their delivery systems. And delivery systems that are being developed in North Korea could spread to other countries, to rogue regimes, and the kind of concerns that the United States has for this are understandable. So I think this has to be treated very seriously. By the same token we have to treat very seriously the impact that this will have on global security. It's not necessarily a negative one.[54]

Off the record, Chrétien's government felt pressure to support NMD for the sake of maintaining the confidence bargain that formed the basis of Canada's security relationship with the US. On the record, Ottawa attempted to put a positive spin on NMD's effect on global stability, and in so doing open the door for Canadian participation.

After the 11 September 2001 terror attacks, and after the Bush administration announced its new National Security Strategy based on the four pillars of pre-eminence, pre-emption, unilateralism, and the promotion of democracy,[55] the use of ballistic missile defence (BMD) to defend against conventional strikes using conventional weapons of mass destruction (albeit from rogue regimes and their terrorist clients) seemed unnecessary, if not obsolete. If the US was going on the offensive against the new asymmetrical terrorist threat, it would need missile defence only if it backtracked on its pre-emptive plans or if those plans failed. Failure to pre-empt or pre-emptive failures would leave the US homeland open to ICBM strikes from rogue states and their terrorist clients if these possessed such firepower. Only the US, Russia, and China had ICBM capability at the time, however. The rationale for the continued pursuit of BMD was therefore more expansive. According to the Missile Defense Agency, "the fundamental goal of the planned BMD system is to defend the forces and territories of the United States, its Allies, and friends as soon as practicable."[56]

BMD would be a layered system (land, sea, space) capable of countering all classes of ballistic missile threats. Shorter-range threats (such as from Scud missiles that rogue states possess) might not directly endanger US homeland security, but they could potentially endanger US troops engaged in pre-emptive actions abroad, or US allies. Expanding the US protective sphere through the deployment of an operational space-based BMD system, and compounding the strike capacity of US forces by making them invulnerable to missile strikes wherever they are on the planet, gives the system less of a defensive posture than an imperial one bent on extending the reach and thrust of American power beyond any previously conceived range.[57]

With this more expansive rationale for BMD coming into focus, and with the Bush administration still smarting after Canada's decision not to formally participate in 2003 invasion of Iraq, Prime Minister Chrétien put off a decision on Canada's role in missile defence as his MPs called for delay and DFAIT recognized that BMD could be a destabilizing force in the world. As Chrétien explained in the House of Commons on 7 May 2003: "We are having a debate. There might be some consultations with the Americans and it will take months before we are in a position to be obliged to make a decision."[58] He said this in an effort to quiet a developing rift in the Liberal caucus. Only twenty-two days later, however, the government announced that it would in fact open talks with the Bush administration regarding possible participation in the BMD system. After taking this tentative step,

Chrétien left office without making a final decision on Canada's role in the missile shield project – leaving doubts as to whether he ever intended to make a firm decision on BMD. Regardless, it is clear that under his leadership, Canada, in the case of BMD, was no more immune to the contrasting structural pressures of hierarchy in anarchy. Known for his decisiveness and shrewd political skills, Chrétien struggled with the BMD decision as Mulroney did before him, and Paul Martin would after him.

Episode III

Once Prime Minister Paul Martin's team took over in January 2004, his defence minister, David Pratt – determined to overcome the difficulties that had plagued his predecessors on this issue – quickly sent a letter to his counterpart in Washington, Donald Rumsfeld, that contained the following emphasis on missile defence cooperation through NORAD:

> A key focus of our cooperation in missile defence should be through NORAD, which has served us well since 1958. NORAD's long-standing global threat warning and attack assessment role can make an important contribution to the execution of the missile defence mission. We believe that our two nations should move on an expedited basis to amend the NORAD agreement to take into account NORAD's contribution to the missile defence mission.[59]

Rumsfeld replied briefly, agreeing that after over fifty years of defence cooperation, "we should seek to expand our cooperation in the area of missile defense."[60] Talks between the two governments followed, and by the summer of 2004 NORAD had been amended to make "its missile warning function – a role it has been performing for the last 30 years – available to the U.S. commands conducting ballistic missile defence."[61] Minister of Foreign Affairs Pierre Pettigrew and Minister of National Defence Bill Graham emphasized that "this amendment safeguards and sustains NORAD regardless of what decision the government of Canada eventually takes on ballistic missile defence."[62] Despite its initial enthusiasm, Martin's government preferred to take this incremental step towards participation in missile defence.

In mid-February 2004, however, the Department of National Defence (DND) divulged plans to participate in testing the shield. It issued tentative contracts worth $700,000 to test "Canadian radar technology in U.S.-run trials of the missile shield this summer," reported Tom Blackwell of the *National Post*. Stephen Staples, a defence researcher at the Polaris Institute in Ottawa, said that the contracts take "Canada into the missile defense program before any decision by the government and any proper debate."[63] Despite this move by DND to force the issue, Ottawa was still hedging on a formal decision almost a year later.

In large part, this had to do with the fact that Canadian participation in Bush's BMD plan had become a source of considerable difficulty for Martin's minority government. Support for missile defence would align Canada with what was widely seen after the 2002 US abrogation of the 1972 ABM Treaty as a destabilizing US foreign policy. As a result, such support could harm Canada's specialized reputation in the broader international community. The prospect of an invincible America, combined with the corrosive effect the pursuit of this lofty goal had on the legal fabric of international society, put missile defence at odds with Canada's interests in a multilateral managed, arms-controlled, anti-nuclear international system. Moreover, a small majority (52 percent) of Canadians felt "passionately" (according to Donna Dasko of the polling firm Environics) that the country should not participate in NMD. In Quebec, the majority was larger: 65 percent were opposed, making the issue one that could have potentially fuelled support for the sovereigntist movement. Sixty-six percent of Newfoundlanders, on the other hand, supported Canadian participation, as did majorities in Atlantic Canada and Alberta.[64]

Like Canada, the US was pushed and pulled in different directions by the contrasting structural environments that came into play on the issue of missile defence. Accordingly, both states agreed to leave the issue off the table during President Bush's visit to Canada in December 2004. Bush, however, could not resist raising the issue at press conferences in both Ottawa and Halifax. Bush urged Canada to join the US in building the missile shield that would defend both countries from potential harm. US ambassador to Canada Paul Cellucci recollected informing Bush, after he did so the first time, of the paradoxical implications of what he had just said, by telling him that "we are now a lot further away than we were five minutes ago."[65]

In a private meeting, Bush allegedly took a more aggressive tone with Martin, leaning across a table and saying: "I'm not taking this position, but some future president is going to say: Why are we paying to defend Canada?" Martin apparently tried to explain the domestic politics constraining him, but Bush interjected, waving his hands and saying, "I don't understand this. Are you saying that if you got up and said this was necessary for the defense of Canada, it wouldn't be accepted?"[66] After the *Washington Post* made this story public, however, a State Department spokesman named Terry Breese tried to play it down, stating that the reporter's account was inaccurate, and that Bush had not been nearly as aggressive as the article had suggested.

One month later, Ambassador Cellucci, on 10 January 2005, told reporters that based on discussions he had had with Canadian government officials, he expected Canada to take part in the missile defence shield.[67] Just over a month after that, however, Martin instructed Pierre Pettigrew to whisper a very different story in the ear of Secretary of State Condoleezza Rice at the

NATO summit in Brussels. In a move of self-assertion, Pettigrew explained to Rice that Canada would not be formally participating in missile defence. In a simultaneous countermove of subordination, however, he explained that the upcoming budget contained $12.8 billion for the military over five years. The idea was to say no to missile defence while at the same time saying yes to a commitment to defend North America. The hike in military spending, Pettigrew explained to Rice, was Canada's largest in twenty years. Meanwhile, the Canadian public was still in the dark about where Canada stood on missile defence.

At the same time that Pettigrew was quietly breaking the bad news to the Americans, Frank McKenna, on his way to Washington to become Canada's ambassador to the United States, told reporters inquiring about his country's role in missile defence that "we're part of it now."[68] McKenna suggested that the NORAD amendment had made more formal participation in the project largely a matter of symbolism. For all practical purposes, Canada was already participating in missile defence. Hours later, the story that Martin was going to reject missile defence was leaked to Radio-Canada. During Question Period in the House of Commons that day, the opposition blasted the Liberal minority government for the contradictory messages it had sent about Canada's role in the missile shield. Opposition MPs accused the government of trying to be "halfway in and halfway out" of the US program. Leader of the Opposition Stephen Harper, less colourfully than Chrétien in 1985, stated that "the government has managed to announce it is in missile defence and not in missile defence in the very same week."[69]

The next day, Martin publicly clarified that Canada would not formally endorse or participate in the missile shield. According to David Rudd, Martin's no was delivered in "a solicitous, almost apologetic fashion. He was careful not to begrudge the United States its right to defend itself, nor did he reject the rationale behind the defence system. This is very significant, in that he conceded the day to BMD-phobic liberals without explicitly endorsing their view that missile defence is a dangerous pursuit – one from which Canada should dissociate itself in thought, word, and deed."[70] Martin's missile defence decision was widely regarded as a reversal of course brought on by domestic politics alone. With a minority in the House, and a possible rebellion in the Liberal Women's and Quebec caucuses, the issue had put the future of the Liberal minority government in jeopardy. That said, it was not long before Pierre Pettigrew was echoing Brian Mulroney in advancing the argument that he would be "very pleased," and in fact saw no contradiction, with Canadian aerospace firms bidding on missile defence contracts.

The politeness of the "no" aside, the Americans were perplexed by the decision. Ambassador Cellucci said: "We simply cannot understand why Canada would in effect give up its sovereignty – its seat at the table – to decide what to do about a missile that might be coming toward Canada. We will deploy. We will defend North America."[71] Participation in BMD means nothing more than that Canada would take part in the decision-making response in the event a missile were ever detected heading towards North America. Without Canadian participation, Cellucci noted, "the United States will make the decision."[72] The *Washington Post* deemed the move a "blunt rebuff to President Bush, who had personally lobbied Canada to join."[73] Dwight N. Mason of the Center for Strategic and International Studies in Washington, DC, wrote: "The decision to opt out of missile defense is an abandonment of some Canadian sovereignty. Canada has put the United States in the position of having to decide independently how to defend North America including Canada from missiles and whether to do so in specific instances."[74] Clearly, the contradiction was not lost on the Americans that Canada's decision to exercise its sovereign right to break ranks with the US had, ultimately, resulted in a loss of its sovereignty.

The decision was indeed puzzling for two reasons. First, Prime Minister Martin had come into power enthusiastic about finally resolving what had been a lingering problem in Canada-US relations. Ever the frugal finance minister, Martin wanted to bring Canada on board with missile defence because: (1) it would not have cost the country a dime; (2) it would have gone some way towards repairing the damage that had been caused to the Canada-US relationship by the decision of the Chrétien government to refrain from symbolically joining the Coalition of the Willing in Iraq; and (3) it would have ensured the continued relevance of NORAD and, accordingly, Canada's voice in continental air defence. Once Martin predictably started to waver, both DND and the Department of Foreign Affairs and International Trade (DFAIT), to varying degrees, became adamant that Canada could not afford to slap the White House in the face on another issue deemed vital to American security. That both DND and DFAIT officials were advising Martin to say yes to missile defence is the second reason his eventual "no" was puzzling. Typically, as we have seen in both the early sections of this chapter and in Chapter 4, on an issue of this nature, DND and DFAIT would be compelled by the opposing structural pressures of hierarchy and anarchy to provide conflicting policy advice to the prime minister. In this case, however, both were nearly desperate not to further damage the relationship with Washington. One of Martin's advisers reflected that "there was a hangover from the Iraq decision that gave a hysterical tone to all the advice that was coming to us. It boiled down to – 'You must do this, for God's sake, or you will alienate the White House.'"[75]

When Martin finally decided not to do what he was being advised to do, the reaction from the White House was anything but as catastrophic as DND and DFAIT officials had predicted. As Janice Stein and Eugene Lang narrate, Defence Minister Bill Graham was instructed to phone Donald Rumsfeld three days after Frank McKenna and Pierre Pettigrew had simultaneously, in different venues, given contradictory answers to the missile defence question. The call was intended to clarify the still ambiguous record. Instead of Rumsfeld, Deputy Secretary of Defense Paul Wolfowitz answered and politely received Graham's news that Canada would not participate in BMD. Wolfowitz apparently conveyed in the most respectful of ways the message that the United States did not "give a damn."[76] He did not imply that there would be consequences for the special relationship, or that the US intended to retaliate in any way, shape, or form. Although perhaps remarkable, this outcome cannot be seen as unprecedented, or even unpredictable, as the Reagan White House reacted in a similar way when Mulroney declined with his "polite no" to participate in SDI.

Paradoxically, according to Stein and Lang, and as we shall see in the following chapter, "despite the evidence that the Canada-U.S. relationship had suffered little or no damage because of Canada's decision not to participate in BMD, the foreign policy and defence establishment in Ottawa felt a renewed sense of urgency to do something significant to offset the negative consequences that they feared. Afghanistan seemed a logical place to start."[77] Indeed, compelled by the structural pressures of the continental hierarchy, Canada would find itself unexpectedly fighting a bloody counterinsurgency war in the dangerous south of Afghanistan largely to compensate for this decision to say no to missile defence.

In the exchanges between the Reagan and Mulroney governments over Canada's participation in SDI, and in the eerily similar repetitions of these moves and countermoves by the US and Canada under Clinton and Chrétien, and again under Bush and Martin, the contrasting structural forces of hierarchy in anarchy are evident across the twenty-five-year time span of this case study. In three separate instances, these paradoxical sequences led to contradictory policy outcomes for both states. This chapter also illuminates evidence in support of the hypothesis regarding Canada's specialized behaviour in the international system. As an advocate for nuclear nonproliferation and disarmament and arms control, Canada repeatedly played a specialized role in opposition to the American missile shield. This, of course, made its participation in the unilateral American pursuit of invincibility challenging, and exacerbated the paradoxical patterns of interaction between Canada and the US throughout the period in question.

This issue between Canada and the US does not appear to have been fully resolved. In its October 2006 interim report entitled *Managing Turmoil*, the Standing Senate Committee on National Security and Defence recommended, among other things, that Canada "enter into discussions with the U.S. Government with the aim of participating in the Ballistic Missile Defence program."[78] Coming on the heels of North Korea's (failed) test of a long-range Taepodong-2 missile, and just before North Korea's first-ever (successful) nuclear test, the report's recommendation suggests that there might be (at least at some point) a reinvigoration of this long-standing debate in Canada over possible participation in the US missile defence program. This chapter suggests that the puzzle of how to square Canada's obligations to the United States as a reliable partner in continental security with its obligations to the international community as a helpful contributor to the cause of peace and stability will confront any future Canadian government faced with an invitation to participate in BMD. This is not, in other words, strictly an issue of domestic politics, nor is the impulse to refrain from participation "based more on emotions than a rational analysis of BMD's potential benefits to Canada,"[79] as the Senate committee's October 2006 report argued.

6
The War on Terror, 2001-9

In the aftermath of the 11 September 2001 terrorist attacks on New York City and Washington, DC, a sense of solidarity and resolve settled in across Western countries. Political leaders denounced the attacks as savage assaults on democracy and freedom, while their peoples mourned the loss and anticipated with anxiety what the future would hold in such a changed world. President George W. Bush immediately vowed a "War on Terror," and punishment for the forces of evil that had harmed his country. His NATO allies stood behind him and invoked the collective defence clause for the first time in that organization's history. This was done on Canada's suggestion, and can be taken as further evidence of the country's propensity for the specialized work of problem-solving in the international system.

"An attack on one is an attack on all" is how NATO Secretary General Lord Robertson characterized the unprecedented move of the nineteen-member alliance. Canadians themselves expressed deeply felt sympathy and compassion for their American neighbours. Vigils were held across the country, and a memorial service in Ottawa on 14 September 2001 was attended by over 100,000 people. Money was raised, the American flag was flown, and Canadian blood was given in dramatic displays of solidarity across the country.[1] In an address to a special session of Parliament on 17 September 2001, Minister of Foreign Affairs John Manley spoke of Canada's sorrow, its sympathy, its solidarity with the United States, and its resolve to respond to the crisis by following the "path of multilateralism"[2] through the United Nations and the Group of Eight (G8). Canada was scheduled to assume the presidency of the G8 in 2002.

The possibility that the US would turn the other cheek and not retaliate was never seriously contemplated. Indeed, President Bush's first words to Vice President Dick Cheney on the morning of 11 September were: "Sounds like we have a minor war going on here, I heard about the Pentagon. We're at war ... somebody's going to pay."[3] Within a day, it was clear that Osama bin Laden's Islamic terrorist network, al-Qaeda, was behind the attacks on

New York and Washington. Bin Laden's group had ties to the Islamic dictatorship in Afghanistan, known as the Taliban. The Taliban had allowed bin
Laden and al-Qaeda to establish training camps in the south of that country,
near the border with Pakistan. The Clinton administration had attempted
to eliminate bin Laden and his henchmen in 1998 with a series of cruise
missile strikes. On 14 September 2001, the Bush administration vowed to
continue the effort to dismantle al-Qaeda. Secretary of State Colin Powell
indicated that once evidence had been gathered and demonstrated to the
world that indeed al-Qaeda had been behind the 9/11 attacks, "we will go
after that group, that network, and those who have harbored, supported
and aided that network, to rip the network up. When we're through with
that network, we will continue with a global assault against terrorism in
general."[4] That same day, President Bush sent a stark message to the rest of
the world: in the new strategic environment brought on by the attacks
against his country, other states were either on the side of the United States
or on the side of the terrorists. There would be no middle path.

In this new, emerging strategic environment, Canada could have been
expected to stand unequivocally in solidarity with the United States. Twenty-
four Canadians had, after all, lost their lives in the collapse of the World
Trade Center towers in New York that fateful morning. A Canadian, Major
General Rick Findlay, was at the helm of NORAD as the organization
scrambled to figure out how to deal with a situation it was neither designed
nor prepared for. And Canadians themselves helped to house the 33,000
passengers of the 224 commercial planes that had been diverted to airport
runways from Goose Bay to Vancouver. Surely, no middle path would be
deemed necessary by a country so closely tied to the US and so directly affected by the terrorist attacks. Indeed, Prime Minister Jean Chrétien stated
that Canada would stand "shoulder to shoulder" with the US, while Foreign
Affairs Minister Manley declared that Canada was indeed "at war with terrorism" within days of 9/11. Yet Canada's involvement in the War on Terror
to date has followed the patterns predicted by structural specialization theory.
Paradoxical exchanges between Canada and the US led to contradictory
policy outcomes for both states. True to form, Canada on a couple of minor
occasions sought out specialized roles in the War on Terror. Importantly,
however, this chapter demonstrates the dangers that emerge when the
country fails to both cultivate and continually pursue a strategy of specialization in the international system.

Afghanistan? "Yes." But ...

After giving the Taliban an ultimatum to surrender bin Laden or share the
fate of his al-Qaeda network, the Bush administration ordered the first wave
of air strikes against specified targets in Afghanistan on 7 October 2001.
Within days, American and British Tomahawk cruise missiles pounded most

of al-Qaeda's terrorist training camps and the Taliban's strongholds in Kabul, Jalalabad, and Kandahar. Cluster bombing of the Taliban's defences continued until the end of the month. Fifteen-thousand-pound Daisy Cutter bombs were also used during this period as a way to demoralize the Taliban with the sheer size and deafening sound of US firepower.

The Daisy Cutters had their intended effect. By early November, US Special Forces and their Afghan Northern Alliance counterparts, a disparate group united only in the aim of ridding Afghanistan of the Taliban, were ready to topple the capital, Kabul. This they did on 7 November, and within twenty-four hours all other Afghan provinces had fallen like dominos, as large numbers of Taliban fighters surrendered, fled, or were captured by the American-led coalition forces. One month later, the remaining Taliban stronghold of Kandahar was left to Northern Alliance forces by Mullah Omar as he escaped into the mountains of Uruzgan province with a band of his fighters in a convoy of motorcycles. The focus of the fighting then turned to the Tora Bora mountains, where residual al-Qaeda forces were still putting up resistance, and where bin Laden and other al-Qaeda leaders were believed to be hiding in caves. Amid intense US bombing, bin Laden escaped from Tora Bora, probably into the tribal regions of Pakistan through the White Mountain range. Despite this mishap, by 22 December Afghanistan had been sufficiently cleared of the Taliban and al-Qaeda that an interim government led by Hamid Karzai, an Afghan tribal leader, could be established.

At a NATO conference held hours before the first air strikes against Afghanistan commenced, Canada was accused by Bruce George, head of the British Parliament's defence committee, of "not pulling its weight" in the alliance. Also that day, a US Congressman appeared on CTV's *Question Period* to say that Canada's lack of defence spending over the past two decades was a concern to "all of the NATO members."[5] The day after the strikes against Afghanistan commenced, Minister of National Defence Art Eggleton announced that Canada would send a third of its naval fleet to the Persian Gulf to assist in the US-led campaign. Canada's elite Joint Task Force 2 (JTF2) commando unit would also depart for Afghanistan and the surrounding area to play an uncertain role in the War on Terror, and 200 Canadian soldiers on exchange with British and American forces would also be cleared to participate in the action.

The deployment was criticized by some as being the equivalent of bringing a knife to a gunfight given that Afghanistan is a landlocked country, but the gesture was a significant one as Canada's troop contributions to Operation Enduring Freedom outweighed that of any other member of the international coalition in Afghanistan after the US and Britain. Defence analysts also pointed out that this was an irresponsible act on the part of the government – to send such a large contingent of the Canadian Forces to the other side of the world after cutting military spending to the bone for decades.[6] The

Canadian troops would be deployed under the auspices of the UN Charter's self-defence provision as well as under Article 5 of NATO – the organization's collective self-defence provision – in response to a direct request made by President Bush to Prime Minister Chrétien on 5 October 2001.

After a month-long 8,000-mile passage, the Canadian Naval Task Group – a destroyer, three frigates, a supply ship, and their *Sea King* air detachments – arrived in the area of operations off the coast of Pakistan on 26 November 2001, almost two months after the start of Operation Enduring Freedom. The US Navy welcomed the Canadians by immediately putting them to work in an interoperable role. Commodore Drew Robertson was appointed Amphibious Support Force Defence Commander, and assigned responsibility for protecting a US Marine Expeditionary Unit engaged in operations close to the twelve-mile limit of Pakistani territorial waters. The main threats to this Amphibious Ready Group that Commodore Robertson and his ships were to protect against were of the new terrorist genre: commercial airplanes used as missiles, fishing vessels packed with explosives, crop dusters filled with deadly chemical or biological agents, and so on.

The task group performed other operations during its tour in the Persian Gulf, including escort of coalition replenishment vessels through the Strait of Hormuz; surveillance of anchored ships in the Gulf of Oman; integration with US Navy carrier battle groups; logistics resupply (the supply ship HMCS *Preserver* carried out over 100 replenishments of coalition vessels); and backfill of higher-capability units dispatched on other tasks.[7]

The task group's role in the Arabian Sea during Operation Apollo – Canada's contribution to the US-led military assault on Afghanistan – was primarily a supporting one. The Canadians, however, also conducted a large number of boarding operations designed to capture al-Qaeda and Taliban leaders as they attempted to flee the region from the port of Jask in Iran on various types of vessels. Most of these were routine and amounted to little action for the Canadians. On one occasion in mid-July 2002, however, HMCS *Algonquin* engaged in a high-speed chase of three "go fasts" – overpowered eight-metre boats – containing illegal migrants (two of whom were suspected al-Qaeda members). Heavily armed Canadians lowered their own high-speed boat from the deck of *Algonquin,* and tracked down and boarded the vessel containing the two suspects. They separated the frantic pair from the rest of the illegal migrants and escorted them back to *Algonquin* at gunpoint. After a night under Canadian armed guard, the al-Qaeda suspects were turned over to US naval forces.[8]

During this time, JTF2 commandos were on the ground in Afghanistan, fighting in units composed primarily of American Special Forces members. The Special Forces units were entirely under American command and control. Initially, the Canadian government refused to discuss the JTF2 and its role in Operation Enduring Freedom, but Minister Eggleton eventually reversed this position and disclosed that indeed the JTF2 was on the ground in Afghanistan, playing a leading part in Canada's contribution to the War on Terror. Although the JTF2 efforts were shrouded in secrecy, it came to light that between forty and fifty of the elite commandos were integrated into American Special Forces units carrying out operations near Kandahar. The operations involved driving around in pickup trucks with Americans and an Afghani translator, hunting the Taliban and al-Qaeda through villages and homes, capturing them, and then transporting them to the Kandahar airport – the primary US base of operations – under cover of darkness, to be held and interrogated.[9]

On 20 January 2002, JTF2 commandos captured a group of suspected Afghan terrorists and handed them over to the US military. Deputy Chief of the Defence Staff Vice Admiral Greg Maddison briefed Eggleton on the matter the following day. The briefing apparently did not register with Eggleton, as he failed to report the incident to the prime minister, who, one week later, when asked what Canadian troops would do with captured al-Qaeda or Taliban operatives, indicated that any answer he gave would be purely hypothetical as Canadian troops had yet to take any prisoners. The following day, Eggleton informed Chrétien and the Cabinet about the JTF2's actions, and informed the House of Commons that he learned about them on 25 January. Following this statement, Maddison and Chief of the Defence Staff General Raymond Henault explained to Eggleton that he had just misled Parliament. The following day, Eggleton explained to the House that he had actually learned of the JTF2's transfer of the prisoners on 21 January. This caused the usual hyperbolic outrage on the opposition benches as NDP, Bloc Québécois, and Conservative members called for Eggleton's resignation. The Liberals opened a four-week inquiry into Eggleton's misstep, which in the end amounted to nothing.

Although Ottawa appeared hesitant to admit it at the time, it was clear that Canada was at war against the Taliban in Afghanistan. This reality caused some prominent Canadians to voice concerns that the country's specialized roles in the international system were being sacrificed as a result. Janice Gross Stein of the University of Toronto's Munk Centre for International Studies argued that "Canada has not been speaking with its traditional voice." Putting "our highly trained and skilled ground forces in harm's way to protect civilians in war is where we can make a difference."[10] Lloyd Axworthy was similarly uneasy with Canada's combat role. He maintained that Ottawa should pursue a uniquely Canadian strategy, one that would work through the channels of multilateralism to "tighten the screws on the terrorists."[11] The responses of Stein and Axworthy, according to analyst Grant Dawson, clearly "reflected the preference of some Canadians for honest-broker diplomacy and norm-building, and their unease with the use of force and close military collaboration with the U.S."[12] Indeed, they reflected the recognition that in taking on a role that was not particularly suited to Canada, Ottawa was acting neither in the national interest nor in the interests of the broader international community. It was, in other words, setting itself on a course for failure that could affect the country in terms of both its international reputation and its internal coherence. Even US ambassador to Canada Paul Cellucci appeared to agree. In answer to a question about the potential role Canada might play in the War on Terror, the ambassador commented, "Maybe one of the contributions that will be long-lasting will be the ability of Canada to continue to do these peacekeeping missions. Because we're probably not going to be in a position to do as much as we have been doing."[13]

Continuing with this apparent departure from Canada's specialization in the international system, Eggleton announced on 7 January 2002 another Canadian deployment in support of the coalition effort in Afghanistan. The deployment included two infantry companies of the 3rd Battalion of the Princess Patricia's Canadian Light Infantry; one reconnaissance squadron from Lord Strathcona's Horse (complete with twelve Canadian-made Coyote reconnaissance vehicles specially requested by the United States); and a logistics group from 1 Service Battalion. In total, 750 members of the Canadian Forces – all out of Edmonton – would be sent to Kandahar as part of Operation Apollo.[14] Specifically, their mission was to engage in offensive combat operations designed to destroy the remnants of the Taliban and al-Qaeda in the dangerous southern region of Afghanistan. Moreover, they were to perform security, site exploration (such as abandoned al-Qaeda camps), and de-mining tasks. All of these efforts were to be under the daily operational control of the US forces.

The decision to have the Canadian Forces fight for the United States in this dangerous counterinsurgency role was not made in a linear, rational manner. In mid-November 2001, the wheels began to turn on a second significant Canadian contribution to the war in Afghanistan. A 1,000-member stabilization force would be placed on the ground to help with the provision of aid and secure transport routes. Within a few days of the troops in Edmonton and Winnipeg being placed on forty-eight-hour standby, however, the deployment was called into question. Prime Minister Chrétien stated on 20 November that "the principal role that we hope they will have if, whenever and if they go there – because there is no final conclusion – will be to make sure [aid gets] to the people who need it." "Of course, we don't want to have a big fight there. We want to bring peace and happiness as much as possible,"[15] Chrétien continued. Eggleton explained that "obviously we are not going to send our people into a condition in which they are unwelcome."[16] And if the fighting got too intense, Eggleton said, he would pull the troops out. Regardless, it became clear that the Northern Alliance was wary of having too many foreign troops on its soil, even for stabilization purposes, so the mission was held up and eventually cancelled altogether.

Further plans to send 1,000 troops as part of the then British-led International Security Assistance Force (ISAF) developed throughout the month of December. European countries, however, decided to use the mission as a way of building solidarity through collaborative foreign engagement, and Canada was asked to provide only minor support. Ottawa ultimately rejected the offer in favour of the more dangerous and less specialized combat role. The decision led columnist Marcus Gee to write a scathing article attempting to expose the "myth" of "Canada's peacekeeper image." The *Toronto Sun* wondered, "Where's Canada?" in a front-page headline above a photograph of other countries' soldiers in Kabul.[17] The *Globe and Mail* printed the front-page headline "Canada Shuns Minor Peace Role" to demonstrate its discontent with the decision.[18] But while Canada's reputation as a "peacekeeper" specializing in the role of postconflict mediation/supervision may have still appeared significant at home, abroad that reputation had waned considerably to that point. Since 1997, Canada has reduced its peacekeeping operations a hundredfold: whereas throughout the history of peacekeeping Canada had contributed an average of about 10 percent of the UN's forces, it currently provides only 0.1 percent.[19] It should not have come as a surprise, then, that Canada found that it could be replaced in one of its cultivated specializations by the up-and-coming European Union forces.

At the same time that the decision was made not to go to Kabul with the Europeans, requests came from the Americans for Canadian ground troops to fight with US soldiers in the southern province of Kandahar. Thinking that Canada needed to demonstrate a greater degree of support for the American efforts in Afghanistan, Ottawa quickly assented to the request, initiating the first deployment of Canadian ground troops for combat since the Korean War and making a decisive break with the country's (however mythologized) peacekeeping tradition.[20]

Detainees

The fact that the Canadian Forces went to Afghanistan to fight under American command became an issue in Canada almost immediately. Opposition MPs and informed members of the public voiced concern over how Canadian soldiers would treat members of the Taliban and al-Qaeda they might capture. The US had decided that these individuals – because they were not fighting for a legitimate international regime – were not covered by the Geneva Convention Relative to the Treatment of Prisoners of War (1949). They could therefore be transported to the US prison facility at Guantanamo Bay, Cuba, to be held and interrogated for indeterminate periods. Once there, they might undergo physical and psychological treatment that would otherwise be illegal under international law.[21] By early 2002, America's treatment of its detainees had come under heavy moral scrutiny in Canada and throughout the international community. Were Canadian troops to participate in the apprehension of such alleged Islamic terrorists, and to hand them over to the Americans (as it was compulsory for them to do, given the rules of Canadian engagement in Afghanistan), the country's international image as an agent of stability and peace might be severely tarnished. Of course, Canadian sailors and JTF2 commandos had already captured and turned over such suspected terrorists to the US military. The Canadian Forces would have to continue to do so throughout their deployment to Kandahar, according to the rules of engagement. Controversy over the proper handling of detainees would continue to plague Canada's involvement in Afghanistan for many years to come.

The Four Pats

On 17 April 2002, four Canadian soldiers were killed and eight others were seriously injured by American friendly fire while conducting an exercise fourteen kilometres south of their base near Kandahar. Sergeant Marc Leger, 29, of Lancaster, Ontario; Corporal Ainsworth Dyer, 25, of Montreal; Private Richard Green, 22, of Mill Cove, Nova Scotia; and Private Nathan Smith, 27, of Tatamagouche, Nova Scotia, were part of the 3rd Battalion of the Princess Patricia's Canadian Light Infantry out of Edmonton. They were the first Canadians in fifty years to die in combat operations. The next day, the story exploded onto the front pages of the major North American newspapers, and all across Canada the soldiers' deaths were mourned.

The mourning mixed with outrage as Canadians learned more about the so-called friendly-fire incident, which significantly cooled public enthusiasm for the Canadian role in Afghanistan. Canadian commanders had given American brigade commanders detailed notification that the Princess Patricia's would be engaged in live-fire night exercises in a US-designated training area called Tarnak Farms. All of the necessary precautions had been taken to ensure the safety of the troops taking part in the ground-to-ground shooting practice. And yet when two F-16 Fighting Falcon fighter pilots flying at 6,400 feet radioed to command that they were taking fire from the ground in that area, they were given permission to go back and mark the target. Pumped up on amphetamines ("go pills") dispensed by the US Air Force, and thinking that they were taking fire for a second time as they passed over to mark the target, Major Harry Schmidt (nicknamed "Psycho") decided that his air partner, Major William Umbach, was under fire and that it was therefore necessary to drop a laser-guided 500-pound bomb on the training area in what he claimed was self-defence – after being told three times to hold his fire.

In Canada, public opinion on the country's role in Afghanistan and in the War on Terror continued to shift. Canadians were upset that President Bush did not make a single comment about the tragedy during his five public appearances the following day. His excuse was that he had, after all, telephoned Prime Minister Chrétien to offer condolences. Apparently, the incident was not worthy of a public statement of regret. Canadians felt disrespected. Less than a week after the incident, 85 percent of Canadians believed that the federal government should demand that the US government pay compensation to the four families who had lost their sons. Forty-five percent of Quebecers polled opposed Canada's continued involvement in the war, as did 33 percent of British Columbians.[22] The deaths of the four "Pats" was voted the top news story of 2002 by the Canadian Press. As Peter Haggert, the managing editor of the Saint John, New Brunswick, *Telegraph-Journal,* said, the deaths of the Canadian soldiers "was truly a shot heard across the country ... this was really the first time one or two generations felt the collective grief of losing Canadian combatants on a world stage."[23] Indeed, the event drove home the reality of Canada's participation in the War on Terror and called it into question, as many started to wonder whether Canada should have stuck with its specialized mediation/supervision role. One month later, Defence Minister Eggleton announced that the Canadian combat troops would be pulled out of Afghanistan at the end of July. This announcement was made without any plan in place for Canada's future involvement in that troubled country.[24] Despite this lack of strategic outlook, and despite repeated calls from officials at National Defence Headquarters for a regenerative pause in Canadian Forces operations, it would not be long before new orders were drawn up for a major deployment of Canadian soldiers to Afghanistan.

The detainee controversy and the deaths of the four "Pats" were early warning signs that Ottawa's failure to define a more specialized contribution to the War on Terror would cost the country in terms of its reputation abroad and its cohesiveness at home.

The War on Iraq? "No." But ...
The unanimous passage of UN Security Council Resolution 1441 on 8 November 2002 gave Saddam Hussein's Baathist dictatorial regime thirty days to disarm his weapons of mass destruction or face, as President Bush put it to the Security Council, "the severest of consequences."[25] The passage of the resolution initiated UN weapons inspections, during which time Iraq was to make a full disclosure of all its weapons programs. Any evidence of omissions or falsities turned up by the UN teams headed by Dr. Hans Blix would have constituted a material breach of the disarmament obligations imposed on Iraq after the Gulf War of 1990-91, and opened the door for serious consequences to be inflicted on Saddam's regime.

Within a week, US Secretary of State Colin Powell was in Ottawa to speak with Defence Minister Bill Graham. The purpose of the meeting was to request Canada's participation in a "like-minded coalition" if force proved the only means of dealing with the Iraq threat.[26] A specific request for a military contribution of naval frigates, reconnaissance vehicles, and JTF2 special forces followed shortly thereafter, but was met with hesitation on Ottawa's part. The request was not immediately assented to; in turn, Canada was cut out of preparations for the war by the US military. Quickly, however, the Canadian government clarified its stand and found itself deeply involved in contingency planning for a possible role for Canada in the impending invasion of Iraq.[27]

On 5 February 2003, Powell, in a globally televised address to the UN Security Council, reiterated the need for the international body to take action against Iraq or risk fading into irrelevance. With charts, maps, and classified audiotapes, he presented evidence that Iraq continued to violate the disarmament obligations it had been violating for twelve years, even after the passage of Resolution 1441, which gave it one final chance to comply. Because of this, any intervention in Iraq by the US would be *implicitly* justified within the UN's multilateral framework, and would therefore not be an act of US unilateralism.[28] Powell demonstrated further that Iraq was harbouring a network of al-Qaeda operatives led by Abu Musab al-Zarqawi, and reminded the Security Council of the sickening human rights abuses that Saddam's regime had perpetrated on its own people in an effort to stay in power.[29] The Security Council had a choice to make: authorize military action against Iraq, or continue to stand by and watch Saddam's dictatorial regime flout its will.

Despite Powell's demonstration of Iraq's attempts to evade and deceive UN weapons inspectors, the foreign ministers of France and Germany, together with their Chinese and Russian counterparts, called for an extension and strengthening of the UN weapons inspection program. Bill Graham, who had been given a "foretaste" of what one Canadian official deemed nothing more than a "PowerPoint slide show" was, according to academic Donald Barry, "not convinced."[30] Justified in their skepticism by future revelations that much of what Powell presented to the Security Council was based on poorly gathered and recklessly cobbled together intelligence,[31] the demands of Germany and France deadlocked the Security Council and sent the United States and the United Kingdom to work on a second UN resolution designed to give an even more explicit ultimatum to Iraq. This was done in an effort to solicit maximum Security Council support for an attack on Iraq. The second resolution was proposed in draft form by the two countries on 25 February, and co-sponsored by Spain. It included a final deadline of 17 March 2003 for Iraqi compliance. France, Germany, Russia, and China, however, remained united in opposition to military action against Iraq without *explicit* UN sanction and without giving UN weapons inspectors more time to complete their work. This opposition made the passage of the follow-up resolution to 1441 impossible.

It appeared that a US-led war on Iraq would go forward without the explicit backing of the Security Council, and the US had made it clear that if this were to happen, Canada would still be asked for military support.[32] This led Canadians to debate the question of whether or not the country should follow the US into battle for the second time in the new millennium. During these tense weeks, Canadian public opposition to the war became evident, as tens of thousands spent their weekends on cold city streets from Vancouver to Halifax taking part in antiwar demonstrations. In a poll taken in the first week of March, 83 percent of Canadians said they would be opposed to Canadian participation in a war that did not have UN sanction. This opposition was especially significant in Quebec, as Premier Bernard Landry's Parti Québécois appeared poised to win another provincial election, and another victory for the sovereigntist movement. In France, Germany, and Australia, opposition to such a war was equally vehement.[33] France's opposition bolstered Quebec's opposition, and seemed to cement in that province the feeling that the US had taken a radical turn with its "you're either with us or against us" doctrine of unilateral pre-emptive war.

With domestic public opinion pushing him one way and the will of the superordinate state pushing him the other, Chrétien was forced to search for a middle path. It is likely that this search was at the heart of a profoundly confused and paradoxical series of statements regarding the government's position on the war from the fall of 2002 until March 2003. As Andrew Richter has written, "throughout this period, the Canadian government's position was poorly articulated and inconsistently applied, some days indicating support for the U.S. while on other days suggesting the opposite."[34] Such a pattern should be familiar to readers by this point. Far from anomalous, this pattern of paradox is rather the norm in high political situations in which Canada confronts the contrasting pressures of the continental hierarchy and the international anarchy.

Buying some time to figure out a strategy, the prime minister eventually insisted in late January that the UN sanction any attack on Iraq, and that no further determination of Canada's policy could be made until at least such time as the UN weapons inspectors' report was presented to the Security Council on 14 February. Following this, a deal was made between Ottawa and Washington to put a Canadian commodore in command of a multinational task force of approximately twenty warships from at least five different navies operating in a region essential to the forthcoming war against Iraq.[35] As American and British troops and military assets were amassing in the Persian Gulf region in preparation for Operation Iraqi Freedom, which would commence in five weeks, Commodore Roger Girouard took command of the newly established Task Force 151 on 7 February. Charged with controlling the waters straddling the Strait of Hormuz and up to the southernmost tip of Kuwait in the Persian Gulf, Girouard had command of the largest operational area of responsibility of any senior Canadian officer since the Second World War.[36] Along with increasing Canada's naval presence in the region, the Canadian government decided not to extract 100 Canadian officers on exchange with American, British, and Australian units preparing for the invasion of Iraq. Moreover, it signed a memorandum of understanding with Qatar that allowed for the presence of Canadian military officers in that Persian Gulf state participating in the planning with US Central Command for the upcoming war on Iraq and the ongoing one in Afghanistan. As far as military preparations went, Canada appeared ready and willing to go to war against Saddam Hussein's regime.

Recognizing, however, that the organization that had facilitated so much of Canada's specialized participation in the international system was in crisis, Chrétien authorized the country's ambassador to the United Nations to present Canada in the role of problem-solver. To this end, Paul Heinbecker distributed a two-page private document to members of the Security Council in mid-February that suggested a series of tests designed to measure Iraqi cooperation and a final deadline of 28 March 2003 to decide on using "all necessary means" to achieve the desired disarmament of Saddam's regime. The Security Council (of which Canada was not a member at the time) met over the proposal and invited Heinbecker to sit in on the discussion, giving Canada the highest profile of any non-Security Council nation in the effort to resolve another UN stalemate. Behind the scenes, however, Bush had already rejected the plan in a phone conversation with Chrétien.[37]

With at least the outward appearance of some momentum behind the proposal and the chance to be seen playing a role in averting a situation that was likely to damage Western solidarity and undermine the efficacy of the United Nations, Chrétien injected some energy into this diplomatic effort to find a compromise that could bridge the chasm in the Security Council. He used his official visit to Mexico in late February 2003 to discuss the Canadian plan with President Vicente Fox, and he telephoned Chilean President Ricardo Lagos to try to generate further diplomatic support for the initiative. Mexico and Chile – two of the nonpermanent members of the Security Council – responded with support for the Canadian proposal, but were feeling the same pressures Canada was feeling as their domestic populations expressed opposition to the prospect of a US-led war on Iraq while Washington continued to utilize persuasive techniques to gain their support for such an effort.[38] Russia also endorsed aspects of the Canadian plan, but would not support the idea of a 31 March 2003 final deadline.

As it became more and more clear that the UN would not be able to endorse a US-led attack on Iraq, it became more and more likely that Canada would have to assert its sovereign autonomy against the will of the superordinate state and decline to participate in the war. With the repercussions of this coming into clear view, two pre-emptive countermoves of subordination were designed to soften the backlash from Washington. The first came as sources in the federal government leaked information about an extra $2 billion being allocated for the depleted Canadian military in the upcoming 18 February budget. Anonymous sources told the *National Post* on 8 February that "this new defence spending is intended to send a strong signal to Washington that the federal government is serious about tackling the decline in Canada's military capabilities."[39]

The second, more significant move came just five days later, as Defence Minister John McCallum announced that a sizable (between 1,500 and 2,000) Canadian troop contribution would be sent to Afghanistan on 18 February. McCallum had discussed this possibility with Defense Secretary Donald Rumsfeld on 8 January, and Rumsfeld had reacted favourably.[40] Indeed, with preparations for the war in Iraq in full swing, Rumsfeld was interested in passing the Afghanistan ball to a willing ally, which would allow American troops to be redeployed to Iraq. Rumsfeld wrongfully believed that the bulk of the fighting in Afghanistan was over, and that all there was left to do was humanitarian work, some training of the Afghan army and police force, and some basic stabilization operations: tasks perfectly suited to Canada![41] He therefore suggested that Canada take the lead of the International Security Assistance Force in Kabul. Contemplating this option and the impending decision about participating in a non-UN-sanctioned war of choice in Iraq, McCallum reminded Rumsfeld that there would be no possibility of Canada sending ground troops for round two of the War on Terror. To this Rumsfeld reportedly replied, "Yeah, I know that."[42]

What Rumsfeld might also have known, and what McCallum absolutely did know, was that in late 2002, the Standing Senate Committee on National Security and Defence had issued a report recommending that all of Canada's troops posted overseas be returned home for a rest period of two years. The Canadian Forces were badly overstretched. Indeed, the commander of Canada's army at the time, Lieutenant General Michael Jeffrey, had told the Chrétien government that his forces were not prepared for another significant overseas mission. He said that he "could see Canadian soldiers dying" and that "the risks were too high."[43] That this further commitment of troops was designed to demonstrate Canada's continued support of the US-led War on Terror just before it declined to support the invasion of Iraq is evident. Inside the Chrétien Cabinet, the decision became known as the "Afghanistan solution." It was, according to Heritage Minister Sheila Copps, "a neat political way of squaring the problem" of how to practically support Washington without symbolically supporting its decision to topple Saddam's regime.[44] Contradictorily, while it freed up American troops to be redeployed for more dangerous duties in Iraq, and while Canadian warships continued to patrol the Persian Gulf throughout, Washington would react with extreme displeasure to the Canadian decision not to formally join the Coalition of the Willing in invading Iraq.

Even in the midst of these subordinate moves, however, Chrétien found it necessary to channel Lester Pearson in an appearance not at Temple University in Philadelphia but at the Council on Foreign Relations in Chicago on 14 February. There, on American soil, he asserted, after assuring the audience that "Canada firmly supports the objectives of the United States" and reminding them of the long history of cooperation and growing interdependence between the two countries, that "the long term interests of the United States will be better served by acting through the United Nations than by acting alone."[45]

In the end, Canada's efforts to find a solution to the UN problem were in vain, and the Bush administration roundly ignored Chrétien's advice. Ambassador Cellucci commented that he did not find Heinbecker's Pearsonian resolution "particularly helpful."[46] Washington was determined to wage war on Iraq, and it did not appreciate the Canadians' last-minute attempt to delay the inevitable with unhelpful meddling.

Shock, Awe, and Canada as a Belligerent?

With the support of only four countries on the Security Council, the United States, Britain, and Spain on 17 March 2003 withdrew their draft resolution authorizing the use of force if Saddam Hussein failed to disarm, and abandoned efforts to win the UN's authorization for a war on Iraq. When the forty-eight-hour window that President Bush gave for Saddam and his sons to leave Iraq had slammed shut, a full-scale air and land invasion of that country commenced. Only Britain and Australia contributed significant ground troops.

With an election pending in Quebec and the provincial Liberals led by Jean Charest behind in the polls, Chrétien, to shouts of "bravo" from the federal Liberal backbenches announced in the House of Commons on 17 March that Canada would not participate in the war on Iraq being led by the country's two closest allies, the United States and Britain. By the spring, Charest's Liberals had come from behind to upset the Parti Québécois. Journalist Chantal Hébert declared that "this morning, Quebec's sovereignty movement is effectively in shambles."[47] According to Chrétien's biographer, Lawrence Martin, the prime minister was eventually able to boast, "My friends, in all modesty, I think that we can state without hesitation that when it comes to the important file of national unity, we can say, 'Mission accomplished.'"[48] The opposition, however, characterized Chrétien's decision to remain formally apart from the Coalition of the Willing as "hypocritical and contradictory."[49] Senior US officials expressed their disappointment. Deputy Prime Minister John Manley said that the Americans would not hold a grudge, even as other Liberal MPs denounced the military strikes as illegal acts and characterized President Bush as a criminal.[50]

Somehow, amid all of this paradox and contradiction, the decision to stand up and say no to the Americans on Iraq is popularly regarded as one of the Chrétien era's greatest moments. The decision has been misconstrued as a triumphant example of when Canada stood defiant in the face of a dominant American state. The reality, however, was that the Chrétien government delegated its decision-making autonomy on this issue to the Security Council, with its one-permanent-member, one-veto voting rule. The government made clear that it would have endorsed the invasion of Iraq had it been sanctioned by the Security Council. Frank Harvey of Dalhousie University was one of the very few who recognized this position for what it was: the precise opposite of multilateralism, the supposed touchstone of Canadian foreign policy. On the contrary, this position was an endorsement of "hyper-unilateralism as the authoritative process through which decisions are made on the UN Security Council, because it assigns to any single member of the Security Council the ultimate authority to kill any multilateral consensus."[51] Aside from falsely draping the ultimate decision to say no to Iraq with the cope of multilateralism, there remains the possibility that Canada could have, despite its formal denunciation of the war, actually gained the status of a belligerent as a result of its practical contributions. Accordingly, the cases of Canada's command of Task Force 151 and of the Canadian exchange officers require further examination.

In order for Commodore Girouard to take up command of Task Force 151 in early February 2003, Canadian warships had to move into the north of the Gulf of Oman (where for over a year they had been commanding a small flotilla of warships), away from Afghanistan and into the Persian Gulf, much closer to Iraq. The destroyer HMCS *Iroquois* and the frigate HMCS *Fredericton* (both with air detachments) were also quickly deployed out of Halifax and eventually joined the three Canadian frigates, HMCS *Regina, Winnipeg,* and *Montréal,* in the area of operations after the four-week transit. With its specialized command-and-control capabilities, *Iroquois* would become the flagship of Task Force 151, taking over from *Montréal,* which was not designed for such a role. The flagship of a naval task force has a range of unique responsibilities and capabilities. Most importantly, it has the capacity to house the commodore and his staff, whose principal responsibility is to coordinate and control the logistics, communications, intelligence, and security operations of the entire task force. In other words, the flagship of a task force is the hub of information, delegation, and decision-making authority on the water.

Throughout his command of Task Force 151, which was formally conducting business under the Operation Enduring Freedom (War on Terror) construct, and not under the Operation Iraqi Freedom (war on Iraq, which the Americans consider to be part of the War on Terror) construct, Commodore Girouard reported to US Vice Admiral Timothy Keating, head of the US Fifth Fleet. Keating and the Fifth Fleet were waging war on Iraq, however. Once the war began in earnest, Girouard was given updated rules of engagement (ROE) by Ottawa, instructing him not to hand over any Iraqi prisoners to the US Navy. These new ROE for the Canadian warships in the Persian Gulf led Keating to cut Canada out of the American, Australian, and British communications and intelligence loop, ultimately diminishing the operational significance of Task Force 151. And while the typical sensationalist stir was created in the House of Commons and the national news media over whether Girouard would be compelled to release Saddam Hussein himself or any other Iraqi escapees if they were captured by a task force warship, this never became an issue in theatre. The task force took no detainees while Girouard was in command. As far as becoming a legal combatant through this form of operational contribution, Canada appeared to stay on the right side of the fine line it was sailing in the Persian Gulf.

When pressed, however, lawyers from both the Department of National Defence and the Department of Foreign Affairs and International Trade said that if Task Force 151 warships were protecting vessels involved in the invasion of Iraq, then Canada could very well be considered a party to the conflict.[52] Since the bulk of what the task force was doing was escorting shipping through the Strait of Hormuz, and since the bulk of that shipping was "feeding the American and British build-up against Iraq," neither Girouard nor the other members of his task force would have been inclined to deny protective escort to ships involved in preparations for the coming war.[53] Once the invasion of Iraq began, the task force engaged in similar escort operations, and once the bulk of the fighting was over, the bulk of its operations consisted in escorting vessels out of Iraq. Whether this made Canada a belligerent is a question that might never be answered. It should suggest strongly, however, that Canada made a significant practical contribution to the war in Iraq. To put this sizable five-ship contribution into some perspective, consider that Canada sent only three warships to the Persian Gulf in August 1990 to fight in the first US-led war against Saddam Hussein, and this was to support a UN-sanctioned effort to repel the Iraqi invasion of Kuwait.[54]

Besides taking up this significant command-and-control responsibility in the Persian Gulf, a role neither lightly nor arbitrarily assigned by the US Navy, Canadian military officers were allowed to remain on exchange with their American, British, and Australian units as they prepared for and went to war with Iraq. One of these exchange officers was Brigadier General Walt Natynczyk, who would eventually become Canada's top-ranked soldier. Natynczyk was directly involved in high-level planning for the war at US military headquarters in Kuwait. Once fighting began, he moved with the portable headquarters into Iraq.[55] One of Canada's top soldiers, in other words, was in uniform on Iraqi soil, participating in Operation Iraqi Freedom, a war in which his government had formally refused to participate. He was not the only soldier wearing a maple leaf to do so. According to Frank Harvey, "some Canadian troops were actually placed in units that saw action in the Iraq campaign ... At least six of them were in battle zones, and one was with the British 7th Armoured Division, which saw heavy fighting around Basra."[56] Other countries that had chosen to opt out of the Coalition of the Willing quickly withdrew their exchange officers who were in similar positions. Canada, for reasons that can only be explained by pressures produced by the continental hierarchy, chose not to do so. Whether this made Canada a belligerent is a matter for international lawyers to debate, but it does suggest a further blurring of the line between Canada's involvement in the War on Terror and its involvement in the war in Iraq. Indeed, as Ambassador Cellucci was keen to recognize in a speech to the Economic Club of Toronto (now the Economic Club of Canada) on 25 March 2003, "ironically, the Canadian naval vessels, aircraft and personnel in the Persian Gulf I mentioned earlier who are fighting terrorism will provide more support indirectly to this war in Iraq than most of the 46 countries that are fully supporting our efforts there."[57] To be precise, Canada's military contribution to the multilateral forces in the Arabian Sea/Persian Gulf region ranked fourth in the coalition behind those of the US, Britain, and Australia.[58]

So significant was this participation that the US military even thanked Canada for its contribution of three transport planes to the Iraq war in a report issued on 30 April 2003 by US Air Force Lieutenant General T. Michael Moseley. In the report, which dealt exclusively with the war in Iraq, Moseley lists thirty-one Canadian troops in a table entitled "Deployed Personnel for OIF," as well as the contribution of three Canadian aircraft engaged in airlift operations, and goes on to acknowledge the input of Canadian and allied officers for their "collection and collation" of the data contained in the unclassified document.[59] After Canadian Forces spokeswoman Major Lynne Chaloux clarified by stating that "we supported Enduring Freedom, the War on Terrorism, not Iraqi Freedom, the war in Iraq,"[60] the US Air Force claimed that it had made an error in reporting.[61] Nevertheless, neither the Canadian nor the American government could deny that a Canadian officer, whose name, rank, and gender remain undisclosed, suffered hearing loss and shrapnel injuries to an arm after the convoy he or she was travelling in was hit by a grenade near the Baghdad airport in April 2003. Canadian officers on exchange continued to serve in Iraq with their American counterparts right through the 2007 "surge" that saw an extra 30,000 American troops deployed in an effort to rescue Baghdad from what had become a condition akin to a Hobbesian state of nature.[62]

Despite significant practical Canadian contributions to Operation Iraqi Freedom, Washington expressed extreme displeasure at Ottawa's lack of symbolic support for the war. President Bush had made it clear in the early days of the War on Terror that countries were either with or against the United States in its quest to make the world safe for freedom. Prime Minister Chrétien's condemnation of the Iraq extension of the War on Terror suggested to the Americans that Canada was against them, despite the fact that for all practical purposes Canada was just as with them as any other country in the Coalition of the Willing. At the level of summit diplomacy, President Bush retaliated by cancelling his trip to Canada scheduled for 5 May 2003, choosing instead to host Australia's Prime Minister John Howard; snubbing Prime Minister Chrétien at an Asia-Pacific Economic Cooperation (APEC) meeting in October 2003; and refusing to visit Canada until after Prime Minister Chrétien had left office. At the level of continental economic relations, trade disputes over softwood lumber and Alberta beef were allowed to fester.

Recognizing that the superordinate state was unhappy with its insubordination, Ottawa announced that it would contribute $100 million to the Iraqi reconstruction project. When this failed to elicit the intended response in Washington, Ottawa announced that it would top up its contribution with an extra $200 million. Even after these subordinate countermoves, however, Washington announced that firms from countries not part of the Coalition of the Willing would not be eligible to bid on $18 billion worth of Iraqi reconstruction contracts. Under the leadership of Paul Martin's Liberal Party, Canada eventually became the first non-coalition country Washington would allow to bid on the reconstruction project. French, German, and Russian companies would become eligible only in the next round of contracts.[63] Canadian firms would, after all, be allowed to profit from the war their government had condemned as illegal.

Under Martin's leadership, Canada quickly sought a specialized role in the Iraq campaign. Following President Bush's trip north in early December 2004, Martin told CNN's Wolf Blitzer that he was willing to send Canadians to Iraq to help train Iraqi election officials. "This is an area in which Canada has a great deal of expertise ... and we're prepared to offer it," Martin told the news anchor. At that point, no official request had been made by Washington for Canada to perform this special function, but Martin indicated to Blitzer that "if we're asked, we will participate ... Canada intends to play a role where it can play a significant one."[64] The next day, it was announced that Canada would sponsor an international conference – the Iraq Election Monitoring Forum – in Ottawa from 18 to 20 December, backed by the UN and attended by the chief electoral officers of up to twenty different countries, with the goal of establishing rules to make Iraq's elections free and fair.

After the conference, it was announced that Canada would establish a sec-
retariat, led by Jean-Pierre Kingsley, for the International Mission for Iraqi
Elections, which was charged with evaluating the three Iraqi votes scheduled
for 2005. After the December 2005 elections in Iraq, Canada praised "the
courage demonstrated by voters and candidates throughout the various
stages of Iraq's transition to democracy. Despite the high level of personal
risk involved, the citizens of Iraq proved their commitment to democratic
change."[65]

Despite this specialized contribution to the cause of stability in Iraq,
Washington continued to pressure Canada to send significant numbers of
Canadian troops to Baghdad to help train Iraqi troops. A small number of
senior Canadian military officers participated in training and mentoring
exercises with Iraqis in Baghdad as part of a NATO mission that was established in August 2004.[66] Despite pressure for a more substantial contribution,
the Martin government offered thirty soldiers and $1 million to help train
Iraqi troops in Jordan. Predictably, Washington was not impressed with this
compromise position, which resulted in the contradictory outcome of Canada's involving itself more deeply in a war from which it had tried (unsuccessfully) to distance itself from the start, and the United States showing little
to no appreciation for its reluctant effort. Also noteworthy in terms of Canada's contribution to Iraqi freedom is its support for a G7-led international
debt reduction program for that country, and the fact that members of the
RCMP have been training Iraqi police in Jordan as well.[67]

Despite Canada's effort to avert the US-led invasion of Iraq through specialized intervention at the United Nations, and despite the Chrétien government's initial denunciation of the war and subsequent efforts on Ottawa's
part to maintain Canada's political distance from Iraq, Canada has been
repeatedly drawn into the conflict by the contrasting pressures of the continental hierarchy and the international anarchy. Paradoxically, despite the
reality of Canada's substantial practical contributions to the Iraq cause, its
political denunciation of the war compelled its deeper involvement in
Afghanistan.

Afghanistan Redux

In the summer of 2003, months after President Bush had declared the toppling of Saddam Hussein's regime to be "mission accomplished," the Canadian Forces began in earnest their contribution to the now NATO-led,
UN-authorized International Security Assistance Force (ISAF) in Kabul, the
capital of Afghanistan. The 2,000-strong contribution made in two six-month
rotations would be the largest to the ISAF mission of any NATO country to
that point. It would culminate in Canada's taking command of the mission
in February 2004.

Under Canadian direction, ISAF made considerable progress in Kabul. In the summer of 2003, many were predicting that the warlords, drug lords, and residual Taliban fighters would push Afghanistan to the brink of chaotic civil war. Instead, under the interim political leadership of Hamid Karzai, the country produced a constitution and held democratic elections. ISAF provided the secure and stable conditions in which this progress could take place. The Canadian Forces contribution included conducting "3800 patrols, 864 vehicle checkpoints, 12 out of area operations, and 9 directed operations to neutralize specific individuals or groups of individuals."[68] Moreover, according to Colonel Alain Tremblay, Canada became the "primary intelligence gathering and data fusion organization and actually the prime feed for the Americans in that area."[69] Indeed, Tremblay reports that "the number and level of forces that were committed for this intelligence gathering in electronic warfare and human intelligence (HUMINT) was tremendous, and was in fact a significant drain on the Canadian Forces resources."[70] This intelligence-oriented war in Kabul was designed to "disrupt terrorist cells trying to interfere with the electoral and political processes, while at the same time facilitating those processes," according to academic Sean Maloney.[71] Ultimately, the goal of the NATO-led ISAF force and the American-led Operation Enduring Freedom forces was and continues to be the consolidation and spread of the Karzai government's authority and control from Kabul in the north all the way down to the most unruly southern provinces.

After the two six-month rotations, Canada's commitment in Kabul was scaled back considerably in preparation for a new mission, one that would involve a range of the country's resources in the stabilization and reconstruction of Kandahar province. The base for the Kabul operation – Camp Julien – was handed over to the Afghan Ministry of Defence shortly thereafter. An inukshuk was left behind in memory of the four "Pats" who were killed in the friendly-fire incident. Also left behind in Kabul was a small group of approximately fifteen military and civilian personnel embedded within departments of the Afghan government as part of Operation Argus. This Strategic Advisory Team – Afghanistan (SAT-A) is a unique feature of the Canadian contribution to the broader development goals of that country. SAT-A combines elements of Canada's problem-solving, intelligence-gathering, and advocacy specializations to help the new Afghan government develop a functioning bureaucracy that is increasingly integrated into and compatible with the norms and rules of the international community and the global economy. No other NATO country has been granted the opportunity to work so closely with the Afghan government. Thus, no other NATO country has the eyes and ears necessary to keep tabs on the billions of dollars of aid money that has flowed into Afghanistan as a result of the international community's compact with that country, which was established at the London Conference on Afghanistan (31 January – 1 February 2006).[72] Along with SAT-A in Kabul, Canada also maintains approximately thirty Canadian Forces officers as part of Operation Archer, which contributes to the training of the Afghan National Army (ANA) in American combat doctrine and the general readying of Afghan security forces. This is part of Canada's contribution to Operation Enduring Freedom under US leadership and command.

Going South

Instead of heading home after closing shop at Camp Julien, the Canadian Forces travelled south across the Afghan desert towards the province of Kandahar, one of the world's most dangerous regions. Kandahar was al-Qaeda's headquarters before the Taliban fell officially on 13 November 2001. It is a region rife with warlords, extremists, and drug smugglers. Bordering Pakistan to the west, Kandahar has remained unstable since the 2001 invasion, and subject to continuing Taliban and al-Qaeda influence. Indeed, the US lost over 100 soldiers to insurgent forces in Kandahar region in 2005. It is unclear to what degree extremist networks based in Pakistan are responsible for inciting insurgent attacks. At the time of this writing, however, it would appear that the war in the south is far from over in any real sense. When it can be expected to end is also far from clear. The 2.6 million ethnic Pashtuns living in exile along the border region of Afghanistan and Pakistan could potentially provide an endless supply of trouble for Western troops in the region. Pakistan's Pashtuns are both ethnically and politically aligned with the Taliban. The Pakistani government retains only nominal control over the Pashtun tribal region, and has demonstrated little effort in cooperating with the Afghan government or with coalition forces to make the area less of a safe haven for the Taliban and a launch pad for their insurgency.[73]

There can be little doubt that Kandahar is, as Canada's former ambassador to Afghanistan once said, "a pivotal province." Afghanistan as a whole has been both devastated and rendered severely stagnant socioeconomically by three decades of war. It is one of the poorest countries in the world and has the lowest female literacy rate on the planet. Eighteen hundred illegally armed gangs roam the country with impunity. Drug addiction, HIV/AIDS, malaria, and malnutrition are ravaging the population. The basic infrastructure needed to develop a market-based economy – banks, roads, power, water for both irrigation and consumption – is either scarce or nonexistent across much of the country. The human infrastructure necessary for development is also severely lacking. Low literacy rates and life expectancy, and poor health and education, have left the Afghan people greatly vulnerable – easy prey for the drug lords and armed gangs that stand in the way of the rule of law and the development of a viable democratic system of government and a market-based economy.[74] Kandahar is widely regarded as being in the worst shape of Afghanistan's thirty-four provinces. And yet, "as Kandahar goes, so goes Afghanistan," according to Chris Alexander.[75]

The decision to send 2,500 Canadian soldiers into this volatile region was influenced primarily, as was argued in the previous chapter, by the necessity felt by Paul Martin's new minority Liberal government to compensate for its controversial "no" to formal participation in the Bush administration's National Missile Defence plans. It is noteworthy that the deployment of a battle group and a Provincial Reconstruction Team (PRT) to Kandahar was announced on 21 March 2005, just two days before Paul Martin's first visit to President Bush's ranch near Crawford, Texas. The decision was also influenced by the enthusiasm and eloquence of the new Chief of Defence Staff, General Rick Hillier, who saw Kandahar as an initiative that would get noticed in Washington.[76] According to Michael Kergin, the Canadian ambassador to the United States who was replaced by Frank McKenna, there was also a lingering sense in Ottawa that Canada had "let the side down" in not formally committing to the Iraq war. "There was the sense that we could be more helpful, militarily, by taking on a role in Afghanistan ... we could make a contribution in a place like Kandahar."[77] No doubt reflecting the pressures of the continental hierarchy after Canada had officially opted out of both the Iraq war and the missile defence initiative, one official who played a role in the decision-making process tellingly noted that "there was what you might call an inevitability about the decision."[78]

In August 2005, Canada took over command of the PRT in Kandahar from the US. The 335-strong PRT is composed primarily of members of the Canadian Forces, although members of the Canadian International Development Agency (CIDA), the Department of Foreign Affairs and International Trade, the RCMP, and the Correctional Service of Canada also fill about twenty spots on the team. The US government also maintains a presence in the Kandahar PRT, with a member of the State Department, an officer from USAID and a handful of US police mentors.[79] The PRT is supported by a 2,000-strong Canadian battalion group, which is primarily responsible for creating the stable and secure conditions within which "reconstruction" can occur. For the most part, this means that the Canadian Forces in Kandahar have been engaged in a very high volume of complex and severe combat operations against Taliban insurgents. The high-risk nature of these operations, and the fact that Canada is attempting to punch somewhat above its military weight, is evidenced by a number of troubling facts. First, analyst David McDonough points out that in 2006-7, Canadian casualties were running a rate five times that of its allies in Afghanistan.[80] Indeed, over 95 percent of the 129 Canadian casualties (at the time of writing) date from the time Canada took command of the PRT in Kandahar. Second, stability and prosperity in Kandahar and in Afghanistan generally appear a long way off, perhaps even further off than in Iraq, as suggested by the fact that battle death tolls of allied forces in Afghanistan exceeded those in Iraq in May and June 2008 (at the time of writing). Finally, a report released by the US

Department of Defense on 27 June 2008 argued that a "Kandahari-based" resurgence of the Taliban combined with a more "complex, adaptive insurgency in the east" were the main threats to Afghanistan's stability and progress.[81] The report was released before its authors could include an analysis of the implications of the prison break that occurred in Kandahar on 13 June 2008, which saw 400 members of the Taliban escape custody among an equal number of common criminals. The prison facility, which Canada had spent $1 million to improve, was attacked from the outside by suicide bombers and Taliban insurgents on motorcycles wielding handheld rocket launchers. This significant incident suggests a major intelligence failure on Canada's part, and the possibility that it may be out of its strategic depth in Kandahar.

The authors of the 2008 report of the Independent Panel on Canada's Future Role in Afghanistan (known popularly as the Manley Report) were clearly aware of this possibility. The report predicted chaos in Kandahar and dark days ahead for NATO were Canada not to extend its mission beyond 2009 and were NATO not to lend a significant helping hand by sending an additional 1,000 troops to the troubled province.[82] Considering that the total number of Canadian troops in Kandahar is approximately 2,500, this suggests that Canada is a significant way from being able to play the part of a principal military power in the international system. As an organization, NATO will have to bail Canada out in Kandahar, at the risk of having to bail itself out of a future credibility crisis. The growing instability in Kandahar province is by no means the fault of the Canadian Forces, but it is suggestive of the implications of Canada's stepping outside its array of specialized roles in order to play a part in international politics that may prove to be tragically beyond its capabilities.

Such are the dangers when a subordinate state overreaches its capabilities and attempts to take on roles in international politics that are more suited to major powers. Had Canada from the outset of the War on Terror defined its roles as being of the postconflict genre – mediating and supervising the establishment of stability and democracy in postregime change states – it may have found itself in less challenging situations with respect to its relations with the US, its reputation abroad, and the confidence and consent of its domestic public. It will be through defining a more specialized role in the War on Terror that Canada will find itself contributing in a way that satisfies these three audiences and thus works to maintain the integrity of its internal and external sovereignty in these difficult times.

As we have seen, the pattern of paradoxical exchange leading to contradictory policy outcomes persists as Canada and the US attempt to combine in their foreign adventures throughout the War on Terror. Indeed, a stunning and tragic example of this pattern is revealed in the nature of Canada's current mission in Afghanistan – fighting a brutal counterinsurgency with one hand, while attempting to construct a life for average Afghans that is enriched enough with the fruits of democracy and capitalism that they will never go back to the tyrannical and fundamentalist ways of the Taliban. The dual logic of the "3-D approach" (Defence, Development, and Diplomacy) can only be described as contradictory. As *Globe and Mail* columnist Jeffrey Simpson put it sympathetically, the Canadian Forces have been asked "to make love and war at the same time."[83]

The reason the Canadian Forces are engaged in such a mission has everything to do with the Canadian state's dual obligations to the superordinate state and to its own people and the international community. The first set of obligations sees Canada carrying out Operation Archer as part of the American war against terrorism. The second set of obligations sees Canada carrying out provincial reconstruction in Kandahar province as part of an international effort to bring peace to a part of the world that has rarely enjoyed it. Canadians themselves (80 percent, according to a recent CBC/Environics poll) are comfortable with seeing the Forces perform peacekeeping/peacebuilding operations. They are less comfortable (only 20 percent) with a combat role for them.[84] The mission in Kandahar is the most significant combat operation Canada has been involved in since the Korean War. Combined with an effort to build peace, stability, and a viable democracy in one of the most chronically underdeveloped and uneducated places in the world, it might prove to be the most risky and deadly situation Canadian troops have been in since the Second World War. While noble, this mission is the direct result of Canada's unwillingness to formally support the American-led invasion of Iraq and the American initiative to create a ballistic missile defence system. "The Afghanistan solution," as it was referred to by members of the Martin Cabinet, with the vast sums of blood and treasure it has cost this country, is thus cold compensation for such moves of self-assertion, and a reminder of the contradictory realities of hierarchy in anarchy.

In the following chapter, we will see how the dynamics of Canada-US relations change once they are removed from the spotlight of the international system.

7
Continental Security after 9/11

Among other things, the immediate aftermath of the 11 September 2001 terror attacks revealed the extent of Canadian economic dependence on access to the American market. Despite all the rhetoric about the special relationship, the US was not about to risk another attack just so that its friend to the north could continue to trade in its massive market. This message was heard loud and clear in Ottawa as soon as Washington decided to put its border inspectors on a level 1 alert. In an instant, this action created a line of trucks thirty-six kilometres long at the Windsor-Detroit border crossing (to cite the most extreme example of many). Typically making the crossing in one or two minutes, these trucks waited ten to fifteen hours. With $1.3 billion worth of goods crossing the border daily in two-way trade, the economic repercussions of such a security crackdown could not be taken lightly by either state in the continental system.

In the abstract, the oft-cited statistics of somewhere between 80 and 90 percent of Canadian exports being sold to American consumers, and between 70 and 80 percent of its imports being bought from American producers, had alerted Canadians for years to this reality. It was the lines of traffic backed up for kilometres trying to cross the Canada-US border in the days following the attacks that drove home the point, however. A prolonged or permanent closure of the 8,900-kilometre border *would* damage the American economy. And numerous US multinational firms with branch plants in Canada, such as Ford and General Motors, *would* protest loudly if Washington ever decided it was necessary to take such drastic measures. But the real devastation would fall on the Canadian economy. Diverting the vast majority of its exports to alternative markets in Europe and Asia, and finding new sources for the nearly equally vast majority of its imports would be next to impossible for Canada. In short, the country would be exposed to an economic depression of such magnitude that its economic survival would be threatened. As Stephen Clarkson put it, "if Washington defined its front line of defence as a Fortress

America by blockading the territorial boundaries along the 49th parallel, Canada's NAFTA-integrated economy would collapse."[1]

This chapter examines the series of moves made by Canada to make its territory, border crossings, ports, and airports secure enough for the United States to remain open to economic flows across the forty-ninth parallel after 9/11. These moves will be shown to have been in response to and in anticipation of moves of domination from the US that threatened Canada's economic prosperity, if not its economic survival. In these instances, the effects of the international anarchy variable are considerably limited, due to the nature of these particular interactions, which were confined to the continental system and had little to do with the broader international system. Instead of the now familiar paradoxical interactions leading to contradictory outcomes between the two states, we will see straightforward exchanges that have led to policy outcomes free from internal incongruity.

National and Transnational Security in the Continental System

The understanding that in the post-Cold War era the calculus of North American security would become as much transnational as international might have been grasped by Ottawa and Washington once Algerian terrorist Ahmed Ressam was apprehended at a border crossing on his way to bomb Los Angeles International Airport on the eve of the new millennium. It was 9/11, however, that was the true harbinger of the new era in transnational security concerns in North America.

In geostrategic terms, Canada and the US were indivisible throughout the Second World War and the Cold War. No rational state aggressor would have attacked one state and not the other, as any attack on Canada would be met with massive retaliation from the US, and any attack on the US would elicit at the very least a non-neutral response from Canada.[2] Threats to the territorial security of the continent were defined first in terms of the Axis Powers, and once they had faded into defeat, in terms of the Soviet empire. Militarily, these threats were met abroad first in collaboration with the Allied Powers, and then, during the Cold War, in collaboration with NATO. During the Cold War, the greatest threat to continental security was from a nuclear strike launched by Soviet bombers and ICBMs crossing the North Pole en route to levelling major North American cities.

After the Cold War, the security calculus began to shift away from rival state actors towards what Peter Andreas has labelled "Clandestine Transnational Actors" (CTAs).[3] With President George H.W. Bush defining illegal drugs as a threat to national security and declaring war on such substances and the criminal elements that profited from them, NORAD was placed at the service of detecting and tracking airborne drug smugglers. As Joseph Jockel writes, however, "NORAD's support for drug interdiction and other anti-smuggling efforts was also mainly focused outwards, largely towards clandestine traffic entering the southern U.S."[4]

After 9/11, a more radical revision of the security calculus took place in the capitals of North America. In Washington, it was clear that the domestic and border policies of America's subordinates could potentially pose as much of a security threat as rogue regimes if they were not in tune with American standards. With security now a transnational issue, a new and far-reaching sphere of Canadian public policy would be subject to US scrutiny, and thus to "defence against help" calculations on the part of the subordinate state. Canada would now be compelled to ensure that an unprecedented array of its domestic policies were up to US standards.

The American Homeland Response to 9/11

The US legislative response to 9/11 was severe and far-reaching. Given that the list of opportune terrorist targets in an open society is virtually without limit – lectures, churches, sporting events, department stores, etc. – this was expected, both by Americans themselves and by the rest of the world. The 9/11 attacks exposed the fatal loophole in liberalism, and the US government's legislative response was an attempt to tighten that loophole without undermining the essence of life in a liberal society.

The US Congress passed the USA PATRIOT Act – formally named "Uniting and Strengthening America by Providing Appropriate Tools Required to Intercept and Obstruct Terrorism," commonly known simply as the Patriot Act – without amendment on 24 October 2001. President Bush officially signed it into law two days later. Controversially, little debate or study went into what was subsequently understood to be an unprecedented piece of legislation, which would amend over twelve pre-existing acts and statutes,[5] and alter, however significantly, the balance between collective and individual rights in the United States.

For example, the Patriot Act significantly broadens the notions of who should be considered a terrorist and of what actions constitute terrorism, and it gives the Attorney General of the United States considerable personal powers in detaining and deporting such people accused of being engaged in such actions. It authorizes denial of access to legal counsel to such terror-related detainees. Moreover, the act provides for potential indefinite confinement of individuals suspected of terrorism. In terms of its effects on individuals not immediately associated with terrorist organizations, it provides substantive new powers of electronic surveillance, search warrants, and detention that remain largely outside the ambit of the legislature and the judiciary.[6] Such powers open suspect personal e-mail, telephone conversations, and other forms of technological communication to new levels of scrutiny in the name of security. The act also creates a number of new crimes, new penalties, and new procedures for dealing with terror-related activities, and establishes lower thresholds for the determination of guilt in such cases.[7] It increases the financial rewards for information related to terrorism, and permits nationwide and perhaps worldwide execution of warrants in terror cases. It also contains a number of provisions designed to enhance border security and to prevent alien terrorists from entering the US, especially from Canada.[8]

The Office of Homeland Security was also established in the immediate aftermath of 9/11, and the governor of Pennsylvania, Tom Ridge, was appointed its director. The office was designed as a precursor to the massive new executive department created by the Homeland Security Act of 2002. The new department, with Ridge as its secretary, was to preside over 150,000 staff and allocate an annual budget of $40 billion towards preventing, reducing, and minimizing the effects of terrorism in the United States, while ensuring that the overall economic security of the nation would not be diminished by such efforts.[9] President Bush announced the creation of the Department of Homeland Security (DHS) in a televised statement in which he outlined the National Strategy for Homeland Security. The DHS would be the grand overseer of the complex task of achieving homeland security in a liberal society. As the strategy document stated:

> American democracy is rooted in the precepts of federalism – a system of government in which our state governments share power with federal institutions. Our structure of overlapping federal, state and local governance – our country has more than 87,000 jurisdictions – provides unique opportunity and challenges for our homeland security efforts. The opportunity comes from the expertise and commitment of local agencies and organizations involved in homeland security. The challenge is to develop interconnected and complementary systems that are reinforcing rather than duplicative and ensure essential requirements are met. A national strategy requires a national effort.[10]

The DHS would therefore have a vast range of powers, including powers over the main border and transportation security agencies. It would also work hand in hand with the Department of the Attorney General and the Federal Bureau of Investigation. Despite the rhetorical references to federalism and the sharing of power between different levels of government, the creation of the DHS constituted a significant centralizing shift in the balance of the American governmental structure.

In April 2002, the Bush administration created the military counterpart to the DHS – US Northern Command (NORTHCOM). The commander of NORTHCOM is in charge of homeland defence, and also has command over

NORAD and US Space Command.[11] NORTHCOM's mandated area of operations includes Canada, Mexico, parts of the Caribbean, and the adjacent waters in the Atlantic and Pacific oceans. Through the establishment of this integrated command structure for the purpose of defending the homeland, sea, air, and space, the US added a military dimension to its security state apparatus to which the Canadian state would in the end be compelled to conform.

In mid-September 2002, the Bush administration published its National Security Strategy. The document formed the basis of the "Bush Doctrine," which adds up to what Robert Jervis has described as a "far reaching program that calls for something very much like an empire."[12] Its four components include (1) a commitment to maintain American pre-eminence, (2) a belief that democracy and capitalism are the cure for terrorism, (3) an understanding that rogue states and terrorists have become the chief security threats to the United States, and (4) a willingness to use unilateral and pre-emptive force if necessary in dealing with either of those threats.

Combined, the passage of the Patriot Act, the creation of the Department of Homeland Security and NORTHCOM, and the articulation of the Bush Doctrine amount to a superordinate state with a new set of more stringent demands for its subordinates. Having transformed itself into a post-9/11 security state, Washington would expect nothing less from Ottawa. The American reaction to 9/11, stark and severe as it was, signalled that serious changes were in the cards for both the continental relationship and Canada itself. No longer could Canada view its domestic policy as outside the scope of American security interests, and no longer could Canada be sure unilateral action to change such policies would not be taken if Washington deemed it necessary. To defend itself against such "help," Canada would have to establish its own doctrine of pre-emption against domination, by actively anticipating or following the American will in terms of changes and innovations in its internal security, its governing structure, its budget allocations, and its border, port, and airport security policies.

The Canadian Homeland Response to 9/11

Canada is on al-Qaeda's hit list. Twice Osama bin Laden has named the country as a target. Terrorists and terrorist networks are operative in Canada, and twenty-four Canadians died as a result of the 9/11 attacks. Terrorists could potentially kill thousands with suicide bombs in the Toronto subway system or hijacked planes crashed into the city's financial district. Such attacks, catastrophic as they would be, would generate in their aftermath a centripetal force of nationalism that would bring the country closer together on a sentimental level than perhaps it has ever been. An American intervention in Canadian domestic politics to actively prevent such an attack, however, would have the exact opposite effect on internal cohesion. The loss of its formal sovereignty would cripple Canada as a political entity in the long run. No terror attack, no matter its magnitude, could achieve that end. Thus, the underlying rationale behind the Canadian response to 9/11 was as much, if not more, based on a "defence against help" calculation as on a rational response to the impending threat of terrorism.

In quick response to the Patriot Act and to UN Security Council Resolution 1373 of 28 September 2001 – which set out the responsibilities of member states for preventing terrorism and requested updates on how they proposed to meet those responsibilities within ninety days – Prime Minister Jean Chrétien's government passed Bill C-36. The 175-page Anti-Terror Act (An Act to Amend the Criminal Code, the Official Secrets Act, the Canadian Evidence Act, the Proceeds of Crime [Money Laundering] Act, and other Acts to Enact Measures Respecting the Registration of Charities in Order to Combat Terrorism) was rammed through Parliament and the Senate, and received royal assent on 18 December 2001, just six weeks after the Patriot Act became law in the United States. Although the bill travelled through the legislative process about as rapidly as it possibly could have, public pressure did result in a five-year sunset clause's being placed on the new police powers of arrest and detention, as well as the rewording of the definition of "terrorist" to guard against undue suppression of legitimate protest.

The aim of the legislation is to give the Canadian state increased powers to combat the threat of terrorism, but it is also intended, as academic Edna Keeble writes, "to allay American fears about their northern border being an unguarded, porous barrier to terrorists."[13] To accomplish this, Bill C-36 amended ten different Canadian statutes, including the Criminal Code, the Official Secrets Act (now the Security of Information Act) and the Proceeds of Crime (Money Laundering) Act. It also ratified two different UN conventions: the International Convention for the Suppression of the Financing of Terrorism, and the International Convention for the Suppression of Terrorist Bombings. As legal scholar Kent Roach succinctly explains, Bill C-36 "introduced new and potentially dangerous legal concepts such as investigative hearings, preventive arrests, broad motive-based crimes based on participation in or contribution to terrorist groups at home or abroad, as well as new powers to list terrorist groups, take their property, and deprive suspected terrorists of sensitive security information in their trials and appeals."[14]

The bill, which was one of the most significant ever to receive royal assent in Canada, realigned the balance in the country between individual rights and collective security. It did so by expanding the criminal law and increasing to extraordinary levels the surveillance and investigative capacity of the state. Despite this, the bill received minimal input from the Canadian public. The Liberal government announced after only four and a half hours of debate that it was presenting a time allocation motion to limit further debate.

A procedure known as pre-consultation was also used in the Senate to push Bill C-36 through the final stages of the legislative process as quickly as possible. Opportunities for interest groups and experts from the general public to voice their views on the new anti-terror legislation were thus limited despite its significance. Funding to help implement this legislation came to $7.7 billion, which was announced to fight terrorism in the December 2001 federal budget. Remarkably, as noted by Stephen Clarkson, this sum was "proportionately larger than the U.S. allocation to the same objectives."[15]

Canada extended its legislative response to the terrorist threat with Bill C-42 (the Public Safety Act), which would ultimately become law as the Public Safety Act, and Bill C-44 (An Act to Amend the Aeronautics Act). Bill C-44 was originally one component of Bill C-42, but was removed and passed separately for purposes of expediency. Despite section 5 of the Personal Information Protection and Electronic Documents Act, it gives aircraft operators the right to provide passenger information to foreign officials during international flights as required by the laws of the foreign state for which the air carrier is bound. It received royal assent on the same day as Bill C-36, exactly one month before section 115 of the US Aviation and Transportation Security Act came into force, which mandates that passenger and crew manifests – including name, date of birth, sex, passport numbers, visa numbers, and any other information deemed necessary to ensure aviation safety – be provided by carriers and foreign air carriers through electronic transmission to the commissioner of customs. The Government of Canada thus had to pass Bill C-44 separately from the rest of the public safety legislation in order for Canadian carriers to comply with the American legislation and not find themselves barred from entry into the United States. As Canadian Alliance MP James Moore explained to the House of Commons on 6 December 2001, "Canadians can thank the United States congress for the bill."[16] Moore was accurately alluding to the similarities between American and Canadian legislative acts, but he might also have thanked the Canadian airlines' dependence on access to the American economic market, since ultimately this compelled Canada's conformity to the American standard on the issue.

Bill C-42 drew significant criticism, and the government chose instead to introduce a streamlined version in the form of Bill C-55, which died on the Order Paper when the first session of the Thirty-Seventh Parliament ended on 16 September 2002. Bill C-55 was replaced by Bill C-17, which was in turn reinstated as Bill C-7 on 10 February 2004. It received royal assent on 6 May 2004, making amendments to twenty-three existing acts. Bill C-7, the Public Safety Act, focuses on the "federal framework for public safety and protection," whereas its counterpart, the Anti-Terror Act (Bill C-36) focuses on the "criminal law aspects of fighting terrorism."[17]

Even in its fourth version, the Canadian Bar Association (CBA) admitted that the Public Safety Act had come some ways towards a "more tailored response" to the terrorist threat. In a letter dated 17 March 2003, however, the CBA urged the Senate not to pass the bill.[18] In a much more distraught tone, the Canadian Association of University Teachers also wrote to the Senate to express its "utmost concern about Bill C-7." It complained about the "wholly inadequate controls" placed on the bill's information-sharing provisions, and declared the bill as a whole to be a "grave risk to Canadians' rights and freedoms, and to Canadian sovereignty."[19] Despite these concerns, which were repeated in more or less the same way with each version of the bill, the government managed with its passage to complete a major transformation of the Canadian legal and federal framework.

Yet it is far from certain whether such sweeping change has made Canadians any more secure against the threat of terrorism. Kent Roach instructively asks the following empirical questions, which might have gone into a more thorough, normal assessment of the potential effectiveness of Canada's anti-terror legislation before it was passed:

> Can peace bonds for terrorists actually prevent terrorism? Are preventive arrests more effective than close surveillance? Will those with knowledge about terrorism tell the truth when compelled to testify before investigative hearings? Do rewards encouraging co-operation work better punishing people for refusing to co-operate at an investigative hearing? Can enhanced penalties deter suicide bombers?[20]

At first glance, the answers to these questions tend towards the negative. They thus introduce a subsequent, more philosophical one: Why, then, was such legislation passed in the first place? According to a number of the academic participants in the Department of Justice's 2004 review of the Anti-Terror Act, "the mere enactment of the Act reassures the United States that Canada is taking the terrorism threat seriously. Such signals to the United States protect Canadian sovereignty, promote intelligence sharing, and maintain the flow of commerce between the two countries."[21] Stuart Farson of the Institute of Governance Studies at Simon Fraser University adds further "that there is a sense among senior intelligence officials that if Canada does not protect US interests in Canada, the US will step in and do so."[22] This suggests an alternative rationale for the Anti-Terror Act, one based on concerns about Canadian sovereignty and economic survival as opposed to the objective threat of terrorism, or to an individual decision-maker, or to bureaucratic interests that might also have been involved in the passage of the legislation.

Besides passing sweeping omnibus legislation and virtually transforming the state and its legal ties to its society, Ottawa also mimicked the state-building response of the US government in its creation of the Department of Public Safety and Emergency Preparedness Canada (PSEPC) in 2003. The new department (which has shortened its name to Public Safety Canada, or PSC) operates with an annual budget of $430 million and has 800 employees. It was created to serve the same type of coordination function as the Department of Homeland Security in the US, ensuring that "all federal departments and agencies responsible for national security and the safety of Canadians" are under central direction.[23] It therefore runs the Government Operations Centre (GOC), which is the central hub bringing together the network of departments and agencies that would play a role in the defence of the nation – RCMP, Health Canada, Foreign Affairs, the Canadian Security Intelligence Service (CSIS), National Defence, and so on. The primary function of the GOC is to provide federal direction to these agencies and departments in the midst of a crisis, and to provide around-the-clock monitoring and surveillance of developing domestic and international situations. The GOC also provides public lists of "entities" associated with terrorism as well as information on those entities, such as their date of founding and a history of their criminal activities. Over thirty such entities are listed on the PSC website. Moreover, the department is responsible for issuing "security certificates" to individuals deemed to be a threat to Canadian society. Once issued, these certificates result in indefinite confinement leading to deportation; five have been issued since 9/11. Public Safety Canada also monitors the use of the provisions of new anti-terror legislation by law enforcement agencies in Canada. This new dimension of the Canadian state is Ottawa's answer to the American Department of Homeland Security. It will never be as large or as well funded, but the fact that it exists demonstrates to the United States that Canada takes terrorism seriously.

The Canadian response to the development of NORTHCOM took somewhat longer to develop. This was largely due to the controversial nature of NORTHCOM itself, and the discussions that took place between the Canadian and American governments regarding how to reconcile the creation of the new command with the previously established joint Canada-US command for the air defence of North America. In the end, the binational planning committee charged with these negotiations came up with minimal results.[24] Canada then moved on its own towards a revolutionary transformation of the structure of the Canadian Forces, bringing them under the central direction of Canada Command for all homeland operations. Canada Command has the immediate authority to respond to any unfolding land, air, or sea crisis, whether of a natural or terrorist variety. Based in the Ottawa/ Hull region, Canada Command controls six regional headquarters: Northern, Pacific, Prairie, Central, East, and Atlantic. It parallels NORTHCOM in that its operational mandate is homeland defence. This, the biggest restructuring of the Canadian Forces in four decades, was announced by General Rick

Hillier on 1 February 2006. About all of this, the defence minister at the time, Bill Graham, commented: "When I go down to the United States and I see Mr. Rumsfeld and go to Congress I'll be able to say: 'Look we're taking steps in Canada. You don't have to worry about Canada.' It sends up comfort levels that we know we're reliable partners in the defence of North America."[25]

Three other commands were established as part of the Canadian Forces transformation. Canadian Expeditionary Force Command (CEFCOM) will oversee all overseas deployments. Canadian Special Operations Forces Command (CANSOFCOM) will oversee the military's elite, covert commando missions. Finally, Canadian Operational Support Command (CANOSCOM) will generate "task-tailored" operational support for the three other new commands.[26]

Prior to the Canadian Forces transformation, Canada unveiled its response to the Bush Doctrine, just in time for Paul Martin's first visit to Washington as prime minister. Canada's *Securing an Open Society* was a northern echo of the Bush administration's 2002 National Security Strategy. The document came on the heels of three reports that had been critical of Canada's efforts to enhance homeland security after 9/11. From Auditor General of Canada Sheila Fraser came criticisms of the government's failure to "achieve improvements in the ability of security information systems to communicate with each other." Moreover, Fraser found deficiencies in the way intelligence was managed across government agencies and departments. In her March 2004 *Report of the Auditor General to the House of Commons,* she wrote: "The government as a whole did not adequately assess intelligence lessons learned from critical incidents such as September 11 or develop and follow up on improvement programs."[27] From the Standing Senate Committee on National Security and Defence came two reports summarized succinctly in their scathing titles: *The Myth of Security at Canada's Airports* (January 2003) and *Canada's Coastlines: The Longest Under-Defended Borders in the World* (October 2003).

It was to these lines of criticism that the Martin government responded with its distinctively entitled document *Securing an Open Society: Canada's National Security Policy.* In realist language, the document begins by listing Canada's three "core national security interests":

1   protecting Canada and Canadians at home and abroad
2   ensuring that Canada is not a base for threats to our allies
3   contributing to international security.[28]

The first of these is the raison d'être of any sovereign state. The second has been entrenched in Canada's defence policy since at least 1938, when Prime Minister Mackenzie King told President Franklin D. Roosevelt that he would do his best to keep a foreign invasion from being launched on the United States from Canadian soil. The third is indicative of the Canadian desire to play a part in the proper functioning of the international system. Indeed, a total of fourteen references are made to Canada's roles in the international system in the sixty-page document. Significantly, three references are made to Canada's role in countering international terrorism. Twice that role is referred to as "important."[29] It is also deemed "significant."[30] The document also states that Canada has played and will "continue to play an important role in preventing the proliferation of weapons of mass destruction, and defusing key intra- and interstate conflicts";[31] "a leading role in strengthening and modernizing international institutions so that they can contribute to international security";[32] "a leading role in the Global Health Security Initiative";[33] "a leading role at the International Civil Aviation Organization";[34] "a leading role at the International Maritime Organization";[35] "a key role in negotiating the implementation of [the United Nations'] twelve international terrorism conventions";[36] "a critical role" in Afghanistan "in helping to restore peace, stabilize the country, and rebuild democratic institutions."[37]

The terrorist theme plays loudly in the tone of the document, despite efforts to group the terrorist threat with other nontraditional security threats such as organized crime, globalized disease outbreak, and natural disasters, and despite the fact that there is not a separate chapter on combating terrorism. It is clear that the reason the strategy was constructed in the first place was to respond to the threat of a terrorist attack on Canada, or one launched on the United States from Canada. In total, terrorism is mentioned thirty-one times in the document's sixty pages. The US also factors heavily into Canada's national security strategy. It is mentioned thirty-four times, almost always in the context of terms such as "cooperation," "close alliance," and "key partner." By contrast, Canada is mentioned only three times in the Bush administration's National Security Strategy, always in lists of different states, while terrorism is mentioned twenty-nine times.

A significant initiative detailed in the Canadian statement is the creation of a National Security Adviser to the Prime Minister for the purpose of improving "coordination and integration of security efforts among government departments."[38] President Eisenhower created the office of National Security Adviser in 1953. In the United States, the National Security Adviser is appointed by the president and is not subject to the approval of the Senate. In Canada, the prime minister appoints the National Security Adviser.

A second significant initiative proposes to establish a new "Integrated Threat Assessment Centre."[39] The purpose of this centre is to create an integrated security model commensurate with those in the United States, the United Kingdom, and Australia. The centre is to be housed within CSIS, and bring together representatives from DFAIT, DND, PSEPC, the RCMP, and the PCO.[40] It will be connected to the network of American, British, and Australian threat assessment centres. Both initiatives, and the overarching themes of integration and coordination woven throughout the document, were deemed by the auditor general to be adequate responses to the criticisms she had levelled against the government in her March 2004 report.

The Martin government pledged $690 million to help facilitate the integration of Canada's security apparatus. Almost half of these funds were allocated to enhance maritime security by increasing the on-water presence of the Coast Guard, RCMP, and Canadian Forces, and tightening security at ports and the St. Lawrence Seaway locks. Maritime security operations would be integrated through the establishment of Marine Security Operations Centres designed to bring together the responsible departments and agencies. This initiative was a clear response to the Standing Senate Committee's criticisms in its 2003 report. In response to the Standing Senate Committee's criticisms of Canada's airport security, the document cites the $1 billion investment that the government made in equipping Canadian airports with advanced explosive detection devices;[41] its establishment of the Air Carrier Protection Program, which places specially trained RCMP officers on selected flights; and its establishment of the Canadian Air Transport Security Authority to enhance the screening of passengers moving through the country's airports.

US Treasury Secretary John Snow "welcomed" the Canadian effort to articulate a security strategy, saying that "it sounded to me very much like what we were doing, so I applauded the development."[42] With all of this President Bush also seemed pleased. In a speech to Nova Scotians in early December 2004, he stated: "Canada has taken a series of critical steps to guard against the danger of terrorism. You created the Department of Public Safety and Emergency Preparedness. You've toughened your anti-terror laws. You're upgrading your intelligence. I want to thank the government for all those constructive and important decisions."[43] But he saved his most significant praise for the Canada-US Smart Border initiative – an enterprise that catalyzed much of the Canadian domestic response to 9/11.

The Longest (Un)defended Border

While these rapid and largely unprecedented changes were taking place inside the United States and Canada, equally rapid and radical changes were taking place along their shared border. "In the decade before September 11, 2001," according to the authors of the *9/11 Commission Report,* "border security – encompassing travel, entry, and immigration – was not seen as a national security matter."[44] This was especially the case with the so-called longest undefended border in the world. After 9/11, this view of border security changed dramatically in the United States. Accordingly, the Canada-US Smart Border Declaration and Action Plan, a thirty-two-point action plan, was signed on 12 December 2001 by Director of the Office of Homeland Security Tom Ridge and Minister of Foreign Affairs John Manley, just three months after the terrorist attacks. The aim of the agreement was to establish what Ridge referred to as a "zone of confidence against terrorist activity."[45] This implied that 9/11 had shaken the confidence Americans had in the longest undefended border in the world. The terrorists might not have come from Canada, but there would nevertheless have to be increased precautions taken against the dire possibility. No longer would it suffice to have just a quarter of the number of US border guards working the Canada-US border as the Mexico-US border. The declaration provided a clear and substantive guide to how the status quo along the forty-ninth parallel would change.

Ridge and Manley were surely aware of the historical confidence bargain that had been struck by their two countries on matters of continental security. Thus, the choice of language for the "zone of confidence" bargain on border security was no accident, and neither were the terms of the eventual accord. Ottawa would do all it could to keep terrorist traffic from crossing the forty-ninth parallel en route to the US, or Washington would either step in and fill the void or unilaterally harden the border – in the former case, causing irreparable harm to Canadian sovereignty, in the latter to the Canadian economy, and either way fundamentally altering the terms of the continental relationship. As Secretary of State Colin Powell said in the early days after 9/11: "Some nations need to be more vigilant against terrorism at their borders if they want their relationship with the U.S. to remain the same."[46] For the Canadian point man in the Smart Border negotiations, then, the implications of 9/11 were crystal-clear. John Manley told the *Toronto Star*: "I felt that the greatest risk to Canada as a result of Sept. 11 ... was to the economy."[47] The urgency with which he negotiated the thirty-two-point border action plan with Tom Ridge was thus motivated by economic necessity, and by a desire to show that Canada would keep up its end of the confidence bargain. Hence the declared goal of the action plan: "To enhance security of our undefended border while facilitating the legitimate flow of people and goods."[48]

In order to accomplish this goal, and thereby keep security from being a nontariff barrier *par excellence,* the border, as the declaration makes clear, has to become smart in terms of (1) the secure flow of people, (2) the secure flow of goods, (3) secure infrastructure, and (4) information sharing and coordination in the enforcement of these objectives.

First, approximately 300,000 people cross the Canada-US border each day. How to distinguish between malignant and benign crossings effectively and efficiently is a problem that is progressively being solved with the implementation of a layered and ultra high-tech system of surveillance and screening techniques. The NEXUS Program, for example, which has become the new status quo at an increasing number of Canada-US border crossings, accomplishes this by predetermining who is eligible to cross the border by land and by air through dedicated lanes subject to minimal inspection.

Frequent crossers apply to be screened and approved for this privilege, which costs Cdn$80. NEXUS users then receive a special identification card that can be scanned electronically as they pass through border inspections in the "fast lane." Biometric technology, which is used to identify persons by their unique biological characteristics – such as irises, fingerprints, faces, hands, and so on – is also being utilized to make borders smarter. Noncitizens in Canada, for example, are issued Permanent Resident Cards equipped with biometric identifiers to eliminate fraud and duplication problems. In tandem with these technological advancements, the two countries moved towards policy harmonization and coordination on a number of issues, including immigration systems and processes, refugee/asylum seekers, and third-country visa exemptions and restrictions.

Second, in terms of securing the flow of goods across the border, a Free and Secure Trade (FAST) program has been established to do for the flow of commercial traffic what NEXUS does for the flow of people. Preapproved importers, carriers, and registered drivers can cross the border with their cargo in designated fast lanes, subject to minimal inspection and information requirements. All major commercial crossings were to be FAST-capable by the end of 2004.[49] In addition, Canada and US customs agencies now participate in joint enforcement teams in each other's main marine ports, targeting container inspection. This inspection work is eased by the requirement of "advance manifest data for incoming ships and the containers they carry."[50]

Third, the above initiatives for securing the flow of people and goods between the United States and Canada necessitated significant improvements to border and port infrastructure. In January 2002, President Bush announced a $2.1 billion spending increase to put hundreds of "additional customs, immigration and border-patrol agents along the 49th parallel."[51] Bush also announced that he wanted to bring annual border control spending up to $10.7 billion by the next fiscal year. The 2006 fiscal year budget, however, included just $6.7 billion for US Customs and Border Protection. In December 2001, the Chrétien government announced that it would spend $1.2 billion on enhanced border security and infrastructure, as part of its $7.7 billion commitment to enhance the overall security of Canada's share of North America. (Notably, one of the summaries of this new spending on the Department of Foreign Affairs and International Trade website described the amounts in US dollar figures.)[52] The Canadian government further established the Border Infrastructure Fund to provide $600 million to support the Smart Border initiatives. Of those funds, nearly half went to improving traffic problems at the Windsor/Detroit border crossing.[53]

Fourth, besides just improved infrastructure and financing, securing the border requires enhanced communication and coordination between Canadian and American officials. Accordingly, Integrated Border Enforcement

Teams (IBETs) have been established to "combine the intelligence and law enforcement expertise of various agencies and use a coordinated approach to identify and stop the high-risk movement of people and goods between the ports of entry on the Canada-United States border."[54] According to PSEPC, "there are IBETs operating in all regions, on land and sea, along the border," and the five core agencies involved in these teams are: (1) Canada Border Services Agency, (2) RCMP, (3) US Customs and Border Protection, (4) US Coast Guard, (5) US Immigration and Customs Enforcement.[55]

Also central to the coordination of the Canada-US response to continental homeland security is the Cross Border Crime Forum, which brings together continental law enforcement agencies annually to discuss

> transnational crime problems including terrorism, organized crime, contra-band smuggling, mass marketing fraud, money laundering, crimes using computers and other emerging cross-border issues such as auto theft. The Forum also focuses on resolving obstacles and impediments – primarily with regards to policy, regulations and legislation – faced by law enforcement and justice officials who work on cross-border crime issues.[56]

The RCMP has also set up Integrated National Security Enforcement Teams to "collect, analyse and share information about national security among partners."[57] One can safely assume that the US is pre-eminent among these partners. The United States has reciprocated this information sharing by making Canada a part of its Foreign Terrorist Tracking Task Force (FTTTF), which exists to "detect, interdict, and remove foreign terrorists."[58] The FBI and the RCMP have agreed – through a Memorandum of Cooperation – to establish a joint electronic database of criminal records information and fingerprint information.[59]

Canada and the United States have jointly developed a risk scoring system for air travellers and the ability to share that information with each other. Little information about the criteria for the risk scoring is available, making this perhaps the most controversial measure taken to date by the Canadian government. Critics charge that it amounts to "profiling Canadian travelers, and expands the state's incursion into the private lives of innocent individuals."[60] In documents released to public interest researcher Ken Rubin under access to information legislation, a summary of the project's cost includes the sum of $35.6 million for computer systems necessary "for Canada to honour commitments made to the United States."[61]

Finally, Canada, the United States, and Mexico announced on 23 March 2005 that they had entered into "an unprecedented trilateral Security and Prosperity Partnership (SPP) to establish a common security strategy and promote economic growth, competitiveness and quality of life."[62] Under the SPP, ministerial-led working groups are to consult with stakeholders in all three countries, and work to develop "measurable and achievable goals" that aim towards continental policy harmonization in the name of both security and prosperity.

Canada and the US moved with urgency and efficiency to smarten the border across these four areas. The progress that has been made in securing the flow of people and goods, in improving border infrastructure, and in integrating communication and information sharing between the two states since 9/11 is significant. Although there are still inefficiencies at the border, the initial post-9/11 moves to increase security while maintaining the flow of commerce and people between the two countries demonstrate that Canada and the US can follow straightforward policy courses towards mutually beneficial policy outcomes free of internal incongruity. This happens when the structural pressures of the continental system bear down on the relationship alone, and are not interfered with by the structural pressures of the broader international system. The pace and form of Canada's transformation into a post-9/11 security state in the American mould – its constitutional, bureaucratic, and defensive changes – is demonstrative of the reality of the continental hierarchy. A made-in-Canada response to the post-9/11 era was never a possibility. Canada was compelled by its subordinate position in North America to mimic the US transformation into a security state.

Conclusion

Through the lens of structural specialization theory, we have seen for the first time how Canada's place in the world is connected to its place in North America, how the predominant patterns of Canada's engagement in the world have been shaped by its relationship with the United States at home, and how this relationship has affected the patterns of interaction between the two states as they have engaged with each another abroad over the last fifty years. Across different eras in international relations, with an array of different leaders in both Ottawa and Washington, and with different regime configurations in both states, the hypothesized patterns of paradox and specialization have persisted. Identifying these patterns and providing a theoretical explanation for them was the primary purpose of this work. Drawing out some of the implications of these findings for the development of the wider body of international relations theory, as well as for the practice of Canada–US relations and Canadian foreign policy, is a task worth doing in conclusion.

This book demonstrates that hierarchy matters in international relations. Canada-US relations do not operate according to the same logic as relations between great powers. Indeed, the case studies of the Vietnam War, the Cuban Missile Crisis, and the War on Terror suggest how remarkably difficult it has been for two states with such a long history of cooperation at home to coordinate their efforts abroad. Even when issues of continental defence take on international significance, as the cases of nuclear weapons and missile defence have demonstrated, the contrasting pressures of hierarchy in anarchy combine to interfere with Canadian and American policy coordination. That the paradoxical and contradictory history of Canada-US high political interaction abroad is due to the hierarchy in their relationship at home has until now remained beyond the grasp of international relations theory. Canada, moreover, has been shown to act in the broader international system in a manner significantly differentiated from that of the great powers. Its behaviour, therefore, cannot be understood through the traditional lenses of international relations theory, which were developed primarily, if not solely, to understand the actions of the great powers themselves.

Given that there is but one great power bestriding the planet, the focus of international relations theory needs to be shifted to the relations of great powers with small states and the role of small states in the international system. These two seemingly disparate features of world politics have appeared to the vast majority of international relations theorists to be minor (epiphenomenal) aspects of their field, unlikely to have any significant determining effects on the major outcomes within the realm of world politics. The case studies presented in this work demonstrate repeatedly the dangers of seeing world politics in such a circumscribed manner. Accordingly, it is time to take hierarchy in international relations seriously. The theory developed in Chapter 1 and tested initially in succeeding chapters suggests a number of avenues for further research and development along these lines.

The first, of course, involves further testing of its two main hypotheses against other hierarchical inter-state relationships. Whether structural specialization theory (SST) holds up as a general theory of hierarchical inter-state relations remains in question until such testing is conducted. The second involves the development of further testable hypotheses from the core of SST. Areas in which such work might be carried out were suggested in Chapter 1. They include further theorizing the effects of structural specialization on the domestic stability of the subordinate state. This book has gone some way towards this by connecting internal cohesion and national morale to the performance of specialized international functions, but it might also be possible to connect other recurring features of the subordinate state/society relationship (such as corruption, low voter turnout, and political apathy) to its position within the inter-state hierarchy. Finally, from a normative perspective, it is important to develop ideas about how inter-state hierarchies, particularly those between the United States and its allies, can be optimized to the benefit of both states involved, and the stability of the broader international system.

In this period of American predominance, what was once thought of as the sideshow of America's relations with its subordinate allies can now be seen to have taken up a place at the centre stage of world politics. How the US manages these relations and the roles of these states in maintaining world order could determine its future position in the system and the continuity and stability of the system itself. If, on the one hand, the US can generate support for its leadership among its allies and effectively delegate specialized aspects of its systemic management role to allies like Canada that possess the requisite attributes and abilities, it is likely that the current world order based on American power and the values of democracy and open markets will continue long into the future. On the other hand, if these relations are managed poorly and the system-ameliorating capabilities of America's subordinate allies are misapplied (as Canada's are in the south of Afghanistan), revisionist powers such as China or Russia could rise (individually or in tandem) to rival the US in influence over the shape of the current world political order.

The current American grand strategy to maintain primacy[1] in the international system seems doomed to failure if it is not combined with a strategy for managing the specialized capacities of its subordinate allies. Failure to recognize the enabling dimension of primacy – how hierarchic inter-state relationships allow subordinate states to alter their strategic approach to pursue specialization – for subordinate states could lead ultimately to a reversion from subordination on the part of allies like Canada, who will be compelled to reject a strategy of specialization for a strategy of balancing against American primacy, or at the very least a lessening of its dependence on the US for its physical and economic survival. Accordingly, it would appear that the US, if it is committed to doing the heavy lifting in the international system – providing security and maintaining a stable and open global economy – also needs to be committed to delegating the more specialized tasks of international system management to its subordinate allies. Creating space and support for such specialized contributions seems key to a successful strategy of primacy, since it is through these contributions that subordinate states maintain their sovereign integrity both at home and abroad.

Importantly, a recent US strategy document, *A Cooperative Strategy for 21st Century Seapower* (2007), suggests that this logic is slowly starting to be embraced by high-level strategic thinkers in US government, military, and academic circles. To quote from the document, which was influenced in its development by a series of "Conversations with the Country" (public forums on the future of American seapower): "Expanded cooperative relationships with other nations will contribute to the security and stability of the maritime domain for the benefit of all. Although our forces can surge when necessary to respond to crises, *trust and cooperation cannot be surged.* They must be built over time so that the strategic interests of the participants are continuously considered while mutual understanding and respect are promoted."[2] This spirit of cooperation, consideration, understanding, and respect needs to be infused with a theoretically informed understanding of how best to manage America's relations with its subordinate allies.

Structural specialization theory suggests that being able to reliably delegate functional tasks to its subordinates would enhance America's systemic management and leadership capabilities.[3] Just as the US, by virtue of its primacy, is bound in some ways to lead, so its subordinate allies are bound in some ways to follow that lead. But the deep paradox of hierarchy in anarchy is that the coordination of the foreign policies of super- and subordinate states is certain to be difficult. An advanced sense of the specialized capabilities of its subordinate allies might help to reduce intra-hierarchical tensions by lessening the number and intensity of US demands for those allies to comply with directives that are out of step with the allies' particular interests in differentiating themselves from US policy and the US role in the world. Here, what Stephen Walt describes as the tactic of "self-restraint"[4] could be exercised by the US in exchange for the promise of specialized contributions on the part of its subordinate allies. For example, before carrying out regime change in Iraq, the Bush administration might have considered the need for democratic elections after Saddam Hussein's removal from power, and the need for advanced democratic countries that were not combatants in the war to step in and show the Iraqi people how to select a representative government. Likewise, Canada might have foreseen this necessity and offered itself for such a role. In this instance, the pressure put on Canada to join the Coalition of the Willing might have been reduced through "self-restraint" on the part of the Bush administration, and the damage to the Canada-US relationship might have been minimized.

This demonstrates that superordinate and subordinate states need to get on the same page with respect to the logic of one another's foreign policy and grand strategy. Each is ultimately after survival, but pursues it through much different means. Superordinate states survive by maintaining their pre-eminent position through the management of a functioning international system built on the foundation of their material capability. Subordinate states survive by fulfilling specialized roles within that system. The specialized roles that are opened up to subordinate states by virtue of their positions in inter-state hierarchies allow for the possibility of a more complex and sophisticated international society, with different states taking up an array of specialized roles, all working towards the same basic end of the smooth functioning, amelioration, and progressive change of the international system. It will not be by great power alone that the United States succeeds in maintaining its position of primacy in the international system. Coordinating its efforts and aims with its subordinate allies and utilizing their specialized capacities and skills will be essential to the longevity and durability of the American unipolar moment.

Not all of the responsibility for this sort of coordination and delegation rests with the US alone, however. America's subordinate allies need to be cognizant of their specialized capabilities and of the fact that their position relative to the US both compels and enables them to perform these particular functions in international politics. Accordingly, they need to both protect and cultivate these capabilities, and cannot, as Canada is currently doing in

Kandahar, risk diminishing them by pursuing roles more suited to great powers. Ideally, America's subordinates would be in constant communication and negotiation with Washington, working to coordinate their particular roles in managing the stability of the international system. Realistically, however, the pressures of the international anarchy would make this difficult, as this sort of coordination would expose the lack of foreign policy autonomy held by America's subordinate allies. This is the essential dilemma posed by the reality of hierarchy in anarchy.

Notes

Introduction

1 Jennifer Welsh, *At Home in the World: Canada's Global Vision for the 21st Century* (Toronto: HarperCollins, 2004), 26.

2 The major exception to this is David B. Dewitt and John Kirton, *Canada as a Principal Power: A Study in Foreign Policy and International Relations* (Toronto: Wiley and Sons, 1983).

3 See Denis Stairs, "The Political Culture of Canadian Foreign Policy," *Canadian Journal of Political Science* 15, 4 (1982): 667-90; J. King Gordon, ed., *Canada's Role as a Middle Power* (Toronto: Canadian Institute of International Affairs, 1966); Peyton V. Lyon and Brian W. Tomlin, *Canada as an International Actor* (Toronto: Macmillan, 1979). For the most recent version of such an argument, see Welsh, *At Home in the World.*

4 See Geoffrey Pearson, *Seize the Day: Lester B. Pearson and Crisis Diplomacy* (Ottawa: Carleton University Press, 1993).

5 See Fen Osler Hampson, Norman Hillmer, and Maureen Appel Molot, eds., *Canada among Nations 2001: The Axworthy Legacy* (Toronto: Oxford University Press, 2001).

6 See David R. Black and Heather A. Smith, "Notable Exceptions? New and Arrested Directions in Canadian Foreign Policy Literature," *Canadian Journal of Political Science* 26, 4 (1994): 745-74.

7 Michael K. Hawes, *Principal Power, Middle Power, or Satellite?* (Toronto: York Research Programme in Strategic Studies, 1984), 2.

Chapter 1: The Special Relationship and Canada as a Specialized Power

1 See Robert O. Keohane, ed., *Neorealism and Its Critics* (New York: Columbia University Press, 1986).

2 Kenneth Waltz, *Theory of International Politics* (Toronto: McGraw-Hill, 1979).

3 Efforts were made to conceive of a structural theory of international politics prior to Waltz (1979). See, for example, Morton Kaplan, *System and Process in International Politics* (New York: Krieger, 1975), and, to a lesser extent, Charles A. McClelland, *Theory and the International System* (New York: Macmillan, 1966).

4 E.H. Carr, *The Twenty Years' Crisis, 1919-1939: An Introduction to the Study of International Relations* (London: Macmillan, 1939, 1962), 1.

5 David Easton, "An Approach to the Analysis of Political Systems," *World Politics* 9, 3 (1957): 386; Waltz, *Theory*, 93; David H. Everson and Joann Poparad Paine, *An Introduction to Systematic Political Science* (Homewood, IL: Dorsey, 1973), 193; David Easton, *The Analysis of Political Structure* (New York: Routledge, 1990), 54.

6 Waltz, *Theory*, 95-97.

7 Ibid., 118.

8 Ibid., 122.

9 Ibid.

10 On this, which amounts to the distinction between offensive and defensive realism, see John J. Mearsheimer, *The Tragedy of Great Power Politics* (New York: Norton, 2001), 21.

11 Ibid., 92.

12 Charles Glaser, "When Are Arms Races Dangerous? Rational versus Suboptimal Arming," *International Security* 28, 4 (2004): 44.

13 Stephen Walt, *The Origins of Alliances* (Ithaca, NY: Cornell University Press, 1987).

14 See John A. Vasquez and Colin Elman, eds., *Realism and the Balancing of Power: A New Debate* (Upper Saddle River, NJ: Prentice Hall, 2003).

15 For examples, see Waltz, *Theory*; John Mearsheimer, "Back to the Future: Instability in Europe after the Cold War," *International Security* 15, 1 (1990): 5-56; and Stephen Van Evera, *Causes of War* (Ithaca, NY: Cornell University Press, 1999).

16 Stephen Krasner, ed., *International Regimes* (Ithaca, NY: Cornell University Press, 1983); see introduction and conclusion by Krasner.

17 See Robert Keohane, "Neoliberal Institutionalism: A Perspective on World Politics," in his collection entitled *International Institutions and State Power* (Boulder, CO: Westview, 1989), 1-20; and David A. Baldwin, ed., *Neorealism and Neoliberalism: The Contemporary Debate* (New York: Columbia University Press, 1993).

18 Alexander Wendt, "Anarchy Is What States Make of It: The Social Construction of Power Politics," *International Organization* 46, 2 (1992): 391-425; see also Emmanuel Adler and Michael Barnett, eds., *Security Communities* (Cambridge: Cambridge University Press, 1998). In particular, Sean M. Shore's article in this volume, "No Fences Made Good Neighbors: The Development of the US-Canada Security Community, 1871-1940," explores the early roots of the North American relationship.

19 John Gerard Ruggie, "What Makes the World Hang Together? Neo-Utilitarianism and the Social Constructivist Challenge," *International Organization* 52, 4 (1998): 887-917; and Emmanuel Adler, "Seizing the Middle Ground: Constructivism in World Politics," *European Journal of International Relations* 3, 3 (1997): 319-63.

20 Kaplan, *System and Process*, 4.

21 See Brian C. Schmidt, *The Political Discourse of Anarchy: A Disciplinary History of International Relations* (Albany, NY: SUNY Press, 1998).

22 Indeed, a number of international relations scholars have begun to chip away at this anarchy assumption. See, for example, Jack Donnelly, "Sovereign Inequalities and Hierarchy in Anarchy: American Power and International Society," *European Journal of International Relations* 12, 2 (2006): 141; Alexander Cooley, *Logics of Hierarchy: The Organization of Empires, States and Military Occupations* (Ithaca, NY: Cornell University Press, 2005); Evelyn Goh, "Great Powers and Hierarchical Order in Southeast Asia: Analyzing Political Security Strategies," *International Security* 32 (Winter 2007/2008), 113-57; David A. Lake, "Anarchy, Hierarchy, and the Variety of International Relations," *International Organization* 50, 1 (1996): 1-33; David A. Lake, "Escape from the State of Nature: Authority and Hierarchy in World Politics," *International Security* 32, 1 (Summer 2007): 47-79.

23 See, for some examples, G. John Ikenberry, "Liberalism and Empire: Logics of Order in the American Unipolar Age," *Review of International Studies* 30 (2004): 609-30; and G. John Ikenberry, ed., *America Unrivaled: The Future of the Balance of Power* (Ithaca, NY: Cornell University Press, 2002); Stephen G. Brooks and William C. Wohlforth, "American Primacy in Perspective," *Foreign Affairs* 81, 4 (2002): 20-33; Charles Kupchan, *The End of the American Era: US Foreign Policy and the Geopolitics of the Twenty-First Century* (New York: Vintage, 2003).

24 Excluding Mexico, Canada claims 9,984,670 square kilometres of the continent, while the United States claims 9,826,629 square kilometres. Barry Turner, ed., *The Statesman's Yearbook: The Politics, Cultures, and Economics of the World* (New York: Palgrave, 2004).

25 Alan Heston, Robert Summers, and Bettina Aten, *Penn World Table Version 6.2,* Center for International Comparisons of Production, Income and Prices at the University of Pennsylvania, September 2006, http://pwt.econ.upenn.edu/php_site/pwt_index.php.

26 See World Bank Group, World Development Indicators Online, 2007, www.worldbank.org.

27 See Information from the Stockholm International Peace Research Institute (SIPRI), http://www.sipri.org/contents/milap/milex/mex_database1.html.

28 President Franklin Roosevelt, Address at Queen's University, Kingston, Ontario, Canada, 18 August 1938, http://www.ibiblio.org/pha/7-2-188/188-09.html.

29 H.L. Keenleyside, "The Canada-United States Permanent Joint Board on Defence, 1940-1945," *International Journal* 16, 1 (1960-61): 52.

30 Nils Ørvik, "The Basic Issue in Canadian National Security: Defence against Help/Defence to Help Others," *Canadian Defence Quarterly* 11, 1 (1981): 9.

31 Statement issued by Prime Minister King and President Roosevelt to their peoples regarding the establishment of the joint defence of North America. Quoted in Keenleyside, "The Canada-United States Permanent Joint Board on Defence," 52.

32 Joseph Jockel, *Canada in NORAD, 1957-2007: A History* (Montreal and Kingston: McGill-Queen's University Press, 2007).

33 Norman Hillmer, ed., *Partners Nevertheless: Canadian-American Relations in the Twentieth Century* (Toronto: Copp Clark, 1989).

34 John P. Warnock, *Partner to Behemoth: The Military Policy of a Satellite Canada* (Toronto: New Press, 1970).

35 James Minifie, *Peacemaker or Powder Monkey: Canada's Role in a Revolutionary World* (Toronto: McClelland and Stewart, 1970).

36 Canada, Department of Foreign Affairs and International Trade, "Canada and the World: A History, 1968-1984: The Trudeau Years," http://www.dfait-maeci.gc.ca/depatment/history/canada9-en.asp.

37 William Henry Pope, *The Elephant and the Mouse: A Handbook on Regaining Control of Canada's Economy* (Toronto: McClelland and Stewart, 1971).

38 US, White House, "President Discusses Strong Relationship with Canada," Halifax, 1 December 2004, http://www.whitehouse.gov/news/releases/2004/12/20041201-4.html.

39 John Gerald Ruggie, "Continuity and Transformation in the World Polity: Toward a Neo-realist Synthesis," in Keohane, *Neorealism and Its Critics,* 135.

40 As Hegel writes: "Without relations with other states, the state can no more be an actual individual than an individual can be an actual person without relationship with other persons. On the other hand, the legitimacy of the state, and more precisely – in so far as it has external relations – of the power of its sovereign, is a purely internal matter (one state should not interfere with the internal affairs of another). On the other hand, it is equally essential that this legitimacy should be supplemented by recognition on the part of other states. But this recognition requires a guarantee that the state will likewise recognize those other states which are supposed to recognize it, i.e., that it will respect their independence; accordingly, these other states cannot be indifferent to its internal affairs": *Elements of the Philosophy of Right,* edited by Allen Wood, translated by H.B. Nisbet (New York: Cambridge University Press, 1991), § 331.

41 On this "push-pull" dynamic under conditions of informal empire, see Alexander Wendt and Daniel Friedheim, "Hierarchy under Anarchy: Informal Empire and the East German State," in *State Sovereignty as Social Construct,* edited by Thomas J. Biersteker and Cynthia Weber (Cambridge University Press, 1996), 252-53.

42 Stephen Walt, "Keeping the World 'Off Balance': Self-Restraint and U.S. Foreign Policy," in *America Unrivaled: The Future of the Balance of Power,* edited by G. John Ikenberry (Ithaca, NY: Cornell University Press, 2002), 121-55.

43 Most prominently, this can be seen in the form of Article 23, which outlines the criteria to be considered for nomination as a nonpermanent member of the Security Council, and in Article 44, which guarantees that any state asked to participate in the application of force for the re-establishment of order will be involved in the decisions of the Security Council leading to that application. As representatives of a trading state with a strong economy, the Canadian delegates also placed strong emphasis on the development of the Economic and Social Council, in which they foresaw significant involvement for Canada.

44 F.H. Soward and Edgar McInnis, "Forming the United Nations, 1945," in *Canadian Foreign Policy: Selected Cases,* edited by Don Munton and John Kirton (Scarborough, ON: Prentice Hall, 1992), 13; see also Adam Chapnick, *The Middle Power Project: Canada and the Founding of the United Nations* (Vancouver: UBC Press, 2005). Chapnick is especially interesting on the American view of the functional principle, 75-76.

45 John J. Kirton, *Canadian Foreign Policy in a Changing World* (Toronto: Thompson-Nelson, 2007), 40-41.

46 Andrew F. Cooper, "In Search of Niches: Saying 'Yes' and Saying 'No' in Canada's International Relations," *Canadian Foreign Policy* 3, 3 (Winter 1995): 1-13; and Duane Bratt, "Niche Making and Canadian Peacekeeping," *Canadian Foreign Policy* 6, 3 (Spring 1999): 73-90.

47 For more on this method, see Alexander L. George and Andrew Bennett, *Case Studies and Theory Development in the Social Sciences* (Cambridge, MA: MIT Press, 2005).

48 Charles F. Hermann, "International Crisis as a Situational Variable," in *International Politics and Foreign Policy,* edited by James N. Rosenau (New York: Simon and Schuster, 1969), 409-21.

Chapter 2: The Vietnam War, 1954-73

1 Douglas Ross, *In the Interests of Peace: Canada and Vietnam, 1954-1973* (Toronto: University of Toronto Press, 1984), 68. This view is supported by a message written to Prime Minister Louis St. Laurent by Secretary of State for External Affairs (SSEA) Lester B. Pearson on 6 May 1954, which stated that "we have, however, through our close contacts with the Americans and the British, been kept completely informed of everything that has been going on, and, indeed, have taken part in a good many of the preliminary and informal discussions": Secretary of State for External Affairs to Prime Minister, Geneva, 6 May 1954, in Department of External Affairs, Documents on Canadian External Relations, edited by Greg Donaghy (Ottawa: Canada Communications Group, 1997), 1668.

2 See Poeliu Dai, "Canada's Role in the International Commission for Supervision and Control in Vietnam," in *The Canadian Yearbook of International Law* (Vancouver: Publications Centre, University of British Columbia, 1966), 164-65.

3 A.J. Langguth, *Our Vietnam: The War, 1954-1975* (Toronto: Simon and Schuster, 2000), 80.

4 John Holmes, "Geneva: 1954," *International Journal* 22, 3 (1967): 464.

5 James Eayrs reports that this was at least what the US Secretary of State in 1967 told his Canadian counterpart: *In Defence of Canada, Indochina: Roots of Complicity* (Toronto: University of Toronto Press, 1983), 60.

6 Ambassador in United States to Secretary of State for External Affairs, Indo-China – International Control Commission, Washington, 20 July 1954, in Department of External Affairs, Documents on Canadian External Relations, 1678.

7 Ambassador in United States to Secretary of State for External Affairs, Indo-China Supervisory Commissions, Washington, 24 July 1954, in Department of External Affairs, Documents on Canadian External Relations, 1686. Further to this point, the Canadian ambassador in Mexico wrote to the SSEA to report: "I had a conversation with Grafstrom, Swedish Minister here, who wished me to let you know in the light of his own experience on official Commissions he believed Canada would be placed in an impossible position were it to agree to serve with India and Poland on the Commission for Indo-China. His view is that the position of Canada would be more difficult than that of Sweden or Switzerland since they, at least, were two to face the intransigency of the Communists and the ambiguity of India. He foresees a serious danger that on many vital issues Canada will be left alone to oppose the two other members of the Commission": Mexico City, 27 July 1954, in Department of External Affairs, Documents on Canadian External Relations, 1689.

8 Ambassador in United States to Secretary of State for External Affairs, Indo-China Supervisory Commissions, Washington, 24 July 1954, in Department of External Affairs, Documents on Canadian External Relations, 1686.

9 John Hilliker and Donald Barry, "Uncomfortably in the Middle: The Department of External Affairs and Canada's Involvement in the International Control Commissions in Vietnam, 1954-1973," paper presented at the Biennial Meeting of the Association for Canadian Studies in the United States, Seattle, WA, 15-19 November 1995, 4.

10 Ross, *In the Interests of Peace,* 94-96.

11 The Geneva Cease-fire Agreement for Vietnam, the Final Declaration of the Geneva Conference on Indochina. Included in Ross, *In the Interests of Peace,* 391.

12 Eayrs, *In Defence of Canada, Indochina,* 163. Eayrs notes further that the *Globe and Mail* ran the story of the minority report under the headline "Ottawa Bares Red Trickery in Indo China" – "a good day's work for Information division" in his estimation.
13 Ibid., 220.
14 J. Blair Seaborn, "Mission to Hanoi: The Canadian Channel, May 1964 – November 1965," in *Canadian Peacekeepers in Indochina, 1954-1973,* edited by Arthur E. Blanchette (Ottawa: Golden Dog, 2002), 92.
15 *The Senator Gravel Edition of the Pentagon Papers: The Defense Department History of United States Decision Making on Vietnam,* vol. 3 (Boston: Beacon, 1971), 164.
16 Ibid., 163.
17 "United States-Vietnam Relations, 1954-1967, VI. C. I. Settlement of the Conflict, History of Contacts, Negotiations, 1965-1966 Vietnam Task Force, Office of the Secretary of Defense, Top Secret – Sensitive," reproduced in *The Canadian Forum,* September 1973, 10.
18 "Memo to: G. Mr U. Alexis Johnson, From S/VN – Josephe A. Medelhall, dated June 1, 1964 (TS) Subject: Instructions for Canadian Interlocutor in Hanoi," reproduced in *The Canadian Forum,* September 1973, 10.
19 "AMEMB Saigon 2212 (S/NODIS), rec'd 15 May 64, 7:20 a.m. for the President from Lodge," ibid., 9.
20 Charles Taylor, *Snow Job: Canada, the United States and Vietnam [1954 to 1973]* (Toronto: Anansi, 1978), 51-53.
21 Daniel Ellsberg, *Secrets: A Memoir of Vietnam and the Pentagon Papers* (New York: Viking, 2002), 17.
22 Taylor, *Snow Job,* 61.
23 Robert Mann, *A Grand Delusion: America's Descent into Vietnam* (New York: Basic Books, 2001), 384.
24 Ellsberg, *Secrets,* 7.
25 Mann, *A Grand Delusion,* 350-51.
26 Ellsberg, *Secrets,* 19.
27 Lyndon Baines Johnson, *The Vantage Point: Perspectives of the Presidency, 1963-1969* (New York: Popular Library, 1971), 67.
28 Diplomatic papers: Butterworth to State Department, 31 January, 2 February 1966, quoted in Taylor, *Snow Job,* 97. Martin would later publicly deny that this was the rationale behind his idea for the Ronning missions.
29 Quoted in Greg Donaghy, *Tolerant Allies: Canada and the United States, 1963-1968* (Montreal and Kingston: McGill-Queen's University Press, 2002), 133.
30 Ibid.
31 Ross, *In the Interests of Peace,* 289.
32 "U.S. Bombed North Week after Assurance: Ronning," *Globe and Mail,* 3 July 1971, 1.
33 Secretary of State Dean Rusk in a cable to the Consulate General in Hong Kong, quoted in Ross, *In the Interests of Peace,* 289.
34 Quoted in John T. Saywell, ed., *Canadian Annual Review for 1965* (Toronto: University of Toronto Press, 1966), 220.
35 Paul Bridle, "Canada and the International Commissions in Indochina, 1954-1972," *Behind the Headlines* 32, 4 (1973): 18.
36 "Extracts from an Address by the Right Honourable Lester B. Pearson, Prime Minister of Canada, to the Canadian Club of Ottawa, February 10, 1965," Canada, Department of External Affairs, Statements and Speeches, 65/3.
37 John H. Sigler and Dennis Goresky, "Public Opinion on United States-Canadian Relations," *International Organization* 28, 4 (1974): 662.
38 There is speculation that US Vice President Hubert Humphrey invited Pearson to make the comments. John English suggests that Humphrey was a dove who could have used Pearson's help in speaking out against the war, but does not go so far as to claim that Humphrey invited Pearson to criticize Johnson's Vietnam policy.
39 Hilliker and Barry, "Uncomfortably in the Middle," 11.
40 Kim Richard Nossal, *The Politics of Canadian Foreign Policy,* 3rd ed. (Scarborough, ON: Prentice Hall, 1997), 210-11.

41 Peter Stursberg, *Lester Pearson and the American Dilemma* (Toronto: Doubleday, 1980), 218.
42 John English, *The Worldly Years: The Life of Lester B. Pearson. Volume II: 1949-1972* (Toronto: A.A. Knopf, 1992), 362.
43 John English, "Speaking Out on Vietnam, 1965," in *Canadian Foreign Policy: Selected Cases,* edited by Don Munton and John Kirton (Scarborough, ON: Prentice Hall, 1992), 141.
44 Lester B. Pearson, *Mike: The Memoirs of the Right Honourable Lester B. Pearson,* Volume 3, 1957-1968, edited by John A. Munro and Alex I. Inglis (Toronto: University of Toronto Press, 1975), 138.
45 J.L. Granatstein, *Yankee Go Home?* (Toronto: HarperCollins, 1996), 176.
46 English, "Speaking Out," 143.
47 Canadian Institute of International Affairs, *Monthly Report* 4, 4 (April 1965): 32.
48 Pearson, *Mike,* 140.
49 Ibid. This rationale was begun on the terrace and followed up in a long letter that Pearson wrote to LBJ on returning to Ottawa. He ended the letter with thanks to LBJ for his "kindness" in speaking to him so "frankly" at Camp David. For the full transcript of the letter, see *Mike,* 142-43.
50 Ross, *In the Interests of Peace,* 262.
51 Sigler and Goresky, "Public Opinion," 662.
52 It might be noted that the Canadians were echoing their American counterparts with this particular protest chant.
53 When the American flag was raised, a hole had been cut out where the stars should have been.
54 FLQ, "Notice to the Population of the State of Quebec," quoted in James Stewart, *Seven Years of Terrorism: The FLQ. A Special Report by the Montreal Star* (Richmond Hill, ON: Simon and Schuster, 1970), 10.
55 Ibid., 52.
56 Taylor, *Snow Job,* 120.
57 The full text of the speech is printed in J.L. Granatstein, ed., *Canadian Foreign Policy since 1945* (Toronto: Copp Clark, 1969), 135-37.
58 Canada, *House of Commons Debates, Official Report, Third Session – Twenty-Eighth Parliament, Volume 7, 1971* (Ottawa: Queen's Printer for Canada), 6803-5.
59 Ibid., 6705-10; 6770-1.
60 Ibid., 6805.
61 Ibid., 6806.
62 Mitchell Sharp, *Foreign Policy for Canadians* (Ottawa: Department of External Affairs, 1970), 10-11.
63 Granatstein, *Yankee Go Home?* 181.
64 Mitchell Sharp, *Which Reminds Me ... A Memoir* (Toronto: University of Toronto Press, 1995), 213.
65 Ottawa to Saigon, 8 May 1973, telegram GPE-495, DEA file 21-13-VIET-ICCS-73, cited in Hilliker and Barry, "Uncomfortably in the Middle," 26.
66 Daniel Molgot, "The Sequel: Canada Does It Again in Vietnam, April 1968–May 1973," in *Canadian Peacekeepers in Indochina, 1954-1973,* edited by Arthur E. Blanchette (Ottawa: Golden Dog, 2002), 183.
67 Hilliker and Barry, "Uncomfortably in the Middle," 25.
68 Ross, *In the Interests of Peace,* 361.
69 Sharp, *Which Reminds Me,* 216.
70 It is interesting to note that Canada's role in ending the Vietnam War is not mentioned by Henry Kissinger in his recent book *Ending the Vietnam War: A History of America's Involvement in and Extrication from the Vietnam War* (Toronto: Simon and Schuster, 2003). Indeed, most histories of the Vietnam War and accounts of it by prominent American actors fail entirely to mention Canada and its involvement in the war.
71 Cited in Ross, *In the Interests of Peace,* 366.
72 Pierre Elliott Trudeau, *Memoirs* (Toronto: McClelland and Stewart, 1993), 218.
73 Sharp, *Which Reminds Me,* 212.

Chapter 3: The Cuban Missile Crisis, 1961-62

1 Examples of such conventional explanations include Lawrence Martin, *The Presidents and the Prime Ministers* (Toronto: Doubleday, 1982), 181-212; Knowlton Nash, *Kennedy and Diefenbaker: Fear and Loathing Across the Undefended Border* (Toronto: McClelland and Stewart, 1990); and Jamie Glazov, *Canadian Policy Toward Khrushchev's Soviet Union* (Montreal and Kingston: McGill-Queen's University Press, 2002), 140-69.
2 Canadian Embassy (Havana) Dispatch, Confidential, "Cuba – Final Impressions," 15 June 1961, http://www.gwu.edu/~nsarchiv/bayofpigs/19610615.pdf.
3 Ibid.
4 See Robert Bothwell, *Alliance and Illusion: Canada and the World, 1945-1984* (Vancouver: UBC Press, 2007), 167, fn. 45.
5 Canada, House of Commons Debates, 19 April 1961, 3795.
6 Quoted in Martin, *The Presidents and the Prime Ministers,* 187.
7 Jocelyn Ghent-Mallet and Don Munton, "Confronting Kennedy and the Missiles in Cuba, 1962," in *Canadian Foreign Policy: Selected Cases,* edited by Don Munton and John Kirton (Scarborough, ON: Prentice Hall, 1991), 80.
8 Quoted in Robert Reford, *Canada and Three Crises* (Toronto: Canadian Institute of International Affairs, 1968), 164.
9 Martin, *The Presidents and the Prime Ministers,* 191.
10 Ibid.
11 "Trends in Canadian Foreign Policy," *National Intelligence Estimate* Number 99-61, 2 May 1961, POF: Countries: Canada Security, JFK Trip to Ottawa, 5/16-18/61, folder (D), Kennedy Papers, quoted in Ghent-Mallet and Munton, "Confronting Kennedy," 80.
12 Peyton Lyon, *Canada in World Affairs, 1961-1963* (Toronto: Oxford University Press, 1968), 28.
13 Indeed, John Herd Thompson and Stephen J. Randall note that "Kennedy had warned Diefenbaker to expect a 'Berlin crisis' before the end of 1961": *Canada and the United States: Ambivalent Allies,* 3rd ed. (Montreal and Kingston: McGill-Queen's University Press, 1994), 222.
14 Graham T. Allison, "Conceptual Models and the Cuban Missile Crisis," in *American Foreign Policy: Theoretical Essays,* 3rd ed., edited by G. John Ikenberry (New York: Longman, 1999), 444.
15 John Warnock, *Partner to Behemoth: The Military Policy of a Satellite Canada* (Toronto: New Press, 1970), 158.
16 James G. Blight, Bruce J. Allyn, and David A. Welch, *Cuba on the Brink: Castro, the Missile Crisis, and the Soviet Collapse* (New York: Pantheon, 1993), 465.
17 Allison, "Conceptual Models," 446.
18 Ibid., 422-24.
19 Timothy Naftali and Philip Zelikow, eds., *The Presidential Recordings, John F. Kennedy: The Great Crises,* vol. 2 (New York: Norton, 2001), 405.
20 JFK message to Diefenbaker, 22 October 1962, POF: Countries: Canada Security, 1961-63, Kennedy Papers, quoted in Ghent-Mallet and Munton, "Confronting Kennedy," 84.
21 Joseph Jockel, *Canada in NORAD, 1957-2007: A History* (Montreal and Kingston: McGill-Queen's University Press, 2007), 55.
22 President John F. Kennedy, "Radio and Television Report to the American People on the Soviet Arms Buildup in Cuba," The White House, 22 October 1962, http://www.jfklibrary.org/ (audio file available).
23 Ibid.
24 Warnock, *Partner to Behemoth,* 161.
25 Canada, House of Commons Debates, 22 October 1962, 806.
26 Ibid.
27 Quoted in Warnock, *Partner to Behemoth,* 162.
28 John J. Kirton, *Canadian Foreign Policy in a Changing World* (Toronto: Thompson-Nelson, 2006), 23.
29 Quoted in Glazov, *Canadian Policy Toward Khrushchev's Soviet Union,* 142.

30 Peter T. Haydon, *The 1962 Cuban Missile Crisis: Canadian Involvement Reconsidered* (Toronto: Canadian Institute for Strategic Studies, 1993), 122-23.
31 Glazov, *Canadian Policy Toward Khrushchev's Soviet Union,* 143.
32 Peter C. Newman, *Renegade in Power: The Diefenbaker Years* (Toronto: McClelland and Stewart, 1963), 339-40.
33 Jon B. McLin, *Canada's Changing Defense Policy: The Problems of a Middle Power in Alliance* (Baltimore: Johns Hopkins University Press, 1967), 156.
34 Henry M. Pachter, *Collision Course: The Cuban Missile Crisis and Coexistence* (New York: Frederick A. Praeger, 1963), 95.
35 Lyon, *Canada in World Affairs,* 36.
36 Peter Stursberg, *Diefenbaker: Leadership Lost, 1962-67* (Toronto: University of Toronto Press, 1976), 16.
37 Kirton, *Canadian Foreign Policy,* 38.
38 Haydon, *The 1962 Cuban Missile Crisis,* 210.
39 Jeffrey V. Brock, *The Thunder and the Sunshine: Memoirs of a Sailor* (Toronto: McClelland and Stewart, 1983), 110.
40 Joel J. Sokolsky, "Canada and the Cold War at Sea, 1945-68," in *The RCN in Transition, 1910-1985,* edited by W.A.B. Douglas (Vancouver: UBC Press, 1988), 209-32.
41 Kirton, *Canadian Foreign Policy,* 39.
42 Vice-Admiral Glenn Davidson, "After the War: Canada's Navy Post-1945," *Starshell* 7, 43 (Summer 2008): 4.
43 Sean Maloney, *Learning to Love the Bomb: Canada's Nuclear Weapons during the Cold War* (Washington, DC: Potomac Books, 2007), 289.
44 Reford, *Canada and Three Crises,* 189.
45 Ibid., 190.
46 Ibid., 194.
47 Patrick Nicholson, *Vision and Indecision* (Don Mills, ON: Longman, 1968), 166.
48 Blight et al., *Cuba on the Brink,* 468-69.
49 John G. Diefenbaker, *One Canada: The Tumultuous Years, 1962-1967,* vol. 3 (Toronto: Macmillan, 1977), 88.
50 Quoted in Nicholson, *Vision and Indecision,* 166.
51 Canada, House of Commons Debates, 25 October 1962, 912.
52 See statement by Prime Minister Harold Macmillan to British House of Commons, 25 October 1962, in David L. Larson, ed., *The Cuban Crisis of 1962: Selected Documents and Chronology* (Boston: Houghton Mifflin, 1963), 123-25.
53 Canada, House of Commons Debates, 25 October 1962, 912.
54 These inspections never took place. The Kennedy administration insisted that, technically, this meant that the non-invasion pledge was null and void. It was subsequently accepted as a de facto commitment, however, and Henry Kissinger later affirmed it in 1973. I thank David Welch for bringing this to my attention.
55 Quoted in Nicholson, *Vision and Indecision,* 171.
56 Ibid.
57 Reford, *Canada and Three Crises,* 191.
58 Walter Grey, "Ottawa Reaction on Cuba One of Cautious Moderation," *Globe and Mail,* 28 October 1962, 1659. Quoted in Glazov, *Canadian Policy Toward Khrushchev's Soviet Union,* 145.
60 Ibid.
61 Canada, House of Commons Debates, 25 January 1963, 3127.
62 Howard Green, "Caribbean Area Vital to Canada," *Ottawa Journal,* 12 October 1963, 10.
63 *Financial Post,* 3 November 1962, quoted in Ghent-Mallet and Munton, "Confronting Kennedy," 91.
64 Diefenbaker, *One Canada,* 79.
65 Importantly, Kim Richard Nossal notes that the Suez crisis of 1956 was a "transformative" moment in Canadian foreign policy, when policymakers in Ottawa, "both then and later," first felt fully justified in their belief that Canada had a specialized role to play as a problem

solver in the international system. See his "Mission Diplomacy and the 'Cult of the Initiative' in Canadian Foreign Policy," in *Worthwhile Initiatives? Canadian Mission-Oriented Diplomacy*, edited by Andrew F. Cooper and Geoffrey Hayes (Toronto: Irwin, 2000), 3-5.

Chapter 4: Nuclear Weapons, 1945-2009

1 For a detailed history of Canada's early advocacy of nuclear disarmament, see Joseph Levitt, *Pearson and Canada's Role in Nuclear Disarmament and Arms Control Negotiations, 1945-1957* (Montreal and Kingston: McGill-Queen's University Press, 1993). It is interesting to note from the outset that, as Levitt argues in his conclusion, "Canada's unique status in the United Nations Atomic Energy Commission and the sub-committee of the Disarmament Commission was the result of a fortuitous circumstance – its possession of uranium deposits and its location next to the United States. Because it was under the latter's security umbrella, Canada had no specific security goals of its own, unlike the chief Western powers which were all great powers" (272).

2 Peter C. Newman makes this argument in *Renegade in Power: The Diefenbaker Years* (Toronto: McClelland and Stewart, 1963), ch. 23; Peyton Lyon also puts his emphasis on Diefenbaker in the chapter entitled "Defence: To Be or Not to Be Nuclear," in his *Canada in World Affairs, 1961-1963* (Toronto: Oxford University Press, 1968), 76-222; Knowlton Nash does as well in *Kennedy and Diefenbaker: Fear and Loathing Across the Undefended Border* (Toronto: McClelland and Stewart, 1990), ch. 7. Howard H. Lentner puts a finer point on this individual-level analysis by arguing that "the explanation of this decision must be sought in a rather complex political process in which personal political style played a large part," in his "Foreign Policy Decision Making: The Case of Canada and Nuclear Weapons," *World Politics* 29, 1 (1976): 30.

3 Canada was the subordinate member of a tripartite coalition, formally established in 1943 at the Quebec Conference, that was led by the United States and (to a somewhat lesser extent) Great Britain. Brian Buckley notes that "Canada's role in the agreement was distinctly subordinate. It was not formally a party to the accord; the document was signed by Churchill and Roosevelt only": *Canada's Early Nuclear Weapons Policy: Fate, Chance, and Character* (Montreal and Kingston: McGill-Queen's University Press, 2000), 29.

4 Ibid., 3.

5 John P. Warnock quotes an estimate by the *Financial Post* "that between 1947 and 1962, Canada sold the United States about $1,370 million worth of uranium": *Partner to Behemoth: The Military Policy of a Satellite Canada* (Toronto: New Press, 1970), 183.

6 John W. Holmes, *The Shaping of Peace: Canada and the Search for World Order, 1943-1957*, vol. 1 (Toronto: University of Toronto Press, 1979).

7 Ibid.

8 Joseph Jockel supports this line of reasoning in his *Canada in NORAD, 1957-2007: A History* (Montreal and Kingston: McGill-Queen's University Press, 2007), 13.

9 H. Basil Robinson, *Diefenbaker's World: A Populist in Foreign Affairs* (Toronto: University of Toronto Press, 1989), 19.

10 Jockel, *Canada in NORAD*, 24.

11 Ibid., 25-35.

12 Douglas Murray, "NORAD and U.S. Nuclear Operations," in *Fifty Years of Canada-United States Defense Cooperation: The Road From Ogdensburg*, edited by Joel J. Sokolsky and Joseph T. Jockel (Lewiston, NY: Edwin Mellen Press, 1992), 209.

13 The estimated unit cost of the plane had also almost quadrupled between 1953 and 1958. Moreover, as Diefenbaker announced to the House of Commons, "the Arrow has been overtaken by events. In recent months it has come to be realized that the bomber threat against which the Arrow was intended to provide a defence had diminished, and alternative means of meeting the threat have been developed much earlier than was expected": Newman, *Renegade in Power*, 455. Robinson further develops the first point: "The issue was basically economic. Because of cost increases, the Arrow was consuming an undue proportion of the defence budget": *Diefenbaker's World*, 85.

14 Nash, *Kennedy and Diefenbaker*, 78.

15 Warnock, *Partner to Behemoth*, 184.
16 Nash, *Kennedy and Diefenbaker*, 75. Sean Maloney has recently suggested that the Bomarc base at North Bay was outfitted with W40 nuclear warheads during the Cuban Missile Crisis. See Maloney, *Learning to Love the Bomb: Canada's Nuclear Weapons during the Cold War* (Washington, DC: Potomac Books, 2007), 287. Jockel confirms that CINCNORAD Gen. John K. Gerhard did request that the Bomarcs be equipped with nuclear warheads on 22 October 1962: *Canada in NORAD*, 57.
17 Lyon, *Canada in World Affairs*, 79.
18 The subordinate move to accept the weapons necessary for the Bomarcs was explicitly recognized as such by Diefenbaker's Cabinet. Nash notes that "the cabinet was aware that in taking the nuclear-tipped U.S. Bomarc weapon, Canada ran the danger of falling under greater U.S. military control in North American air defence." In support of this argument, he quotes the summary of a 23 February 1959 Cabinet meeting: "It should be remembered that maintaining freedom from U.S. control was a continuous struggle. It might appear that the present decision is a retrograde step. But there would be other opportunities to assert Canadian sovereignty and independence": *Kennedy and Diefenbaker*, 76.
19 Jon B. McLin, *Canada's Changing Defense Policy: The Problem of a Middle Power in Alliance* (Baltimore: Johns Hopkins University Press, 1967), 90-97.
20 Quoted in Nash, *Kennedy and Diefenbaker*, 77.
21 Indeed, Don Munton reports that Robert McNamara, when asked by a congressional sub-committee in 1963 whether the Bomarcs were a waste of money, could only offer the arguments that they didn't cost much to keep in place, and "at least served the purpose of drawing Soviet fire away from other targets": "Going Fission: Tales and Truths about Canada's Nuclear Weapons," *International Journal* (Summer 1996): 518.
22 Jocelyn Ghent-Mallet, "Deploying Nuclear Weapons, 1962-63," in *Canadian Foreign Policy: Selected Cases*, edited by Don Munton and John Kirton (Scarborough, ON: Prentice Hall, 1992), 101-2.
23 Lyon, *Canada in World Affairs*, 223.
24 Peter Stursberg, *Diefenbaker: Leadership Lost, 1962-67* (Toronto: University of Toronto Press, 1976), 23.
25 Lyon, *Canada in World Affairs*, 225. E.A. Goodman further substantiates this, commenting that Green "said that Canada was taking a leading role in certain disarmament discussions, and he was very strongly against the resolution, as he said it would spoil our attempts to play the honest broker": Stursberg, *Diefenbaker*, 30.
26 *Toronto Daily Star*, "An Inspired Nag at Geneva," 20 March 1962, quoted in Lyon, *Canada in World Affairs*, 227.
27 See John T. Saywell, ed., *Canadian Annual Review for 1962* (Toronto: University of Toronto Press, 1963), 96.
28 Stursberg, *Diefenbaker*, 24.
29 Ghent-Mallet, "Deploying Nuclear Weapons," 103.
30 Minister of National Defence Douglas Harkness recalls that "these were all impractical schemes. However the Americans were very patient over the whole matter, in my view, and in each case they said they would look into this, and they made cost analyses to show what the cost of this would be and analyses as to how much time would be required, how many planes would be required to be kept always on the alert for this purpose, and so on – and the costs were extremely large. Also it was quite apparent that the way the crisis was likely to come on there just wouldn't be time to do this sort of thing. So these were not practical propositions. Nevertheless the negotiations dragged on. In my view, these were delaying tactics again on the part of the External Affairs people": quoted in Stursberg, *Diefenbaker*, 27.
31 Nash, *Kennedy and Diefenbaker*, 145.
32 Ghent-Mallet, "Deploying Nuclear Weapons," 106.
33 Nash has Donald Fleming referring to the speech as "without exception the most equivocal" he had ever heard, and Basil Robinson as calling it an "indigestible stew": *Kennedy and Diefenbaker*, 236-37.

34 Ghent-Mallet, "Deploying Nuclear Weapons," 110.
35 John Clearwater, *Canadian Nuclear Weapons: The Untold Story of Canada's Cold War Arsenal* (Toronto: Dundurn, 1998), 23.
36 See the follow-up volume by John Clearwater, *US Nuclear Weapons in Canada* (Toronto: Dundurn, 1998), 17-44.
37 In the April 1963 issue of *Cité Libre,* Trudeau wrote of the American pressure that he believed was behind Pearson's change of heart. "Fate had it that the final thrust came from the Pentagon and obliged Mr. Pearson to betray his party's platform as well as the ideal with which he had always identified himself. Power presented itself to Mr. Pearson; he had nothing to lose but honour. He lost it. And his whole party lost it with him." Quoted in Walter Gordon, "The Liberal Leadership and Nuclear Weapons," in *Canada and the Nuclear Arms Race,* edited by Ernie Regehr and Simon Rosenblum (Toronto: James Lorimer, 1983).
38 Pierre Elliott Trudeau, *Lifting the Shadow of War* (Edmonton: Hurtig, 1987), 27.
39 See Harold Von Riekhoff and John Sigler, "The Trudeau Peace Initiative: The Politics of Reversing the Arms Race," in *Canada among Nations, 1984: A Time of Transition,* edited by Brian W. Tomlin and Maureen Molot (Toronto: James Lorimer, 1985), 50-69; Christina McCall and Stephen Clarkson, *Trudeau and Our Times. Volume 2: The Heroic Delusion* (Toronto: McClelland and Stewart, 1994), 363-72. See also Geoffrey Pearson, "Trudeau Peace Initiative Reflections," *International Perspectives* (March/April 1985): 3-6, and Beth A. Fischer, "The Trudeau Peace Initiative and the End of the Cold War: Catalyst or Coincidence?" *International Journal* 49, 3 (1994): 613-34.
40 See Ron Finch, *Exporting Danger* (Montreal: Black Rose, 1986), 47-70.
41 See David Cox, "The Cruise Testing Agreement," *International Perspectives* (July/August 1983): 3-5.
42 Peter C. Newman noted at the time that the "proposed overflights [of the cruise missiles over Canadian territory] have roused deeply-felt indignation, even among Canadians who haven't given the country's defence matters a second thought for a generation": *The True North: Not Strong and Free* (Toronto: McClelland and Stewart, 1983), 113. Eighty thousand Canadians also took to the streets in protest against their government's decision to allow the tests: Canada, House of Commons Debates, 25 April 1983, 24808.
43 Howard Peter Langille, *Changing the Guard: Canada's Defence in a World in Transition* (Toronto: University of Toronto Press, 1990), 45.
44 Ibid., 47.
45 Ibid., 56.
46 Jeff Sallot, "U.S. Subs to Sail in Strait. Nuclear Vessels Cause Uproar," *Globe and Mail,* 31 October 1991, A1.
47 Marianne Hanson, *Advancing Disarmament in the Face of Great Power Reluctance: The Canadian Contribution,* Working Paper 37 (Vancouver: Institute of International Relations, University of British Columbia, June 2001), 6.
48 Canada, House of Commons, "Canada and the Nuclear Challenge: Reducing the Political Value of Nuclear Weapons for the Twenty-First Century," Report of the Standing Committee on Foreign Affairs and International Trade, Bill Graham, MP, Chair, December 1998, 91.
49 For a more elaborate exposition of this evolving mode of participation in the global political system, see Robert Lawson, "The Ottawa Process: Fast-Track Diplomacy and the International Movement to Ban Anti-Personnel Landmines," in *Canada among Nations, 1998: Leadership and Dialogue,* edited by Fen Osler Hampson and Maureen Appel Molot (Toronto: Oxford University Press, 1998), 81-99; Lloyd Axworthy, "Lessons from the Ottawa Process," *Canadian Foreign Policy* 3, 5 (1998); and Alison Van Rooy, "Civil Society and the Axworthy Touch," in *Canada among Nations, 2001: The Axworthy Legacy,* edited by Fen Osler Hampson, Norman Hillmer, and Maureen Appel Molot (Don Mills, ON: Oxford University Press, 2001), 253-70.
50 House of Commons, *Canada and the Nuclear Challenge,* 95.
51 Lloyd Axworthy, *Navigating a New World: Canada's Global Future* (Toronto: A.A. Knopf, 2003), 362.
52 Ibid., 363.

53 Douglas Roche, "How Canada Bucked the U.S. Line on Nuclear Arms," *Globe and Mail,* 23 November 1998, A21.
54 Axworthy, *Navigating a New World,* 363.
55 Canada, Department of Foreign Affairs and International Trade, Government Statement on "Nuclear Disarmament and Non-Proliferation: Advancing Canadian Objectives," http://www.dfait-maeci.gc.ca/nucchallenge/POLICY-en.asp.
56 Jeff Sallot, "Axworthy Blasts U.S. on Nuclear Policy," *Globe and Mail,* 23 October 1999, A12.
57 Axworthy, *Navigating a New World,* 364.

Chapter 5: Missile Defence, 1983-2009
1 Excerpts from President Reagan's 23 March 1983 speech were printed in *Survival* 25, 3 (1983): 129-30.
2 See Donald R. Baucom, *The Origins of SDI, 1944-1983* (Lawrence: University Press of Kansas, 1992). For a more succinct rendition, see Michael Krepon, *Cooperative Threat Reduction, Missile Defense, and the Nuclear Future* (New York: Palgrave, 2003), 85-103.
3 Frances Fitzgerald, *Way Out There in the Blue: Reagan, Star Wars, and the End of the Cold War* (Toronto: Simon and Schuster, 2000), 18.
4 Barry R. Schneider and Colin S. Gray, "Defending versus Avenging: A Critical Assessment of SDI and MAD Policies," in *Space Weapons and International Security,* edited by Bhupendra Jasani (Toronto: Oxford University Press, 1987), 107.
5 Ibid.
6 P.L. Meredith, "The Legality of a High-Technology Missile Defense System: The ABM and Outer Space Treaties," *American Journal of International Law* 78, 2 (1984): 419.
7 Yao Wenbin, "The Impact of SDI in International Security," in Jasani, *Space Weapons and International Security,* 263.
8 SDI, however, was not technically prohibited by the ABM Treaty, which did not limit "research," only development. On this controversial distinction, see John B. Rhinelander, "Implications of US and Soviet BMD Programmes for the ABM Treaty," in Jasani, *Space Weapons and International Security,* 145-61.
9 See Jean Chrétien's reference to this previous motion in his discussion of the issue in Canada, House of Commons Debates, 19 March 1985, 3157.
10 See remarks by Hon. Lloyd Axworthy in House of Commons Debates, 22 January 1985, 1551.
11 David Bercuson, J.L. Granatstein, and W.R. Young, *Sacred Trust? Brian Mulroney and the Conservative Party in Power* (Toronto: Doubleday, 1986), 243.
12 House of Commons Debates, 21 January 1985, 1502.
13 Bercuson et al., *Sacred Trust?* 243-44.
14 Ibid.
15 James Rusk, "PM Support on Star Wars Pleases US," *Globe and Mail,* 2 February 1985, 1.
16 Bercuson et al., *Sacred Trust?* 244.
17 Ibid.
18 Ibid.
19 Stephen Clarkson, *Canada and the Reagan Challenge: Crisis and Adjustment, 1981-1985* (Toronto: James Lorimer, 1985), 357.
20 Joseph Jockel, *Canada in NORAD, 1957-2007: A History* (Montreal and Kingston: McGill-Queen's University Press, 2007), 126-27.
21 Joseph Jockel, *Security to the North: Canada-U.S. Defense Relations in the 1990s* (East Lansing: Michigan State University Press, 1991), 99.
22 Fitzgerald, *Way Out There in the Blue,* 18.
23 Steven A. Hildreth, "Ballistic Missile Defense: Historical Overview," CRS Report for Congress, 22 April 2005, http://www.fas.org/sgp/crs/weapons/RS22120.pdf.
24 Fitzgerald, *Way Out There in the Blue,* 18.
25 Coleman Romalis, "What Is Star Wars Doing to Canada?" *Peace Magazine,* June 1985, 11-14, http://www.peacemagazine.org/archive/v01n4p11.htm. See also Jeffrey Simpson, "The Canadian Connection," *Globe and Mail,* 16 January 1985, 6. On that day, the cartoon on

the editorial page of the *Globe and Mail* depicted Reagan as Darth Vader standing over R2D2 (the garbage pail-shaped droid of the Star Wars movie series by George Lucas) beside the Grim Reaper standing over a garbage pail with a smouldering globe sticking out the top. This was all under the heading "Star Wars." The paper's position could not have been put more absolutely. This message was followed up on 23 January with an editorial entitled "Complacent to a Fault," which criticized Clark's inability or unwillingness to take a stand against the Star Wars project: *Globe and Mail*, 23 January 1985, 6.

26 Roy MacGregor, "Mixed Signals on Star Wars," *Maclean's*, 8 April 1985, 10.
27 Ibid.
28 Ibid., 11.
29 "Star Wars Endangers Peace Role, Tories Told," *Globe and Mail*, 17 July 1985, P1.
30 Ibid.
31 To Peter Newman, Mulroney allegedly said: "I don't think Star Wars is a big deal. I've never been impressed with the whole concept. I can't see how we'd gain anything from it. I don't think we'd participate. It doesn't make sense to me": Peter Newman, *The Secret Mulroney Tapes: The Unguarded Confessions of a Prime Minister* (Toronto: Random House, 2005), 307-8.
32 House of Commons Debates, 26 September 1985, 7080.
33 Jockel, *Security to the North*, 102.
34 Roche would later comment that "the biggest shock that I got was to learn the influence that the United States government has on the Canadian government on the issues of disarmament and security. That influence operates in varying degrees, from subtlety and politesse to crude threats." Quoted in Howard Peter Langille, *Changing the Guard: Canada's Defence in a World in Transition* (Toronto: University of Toronto Press, 1990), 56-57.
35 Bercuson et al., *Sacred Trust?* 250.
36 Peter Goodspeed, "Ottawa Will Support Missile Defense: Experts: 'It's Just a Question of Timing,' Seminar Told," *National Post*, 12 May 2001, A11.
37 Andrew Richter, "North American Aerospace Defence Cooperation in the 1990s: Issues and Prospects," Department of National Defence, Canada, *Operational Research and Analysis Establishment (ORAE) Extra-Mural Paper 57* (Ottawa: Department of National Defence, 1991), 25.
38 Joel J. Sokolsky, "Arms Control Negotiations: Confronting the Paradoxes," in *Canada among Nations, 1985: The Conservative Agenda*, edited by Maureen Appel Molot and Brian W. Tomlin (Toronto: James Lorimer, 1986), 62.
39 David Leyton Brown, "A Refurbished Relationship with the United States," in *Canada among Nations, 1988: The Tory Record*, edited by Brian W. Tomlin and Maureen Appel Molot (Toronto: James Lorimer, 1989), 178.
40 Commission to Assess the Ballistic Missile Threat to the United States, Report of the Commission to Assess the Ballistic Missile Threat to the United States, 15 July 1998, 5, http://www/fas/org/irp/threat/missile/rumsfeld/to.htm.
41 Ivan Eland with Daniel Lee, "The Rogue State Doctrine and National Missile Defense," Cato Institute Foreign Policy Briefing 65 (29 March 2001), http://www.cato.org/pubs/fpbriefs/fpb65.pdf.
42 See Andrew Richter, "A Question of Defense: How American Allies Are Responding to the US Missile Defense Program," *Comparative Strategy* 23 (2004): 153.
43 On the Axworthy era of Canadian foreign policy, see Fen Osler Hampson and Dean F. Oliver, "Pulpit Diplomacy: A Critical Assessment of the Axworthy Doctrine," *International Journal* (Summer 1998): 379-406; and Kim Richard Nossal, "Pinchpenny Diplomacy: The Decline of 'Good International Citizenship' in Canadian Foreign Policy," *International Journal* (Winter 1998-99): 87-105.
44 "U.S. Backs Away from We-Won't-Protect-You Stance of Admiral: Anti-Missile Shield: 2's Comments Do Not Reflect Official Policy, Washington," *National Post*, 4 May 2000, A11.
45 Richter, "A Question of Defense," 155.
46 Robert Russo, "Canada Feels Heat to Back Star Wars II," *Winnipeg Free Press*, 16 March 2000, B1.

47 Robert Fife and Peter Morton, "Missile Plan Splits Canada, U.S.: Shock in Washington: Putin Nominates Ottawa as Mediator in Shield Stand Off," *National Post,* 19 December 2000, A1.

48 Russo, "Canada Feels Heat," B1.

49 Fife and Morton, "Missile Plan Splits Canada, U.S.," A1.

50 Project for a New American Century, "Rebuilding America's Defenses: Strategy, Forces, and Resources for a New Century," September 2000, 8, http://www.newamericancentury.org/ RebuildingAmericasDefenses.pdf. Signatories to PNAC's original Statement of Principles who would later become key players in the Bush administration included Dick Cheney, Donald Rumsfeld, Paul Wolfowitz, and I. Lewis Libby.

51 Ibid., 12.

52 Robert Fife, "Canada to Back Missile Shield: Chrétien Cabinet Prepares Public Opinion for Policy Switch on High-Tech Defense," *National Post,* 14 May 2001, A1.

53 Nils Ørvik, "The Basic Issue in Canadian National Security: Defence against Help/Defence to Help Others," *Canadian Defence Quarterly* 11, 1 (1981).

54 Fife, "Canada to Back Missile Shield."

55 US, White House, "Transform America's National Security Institutions to Meet the Challenges and Opportunities of the Twenty-First Century," The National Security Strategy of the United States of America, September 2002, http://www.whitehouse.gov/nsc/nss.pdf.

56 Missile Defense Agency, "Ballistic Missile Defense Approach," Fact Sheet, March 2002, http://www.acq.osd.mil/bmdo/bmdolink/pdf/approach.pdf.

57 See The Project for a New American Century, "Rebuilding America's Defenses," as well as Charles V. Pena, "Missile Defense: Defending America or Building Empire?" CATO Institute Foreign Policy Briefing 77, 28 May 2003, 8, http://www.globalpolicy.org/empire/ intervention/2004/0528missdef.pdf.

58 Sheldon Alberts, "Liberal Rift Delays Entry to Arms Plan," *National Post,* 8 May 2003, A1.

59 Canada, Department of National Defence, "Letter from Minister Pratt to Secretary Rumsfeld," 15 January 2004, http://www.forces.gc.ca/site/Focus/Canada-us/letter_e.asp.

60 Canada, Department of National Defence, "Reply from Secretary Rumsfeld to Minister Pratt," http://www.forces.gc.ca/site/Focus/Canada-us/letter_e.asp.

61 Canada, Department of National Defence, "Canada-.U.S. Amend NORAD Agreement," 5 August 2004, http://www.forces.gc.ca/site/Newsroom/view_news_e.asp?id=1422.

62 Ibid.

63 Tom Blackwell, "Contract 'Takes Canada into Missile Program': $700,000 Radar Testing: Defense Accused of Pushing Ahead before Issue Debated," *National Post,* 16 February 2004, A2.

64 Centre for Research and Information on Canada, "Canadians Oppose US Missile Defence System by a Small Majority," 4 November 2004, http://www.cric.ca/pdf/cric_poll/portraits/ portraits_2004/eng_can_us_2004.pdf.

65 Quoted in Janice Gross Stein and Eugene Lang, *The Unexpected War: Canada in Kandahar* (Toronto: Viking, 2007), 164.

66 Peter Baker, "Bush Doctrine Is Expected to Get Chilly Reception," *Washington Post,* 23 January 2005, A1.

67 "Missile Defence Approval Expected. U.S. Ambassador Optimistic Canada to Join Shield Plan," *Winnipeg Free Press,* 10 January 2005, A1.

68 Michael Den Tandt and Daniel Leblanc, "PM Set to Reject Missile Defense: After McKenna Says Canada Is in, Martin Will Announce that It's Out," *Globe and Mail,* 23 February 2005, A1.

69 Doug Struck, "Canada Rejects Missile Shield Plan; Decision Is a Snub to Bush, Who Had Sought Partnership," *Washington Post,* 25 February 2005, A18.

70 David Rudd, "Muddling through on Missile Defence: The Politics of Indecision," *Policy Options* (May 2005): 30.

71 Clifford Krauss, "Divergent Paths: Canada Breaks with U.S. Over Missile Shield," *New York Times,* 27 February 2005, 3.

72 Michael Den Tandt and Paul Koring, "Opposition Rakes Liberals over Missile-Defence Coals; but 'Unprecedented Spectacle' of Confusion on Issue Causes Little Stir in Washington," *Globe and Mail,* 24 February 2005, A4.

73   Struck, "Canada Rejects Missile Shield Plan," A18.
74   Dwight N. Mason, "A Flight from Responsibility: Canada and Missile Defense of North America," Center for Strategic and International Studies, 25 February 2005, http://www.csis.org/americas/canada/050225_Mason.pdf.
75   Stein and Lang, *Unexpected War*, 165-66.
76   Ibid., 175-76.
77   Ibid., 177.
78   Canada, Standing Senate Committee on National Security and Defence, "Managing Turmoil: The Need to Upgrade Canadian Foreign Aid and Military Strength to Deal with Massive Change," Interim Report of the Standing Senate Committee on National Security and Defence (October 2006), 93, http://www.parl.gc.ca/39/1/parlbus/commbus/senate/com-e/defe-e/rep-e/RepOct06-e.pdf.
79   Ibid., 90.

Chapter 6: The War on Terror, 2001-9

1   Andrew Cohen, "Canadian-American Relations: Does Canada Matter in Washington? Does It Matter if Canada Doesn't Matter?" in *Canada among Nations, 2002: A Fading Power*, edited by Norman Hillmer and Maureen Appel Molot (Don Mills, ON: Oxford University Press, 2002), 36.
2   Canada, Department of Foreign Affairs and International Trade, "Notes for an Address by the Honourable John Manley, Minister of Foreign Affairs, to a Special Session of Parliament," 17 September 2001, http://w01.international.gc.ca/minpub/Publication.asp?FileSpec=/Min_Pub_Docs/104518.htm.
3   National Commission on Terrorist Attacks upon the United States, *The 9/11 Commission Report: Final Report of the National Commission on Terrorist Attacks upon the United States* (New York: Norton, 2004), 39.
4   R.W. Apple Jr., "No Middle Ground," *New York Times*, 14 September 2001, 1.
5   Steven Chase, "Spend More on Military, Ottawa Told," *Globe and Mail*, 8 October 2001, A13.
6   On this last point, see J.L. Granatstein, *Who Killed the Canadian Military?* (Toronto: Harper-Flamingo, 2004). David Bercuson notes that this deployment – "heavy on naval forces, extremely light on air assets" – was "the best Ottawa could do with the nation's badly depleted military": "Canada-U.S. Defence Relations Post-11 September," in *Canada among Nations, 2003: Coping with the American Colossus*, edited by David Carment, Fen Osler Hampson, and Norman Hillmer (Don Mills, ON: Oxford University Press, 2003), 133.
7   Richard Gimblett, *Operation Apollo: The Golden Age of the Canadian Navy in the War against Terrorism* (Ottawa: Magic Light, 2004), 44-55.
8   Mike Trickey, "Canadian Destroyer Nabs Two al-Qaeda Suspects: Gulf of Oman Chase," *National Post*, 16 July 2002, A6.
9   Mark MacKinnon, "Secrecy Surrounds Canadian Missions," *Globe and Mail*, 7 February 2002, A15.
10   Quoted in Grant Dawson, "'A Special Case': Canada, Operation Apollo, and Multilateralism," in Carment et al., *Canada among Nations*, 2003, 181.
11   Quoted in ibid.
12   Ibid.
13   Paul Knox, "Cellucci Urges Canada to Hike Defence Budget," *Globe and Mail*, 3 October 2001, A8.
14   Canada, Department of National Defence, "Operations Briefing – Defence Minister Art Eggleton and Chief of Staff Ray Henault Give a News Conference on Deployment of Canadian Forces in Afghanistan," 7 January 2002, http://www.forces.gc.ca/site/Newsroom/view_news_e.asp?id=352.
15   Sheldon Alberts, with files from Chris Wattie, "War Planners Get Cold Feet: Canada Reconsiders Role," *National Post*, 20 November 2001, A01.
16   Brian Laghi and Jill Mahoney, "Troops Won't Go if They're 'Unwelcome,'" *Globe and Mail*, 20 November 2001, A1.
17   Marcus Gee, "Canada's Peacekeeper Image a Myth," *Globe and Mail*, 4 January 2002, A6.
18   Allan Freeman, "Canada Shuns Minor Peace Role," *Globe and Mail*, 4 January 2002, A1.

19 Walter Doern, "Canadian Peacekeeping: No Myth – but Not What It Once Was," SITREP 67, 2 (2007): 6.
20 Janice Stein and Eugene Lang, *The Unexpected War: Canada in Kandahar* (Toronto: Viking, 2007), 18-19.
21 See Jane Mayer, "The Experiment," *New Yorker*, 11 July 2005.
22 Wallace Immen, "85% Want U.S. to Pay for Tragedy," *Globe and Mail*, 22 April 2002, A1.
23 Scott White, "Canadian Soldiers in Afghanistan Top Story – CP Members Pick 1 News Event; Four Deaths Touched a Nerve," *Toronto Star*, 2 January 2003, A18.
24 Stein and Lang, *Unexpected War*, 20.
25 Julia Preston, "Security Council Votes, 15-0, for Tough Iraq Resolution," *New York Times*, 9 November 2002, 1.
26 Sheldon Alberts, "Powell Urges Canada to Join Iraq Coalition," *National Post*, 15 November 2002, A16.
27 Allan Thompson, "Canada Lines Up Military Muscle for War on Iraq," *Toronto Star*, 9 January 2003, A1.
28 Jutta Brunnee and Adrian Di Giovanni, "Iraq: A Fork in the Road for a Special Relationship?" *International Journal* 60, 2 (2005): 378.
29 A full transcript of the address was published under the headline "Powell's Address, Presenting 'Deeply Troubling' Evidence on Iraq," *New York Times*, 6 February 2003, 18.
30 Donald Barry, "Chrétien, Bush, and the War in Iraq," *American Review of Canadian Studies* (Summer 2005): 223.
31 Senate Committee on Intelligence, "Report on the U.S. Intelligence Community's Pre-War Intelligence Assessments on Iraq," 2004, http://www.gpoaccess.gov/serialset/creports/iraq.html.
32 Jeff Sallot, "U.S. Wants Troops for Iraqi War," *Globe and Mail*, 15 November 2002, A1.
33 Peter Morton, "U.S. Citizens at Odds with World on War: Nearly 60% of Americans Support Attack on Iraq," *National Post*, 12 March 2003, A15.
34 Andrew Richter, "From Trusted Ally to Suspicious Neighbor: Canada-U.S. Relations in a Changing Global Environment," *American Review of Canadian Studies* 35, 3 (Autumn 2005): 477.
35 Paul Koring and Daniel Leblanc, "Canadian Will Run Persian Gulf Naval Task Force," *Globe and Mail*, 11 February 2003, A1.
36 Gimblett, *Operation Apollo*, 111.
37 Barry, "Chrétien, Bush, and the War in Iraq," 225.
38 Tonda MacCharles, "Small Countries Look to Canada: Feeling Pressured over Iraq Stance Council Members Want Compromise," *Toronto Star*, 3 March 2003, A1.
39 Anne Dawson, "Budget to Add $2B for Military: Forces Pushing for Major Role in Iraq War," *National Post*, 8 February 2003, A1.
40 Barry, "Chrétien, Bush, and the War in Iraq," 224.
41 Stein and Lang, *Unexpected War*, 48-49.
42 Ibid., 50.
43 "Chrétien Government Rejected Military's Advice on Afghan Deployment: Ex-Army Chief," CBC News, 18 October 2006, http://www.cbc.ca/canada/story/2006/10/18/afghan-military-advice.html.
44 Stein and Lang, *Unexpected War*, 73.
45 Jean Chrétien, "Don't Act Alone," *Globe and Mail*, 14 February 2003, A17.
46 Colin Perkel, "U.S.-Canada Relationship Could Suffer, Cellucci Says," *Globe and Mail*, 1 March 2003, A9.
47 Chantal Hébert, "Quebecers Have Moved on," *Toronto Star*, 15 April 2003, A1.
48 Lawrence Martin, *Iron Man: The Defiant Reign of Jean Chrétien*, vol. 2 (Toronto: Viking, 2003), 420.
49 Sheldon Alberts, "PM Maintains War in Iraq Is 'Not Justified': 'Case Was Not Made'," *National Post*, 19 March 2003, A12.
50 Ibid.
51 Frank P. Harvey, *Smoke and Mirrors: Globalized Terrorism and the Illusion of Multilateral Security* (Toronto: University of Toronto Press, 2004), 203.

52 Stein and Lang, *Unexpected War,* 82.
53 Gimblett, *Operation Apollo,* 112.
54 It should be noted that the presence of five Canadian warships in the Persian Gulf during this period was short-lived. *Halifax* and *Montréal* sailed home shortly after the arrival of *Iroquois* and *Fredericton.*
55 Stein and Lang, *Unexpected War,* 88-90.
56 Harvey, *Smoke and Mirrors,* 235.
57 A. Paul Cellucci, "Speech to the Economic Club of Toronto," 25 March 2003, http://ottawa.usembassy.gov/content/content.asp?section=embconsul&document=cellucci_030325.
58 Richard Sanders, "Who Says We're Not at War?" *Globe and Mail,* 31 March 2003, A15.
59 T. Michael Moseley, Lt. Gen. USAF, Operation Iraqi Freedom – by the Numbers, 30 April 2003, 3, 16, http://www.globalsecurity.org/military/library/report/2003/uscentaf_oif_report_30apr2003.pdf.
60 David Pugliese, "U.S. Thanks Canada for Role in Iraq War: But Ottawa Insists It Did Nothing to Help," *National Post,* 14 June 2003, A1.
61 "U.S. Admits Its Mistake over Canada's Role in War," *Toronto Star,* 23 June 2003, A18.
62 On this issue of Canadian exchange officers serving in Iraq, see Mark MacKinnon, "For Canadian Serving in Iraq Is a Source of Pride," *Globe and Mail,* 21 March 2008, A3.
63 Mike Allen, "Cheney Reaches Out to Iraq War Critics; Anti-Terror Efforts Need 'Many Hands,'" *Washington Post,* 25 January 2004, A17.
64 Jane Taber, "Ottawa Torn by Turbulent Elections; Iraq; Martin Says Yes to Training Workers, but No to Troops," *Globe and Mail,* 6 December 2004, A1.
65 Canada, Department of Foreign Affairs and International Trade, "Statement by the Government of Canada on Iraq's Parliamentary Elections," 15 December 2005, http://w01.international.gc.ca/MinPub/Publication.asp?Language=E&publication_id=383558.
66 Mike Blanchfield, "Canadian Soldiers Based in Baghdad: Senior Officers Part of NATO Training Program," *National Post,* 19 February 2005, A6.
67 Canadian International Development Agency, "Iraq Overview," http://www.acdi-cida.gc.ca/iraq.
68 Col. Alain Tremblay, "The Canadian Experience in Afghanistan," in *The New World of Robust International Peacekeeping Operations: What Roles for NATO and Canada?* edited by Brian S. MacDonald and David S. McDonough (Toronto: Royal Canadian Military Institute, 2005), 49.
69 Ibid., 46.
70 Ibid.
71 Sean M. Maloney, "Canada's New and Dangerous Mission in Afghanistan," *Policy Options* (March 2006): 98.
72 See London Conference on Afghanistan, "The Afghanistan Compact," London, 31 January–1 February 2006, http://www.unama-afg.org/news/_londonConf/_docs/06jan30-AfghanistanCompact-Final.pdf.
73 Ahmed Rashid, "Who's Winning the War on Terror?" *Yale Global,* 5 September 2003, http://yaleglobal.yale.edu/display.article?id=2384.
74 Islamic Republic of Afghanistan, Afghanistan National Development Strategy, Summary Report: An Interim Strategy for Security, Governance, Economic Growth and Poverty Reduction, http://www.unama-afg.org/news/_londonConf/_docs/ANDS-SummaryReport-eng.pdf.
75 Stein and Lang, *Unexpected War,* 133.
76 Ibid., 181. It is worth noting that a competing account of this decision has been offered by a number of authors, which suggests that the choice of Kandahar as a place for Canada to set up a PRT was almost accidental. After a period of prolonged indecision and procrastination, Kandahar was the only option left to the Canadians. See David S. McDonough, "The Paradox of Afghanistan: Stability Operations and the Renewal of Canada's International Security Policy?" *International Journal* 62, 3 (Summer 2007): 626; and Maloney, "Canada's New and Dangerous Mission," 101.
77 Quoted in Bill Schiller, "The Road to Kandahar," *Toronto Star,* 9 September 2006, F01.
78 Quoted in ibid.

79 John Manley, Derek H. Burney, Jake Epp, Paul Tellier, and Pamela Wallin, *Independent Panel on Canada's Future Role in Afghanistan,* January 2008, http://dsp-psd.pwgsc.gc.ca/collection_2008/dfait-maeci/FR5-20-1-2008E.pdf.
80 McDonough, "The Paradox of Afghanistan," 633.
81 US, Department of Defense, "Report on Progress toward Security and Stability in Afghanistan," 27 June 2008, http://www.defenselink.mil/pubs/Report_on_Progress_toward_Security_and_Stability_in_Afghanistan_1230.pdf.
82 Manley et al., *Independent Panel on Canada's Future Role in Afghanistan.*
83 Jeffrey Simpson, "Trying to Make Love and War in Afghanistan," *Globe and Mail,* 7 March 2006, A15.
84 In-depth Afghanistan: CBC-Environics Public Issues Poll, November 2006, http://www.cbc.ca/news/background/afghanistan/afghanistan-survey2006.html.

Chapter 7: Continental Security after 9/11
A version of this chapter was published as "From Golden Straitjacket to Kevlar Vest: Canada's Transformation to a Security State," *Canadian Journal of Political Science* 40, 4 (2007): 1017-38. Copyright 2007, Cambridge University Press, New York. Reprinted with permission.
1 Stephen Clarkson, *Uncle Sam and Us: Globalization, NeoConservatism, and the Canadian State* (Toronto: University of Toronto Press, 2002), 401.
2 Nils Ørvik, "The Basic Issue in Canadian National Security: Defence against Help/Defence to Help Others," *Canadian Defence Quarterly* 11, 1 (1981): 9.
3 Peter Andreas, "Redrawing the Line: Borders and Security in the 21st Century," *International Security* 28, 2 (Fall 2003): 78-111.
4 Joseph Jockel, "After the September Attacks: Four Questions about NORAD's Future," *Canadian Military Journal* (Spring 2002), http://www.journal.forces.gc.ca/engraph/Vol3/no1/pdf/11-16_e.pdf.
5 Of these were the following: the Wiretap Statute, the Electronic Communications Privacy Act, the Computer Fraud and Abuse Act, the Foreign Intelligence Surveillance Act, the Family Education Rights and Privacy Act, the Pen Register and Trap and Trace Statute, the Money Laundering Act, the Bank Secrecy Act, the Right to Financial Privacy Act, and the Fair Credit Reporting Act.
6 Daniel Drache, *Borders Matter: Homeland Security and the Search for North America* (Halifax: Fernwood, 2004), 7.
7 Matthew Purdy, "A Nation Challenged: The Law; Bush's New Rules to Fight Terror Transform Legal Landscape," *New York Times,* 25 November 2001, 1.
8 Charles Doyle, "The USA Patriot Act: A Sketch," *CRS Report for Congress,* 18 April 2002, http://www.fas.org/irp/crs/RS21203.pdf.
9 US Congress, *Homeland Security Act of 2002,* http://news.findlaw.com/hdocs/docs/terrorism/hsa2002.pdf.
10 US, Office of Homeland Security, *The National Strategy for Homeland Security* (July 2002), vi, http://www.dhs.gov/xlibrary/assets/nat_strat_hls.pdf.
11 Dwight N. Mason, "US-Canada Defence Relations: A View from Washington," in *Canada among Nations, 2003: Coping with the American Colossus,* edited by David Carment, Fen Osler Hampson, and Norman Hillmer (Don Mills, ON: Oxford University Press, 2003), 146.
12 Robert J. Jervis, "Understanding the Bush Doctrine," in *American Foreign Policy: Theoretical Essays,* 5th ed., edited by G. John Ikenberry (New York: Pearson-Longman, 2004), 576.
13 Edna Keeble, "Immigration, Civil Liberties, and National/Homeland Security," *International Journal* 60 (Spring 2005): 360.
14 Kent Roach, "Did September 11 Change Everything? Struggling to Preserve Canadian Values in the Face of Terrorism," *McGill Law Journal* 47 (2002): 895.
15 Stephen Clarkson, "Uncle Sam and Canada after September 11th," in *The Canadian Forces and Interoperability: Panacea or Perdition?* edited by Ann L. Griffiths (Halifax: Dalhousie University, Centre for Foreign Policy Studies, 2002), 85.
16 Canada, House of Commons Debates, 6 December 2001, http://www.parl.gc.ca/37/1/parlbus/chambus/house/debates/126_2001-12-06/han126_1135-E.htm.

17 Transport Canada, "Public Safety Act Receives Royal Assent," 6 May 2004, http://www.tc.gc.ca/mediaroom/releases/nat/2004/04-gc004ae.htm.
18 Canadian Bar Association, Office of the President, "Re: Bill C-7 – Public Safety Act, 2002," http://www.cba.org/CBA/submissions/pdf/04-09-eng.pdf.
19 Canadian Association of University Teachers (CAUT), Letter to Senators Expressing Concern over Bill C-7: Public Safety Act, 4 March 2004, http://www.caut.ca/en/issues/civil_liberties/2004mar_CAUTbillc7.pdf.
20 Roach, "Did September 11 Change Everything?" 915-16.
21 Thomas Gabor, *The Views of Canadian Scholars on the Impact of the Anti-Terrorism Act* (Ottawa: Research and Statistics Division, Department of Justice Canada, 2004), 7.
22 Ibid.
23 Public Safety and Emergency Preparedness Canada, "About Us," http://www.psepc-sppcc.gc.ca/abt/index-en.asp.
24 Bernard Stancati, "The Future of Canada's Role in Hemispheric Defense," *Parameters* 36 (2006): 110.
25 Quoted in Chris Wattie, "Canada's Homeland Defence Team Names Its First Commander," *National Post,* 29 June 2005, A6.
26 Canada, Department of National Defence, "Backgrounder – Canadian Operational Support Command," 31 January 2006, http://www.forces.gc.ca/site/newsroom/view_news_e.asp?id=1853.
27 Office of the Auditor General of Canada, "National Security in Canada – The 2001 Anti-Terrorism Initiative," in *Report of the Auditor General to the House of Commons,* March 2004, http://www.oag-bvg.gc.ca/internet/English/parl_oag_200403_e_1123.html.
28 Canada, Privy Council Office, *Securing an Open Society: Canada's National Security Policy, April 2004,* http://www.pco-bcp.gc.ca/docs/information/publications/natsec-secnat/natsec-secnat-eng.pdf, vii.
29 Ibid., xi, 47.
30 Ibid., 2.
31 Ibid., xi.
32 Ibid., 6.
33 Ibid., 30.
34 Ibid., 36.
35 Ibid., 37.
36 Ibid., 48.
37 Ibid., 4938, 9.
39 Ibid., 18.
40 Ibid.
41 Ibid., 36.
42 Quoted in Barrie McKenna, "U.S. Praises Security Blueprint," *Globe and Mail,* 26 April 2004, A7.
43 US, White House, "President Discusses Strong Relationship with Canada," Halifax, 1 December 2004, http://www.whitehouse.gov/news/releases/2004/12/20041201-4.html.
44 National Commission on Terrorist Attacks upon the United States, *The 9/11 Commission Report: Final Report of the National Commission on Terrorist Attacks upon the United States* (New York: Norton, 2004), 383-84.
45 Quoted in Ben Rowswell, "McLellan's U.S. Challenge," *Toronto Star,* 18 December 2003, A31.
46 Quoted in Greg Weston, "Fix Leaky Borders: U.S.," *Toronto Sun,* 20 September 2001, 7.
47 Quoted in Allan Thompson, "Can Canada Still Lay Claim to Being Glorious and Free?" *Toronto Star,* 9 September 2002, A6.
48 US, White House, "Summary of the Smart Border Action Plan Status," 9 September 2002, http://www.whitehouse.gov/news/releases/2002/09/20020909.html.
49 Canada Border Services Agency, "The Free and Secure Trade Program," http://www.cbsa-asfc.gc.ca/import/fast/menu-e.html#what.
50 US, White House, "U.S.-Canada Smart Border/30-Point Action Plan Update," 6 December 2002, http://www.whitehouse.gov/news/releases/2002/12/20021206-1.html.

51 Paul Koring, "Bush Adds $2-Billion to Border Pot," *Globe and Mail*, 26 January 2002, A13.
52 Thompson, "Can Canada Still Lay Claim to Being Glorious and Free?" A20.
53 Deborah Waller Myers, "Does 'Smarter' Lead to Safer? An Assessment of the US Border Accords with Canada and Mexico," *International Migration* 41, 4 (2003): 14.
54 Canada Border Services Agency, "Canada-United States Integrated Enforcement Teams," http://www.cbsa-asfc.gc.ca/general/enforcement/ibet-eipf-e.html.
55 Public Safety and Emergency Preparedness Canada, "Integrated Border Enforcement Teams," http://www.psepc-sppcc.gc.ca/prg/le/bs/ibet-en.asp.
56 Public Safety and Emergency Preparedness Canada, "Canada-United States Cross Border Crime Forum," http://www.psepc-sppcc.gc.ca/prg/le/oc/cbc-en.asp.
57 Canada, Privy Council Office, *Securing an Open Society*, 42-43.
58 US, Department of Homeland Security, "US-Canada Smart Border/30-Point Action Plan Update," 6 December 2002, http://www.dhs.gov/dhspublic/display?content=128.
59 Ibid.
60 Tonda MacCharles, "Air Travelers Face Screening," *Toronto Star*, 17 January 2004, A1.
61 Ibid.
62 US, Department of Homeland Security, "Fact Sheet: Security and Prosperity Partnership," 27 June 2005, http://www.dhs.gov/xnews/releases/press_release_0695.shtm.

Conclusion

1 For a theoretical exposition of this strategy and other leading alternatives, see Barry R. Posen and Andrew L. Ross, "Competing Visions for U.S. Grand Strategy," *International Security* 21 (Winter 1996-97): 5-53. For what each of the four competing visions means for America's allies, particularly Canada, see Douglas A. Ross and Christopher N.B. Ross, "From Neo-Isolationism to Neo-Imperialism: Grand Strategy Options in the American International Security Debate and the Implications for Canada," in *The Dilemmas of American Strategic Primacy: Implications for the Future of Canadian-American Cooperation*, edited by David S. McDonough and Douglas A. Ross (Toronto: Royal Canadian Military Institute, 2005), 165-219. The strategy of maintaining primacy was one of the four essential elements of the Bush Doctrine as outlined in the National Security Strategy of 2002. For a description of the other three elements and an analysis of the Bush Doctrine, see Robert J. Jervis, "Understanding the Bush Doctrine," in *American Foreign Policy: Theoretical Essays*, 5th ed., edited by G. John Ikenberry (New York: Pearson-Longman, 2004).
2 United States Navy, *A Cooperative Strategy for 21st Century Seapower*, October 2007, http://www.navy.mil/maritime/MaritimeStrategy.pdf.
3 On this important and related issue of leadership and followership, see Andrew Fenton Cooper, Richard A. Higgott, and Kim Richard Nossal, "Bound to Follow? Leadership and Followership in the Gulf Crisis," *Political Science Quarterly* 106 (Autumn 1991): 391-410.
4 Stephen Walt, "Keeping the World 'Off Balance': Self-Restraint and U.S. Foreign Policy," in *America Unrivaled: The Future of the Balance of Power*, edited by G. John Ikenberry (Ithaca, NY: Cornell University Press, 2002), 121-55.

Bibliography

Books and Journal Articles

Adler, Emmanuel. "Seizing the Middle Ground: Constructivism in World Politics." *European Journal of International Relations* 3, 3 (1997): 319-63.

Adler, Emmanuel, and Michael Barnett, eds. *Security Communities.* Cambridge: Cambridge University Press, 1998.

Allison, Graham T. "Conceptual Models and the Cuban Missile Crisis." In *American Foreign Policy: Theoretical Essays,* 3rd ed., edited by G. John Ikenberry. New York: Longman, 1999.

Andreas, Peter. "Redrawing the Line: Borders and Security in the 21st Century." *International Security* 28, 2 (Fall 2003): 78-111.

Axworthy, Lloyd. "Lessons from the Ottawa Process." *Canadian Foreign Policy* 3, 5 (1998): 1-13.

–. *Navigating a New World: Canada's Global Future.* Toronto: A.A. Knopf, 2003.

Baldwin, David A., ed. *Neorealism and Neoliberalism: The Contemporary Debate.* New York: Columbia University Press, 1993.

Barry, Donald. "Chrétien, Bush, and the War in Iraq." *American Review of Canadian Studies* (Summer 2005): 215-45.

Baucom, Donald R. *The Origins of SDI, 1944-1983.* Lawrence: University Press of Kansas, 1992.

Bercuson, David. "Canada-U.S. Defence Relations Post-11 September." In *Canada among Nations, 2003: Coping with the American Colossus.* Edited by David Carment, Fen Osler Hampson, and Norman Hillmer. Don Mills, ON: Oxford University Press, 2003.

Bercuson, David, J.L. Granatstein, and W.R. Young. *Sacred Trust? Brian Mulroney and the Conservative Party in Power.* Toronto: Doubleday, 1986.

Black, David R., and Heather A. Smith. "Notable Exceptions? New and Arrested Directions in Canadian Foreign Policy Literature." *Canadian Journal of Political Science* 26, 4 (1994): 745-74.

Blight, James G., Bruce J. Allyn, and David A. Welch. *Cuba on the Brink: Castro, the Missile Crisis, and the Soviet Collapse.* New York: Pantheon, 1993.

Bothwell, Robert. *Alliance and Illusion: Canada and the World, 1945-1984.* Vancouver: UBC Press, 2007.

Bratt, Duane. "Niche Making and Canadian Peacekeeping." *Canadian Foreign Policy* 6, 3 (Spring 1999): 73-90.

Bridle, Paul. 1973. "Canada and the International Commissions in Indochina, 1954-1972." *Behind the Headlines* 32, 4: 18.

Brock, Jeffrey V. *The Thunder and the Sunshine: Memoirs of a Sailor.* Toronto: McClelland and Stewart, 1983.

Brooks, Stephen G., and William C. Wohlforth. "American Primacy in Perspective." *Foreign Affairs* 81, 4 (2002): 20-33.

Brown, David Leyton. "A Refurbished Relationship with the United States." In *Canada among Nations, 1988: The Tory Record*. Edited by Brian W. Tomlin and Maureen Appel Molot. Toronto: James Lorimer, 1989.

Brunnee, Jutta, and Adrian Di Giovanni. "Iraq: A Fork in the Road for a Special Relationship?" *International Journal* 60, 2 (2005): 375-85.

Buckley, Brian. *Canada's Early Nuclear Weapons Policy: Fate, Chance, and Character*. Montreal and Kingston: McGill-Queen's University Press, 2000.

Canada. House of Commons. *Canada and the Nuclear Challenge: Reducing The Political Value of Nuclear Weapons for the Twenty-First Century*. Report of the Standing Committee on Foreign Affairs and International Trade, Bill Graham, MP, Chair. December 1998.

Canada. *House of Commons Debates, Official Report, Third Session – Twenty-Eighth Parliament, Volume 7, 1971*. Ottawa: Queen's Printer for Canada.

Canadian Institute of International Affairs. *Monthly Report* 4, 4 (April 1965).

Carr, E.H. *The Twenty Years' Crisis, 1919-1939: An Introduction to the Study of International Relations*. London: Macmillan, 1939, 1962.

Chapnick, Adam. *The Middle Power Project: Canada and the Founding of the United Nations*. Vancouver: UBC Press, 2005.

Clarkson, Stephen. *Canada and the Reagan Challenge: Crisis and Adjustment, 1981-1985*. Toronto: James Lorimer, 1985.

–. *Uncle Sam and Us: Globalization, NeoConservatism, and the Canadian State*. Toronto: University of Toronto Press, 2002.

–. "Uncle Sam and Canada after September 11th." In *The Canadian Forces and Interoperability: Panacea or Perdition?* Edited by Ann L. Griffiths. Halifax: Dalhousie University, Centre for Foreign Policy Studies, 2002.

Clearwater, John. *Canadian Nuclear Weapons: The Untold Story of Canada's Cold War Arsenal*. Toronto: Dundurn, 1998.

–. *U.S. Nuclear Weapons in Canada*. Toronto: Dundurn, 1998.

Cohen, Andrew. "Canadian-American Relations: Does Canada Matter in Washington? Does It Matter if Canada Doesn't Matter?" In *Canada among Nations, 2002: A Fading Power*. Edited by Norman Hillmer and Maureen Appel Molot. Don Mills, ON: Oxford University Press, 2002.

Cooley, Alexander. *Logics of Hierarchy: The Organization of Empires, States and Military Occupations*. Ithaca, NY: Cornell University Press, 2005.

Cooper, Andrew F. "In Search of Niches: Saying 'Yes' and Saying 'No' in Canada's International Relations." *Canadian Foreign Policy* 3, 3 (Winter 1995): 1-13.

Cooper, Andrew Fenton, Richard A. Higgott, and Kim Richard Nossal. "Bound to Follow? Leadership and Followership in the Gulf Crisis." *Political Science Quarterly* 106 (Autumn 1991): 391-410.

Cox, David. "The Cruise Testing Agreement." *International Perspectives* (July/August 1983): 3-5.

Dai, Poeliu. "Canada's Role in the International Commission for Supervision and Control in Vietnam." In *The Canadian Yearbook of International Law*. Vancouver: Publications Centre, University of British Columbia, 1966.

Davidson, Vice-Admiral Glenn. "After the War: Canada's Navy Post-1945." *Starshell* 7, 43 (Summer 2008): 3-6.

Dawson, Grant. "'A Special Case': Canada, Operation Apollo, and Multilateralism." In *Canada among Nations, 2003: Coping with the American Colossus*. Edited by David Carment, Fen Osler Hampson, and Norman Hillmer. Don Mills, ON: Oxford University Press, 2003.

Department of External Affairs, *Documents on Canadian External Relations*, 20 (1954). Edited by Greg Donaghy. Ottawa: Canada Communication Group, 1997.

Dewitt, David B., and John Kirton. *Canada as a Principal Power: A Study in Foreign Policy and International Relations*. Toronto: Wiley and Sons, 1983.

Diefenbaker, John G. *One Canada: The Tumultuous Years, 1962-1967*, vol. 3. Toronto: Macmillan, 1977.

Doern, Walter. "Canadian Peacekeeping: No Myth – but Not What It Once Was." *SITREP* 67, 2 (2007): 6.

Donaghy, Greg. *Tolerant Allies: Canada and the United States, 1963-1968*. Montreal and Kingston: McGill-Queen's University Press, 2002.

Donnelly, Jack. "Sovereign Inequalities and Hierarchy in Anarchy: American Power and International Security." *European Journal of International Relations* 12, 2 (2006): 139-70.

Drache, Daniel. *Borders Matter: Homeland Security and the Search for North America*. Halifax: Fernwood, 2004.

Easton, David. "An Approach to the Analysis of Political Systems." *World Politics* 9, 3 (1957): 383-400.

–. *The Analysis of Political Structure*. New York: Routledge, 1990.

Eayrs, James. *In Defence of Canada, Indochina: Roots of Complicity*. Toronto: University of Toronto Press, 1983.

Ellsberg, Daniel. *Secrets: A Memoir of Vietnam and the Pentagon Papers*. New York: Viking, 2002.

English, John. "Speaking Out on Vietnam, 1965." In *Canadian Foreign Policy: Selected Cases*. Edited by Don Munton and John Kirton. Scarborough, ON: Prentice Hall, 1992.

–. *The Worldly Years: The Life of Lester B. Pearson. Volume II: 1949-1972*. Toronto: A.A. Knopf, 1992.

Everson, David H., and Joann Poparad Paine. *An Introduction to Systematic Political Science*. Homewood, IL: Dorsey, 1973.

Finch, Ron. *Exporting Danger*. Montreal: Black Rose, 1986.

Fischer, Beth A. "The Trudeau Peace Initiative and the End of the Cold War: Catalyst or Coincidence?" *International Journal* 49, 3 (1994): 613-34.

Fitzgerald, Frances. *Way Out There in the Blue: Reagan, Star Wars, and the End of the Cold War*. Toronto: Simon and Schuster, 2000.

Gabor, Thomas. *The Views of Canadian Scholars on the Impact of the Anti-Terrorism Act*. Ottawa: Research and Statistics Division, Department of Justice Canada, 2004.

George, Alexander L., and Andrew Bennett. *Case Studies and Theory Development in the Social Sciences*. Cambridge, MA: MIT Press, 2005.

Ghent-Mallet, Jocelyn. "Deploying Nuclear Weapons, 1962-63." In *Canadian Foreign Policy: Selected Cases*. Edited by Don Munton and John Kirton. Scarborough, ON: Prentice Hall, 1991.

Ghent-Mallet, Jocelyn, and Don Munton. "Confronting Kennedy and the Missiles in Cuba, 1962." In *Canadian Foreign Policy: Selected Cases*. Edited by Don Munton and John Kirton. Scarborough, ON: Prentice Hall, 1991.

Gimblett, Richard. *Operation Apollo: The Golden Age of the Canadian Navy in the War against Terrorism*. Ottawa: Magic Light, 2004.

Glaser, Charles. "When Are Arms Races Dangerous? Rational versus Suboptimal Arming." *International Security* 28, 4 (2004): 44-84.

Glazov, Jamie. *Canadian Policy Toward Khrushchev's Soviet Union*. Montreal and Kingston: McGill-Queen's University Press, 2002.

Goh, Evelyn. "Great Powers and Hierarchical Order in Southeast Asia: Analyzing Political Security Strategies." *International Security* 32 (Winter 2007/2008): 113-57.

Gordon, J. King, ed. *Canada's Role as a Middle Power*. Toronto: Canadian Institute of International Affairs, 1966.

Gordon, Walter. "The Liberal Leadership and Nuclear Weapons." In *Canada and the Nuclear Arms Race*. Edited by Ernie Regehr and Simon Rosenblum. Toronto: James Lorimer, 1983.

Granatstein, J.L., ed. *Canadian Foreign Policy since 1945*. Toronto: Copp Clark, 1969.

–. *Who Killed the Canadian Military?* Toronto: Harper-Flamingo, 2004.

–. *Yankee Go Home?* Toronto: HarperCollins, 1996.

Hampson, Fen Osler, and Dean F. Oliver. "Pulpit Diplomacy: A Critical Assessment of the Axworthy Doctrine." *International Journal* (Summer 1998): 379-406.

Hampson, Fen Osler, Norman Hillmer, and Maureen Appel Molot, eds. *Canada among Nations 2001: The Axworthy Legacy*. Toronto: Oxford University Press, 2001.

Hanson, Marianne. *Advancing Disarmament in the Face of Great Power Reluctance: The Canadian Contribution.* Working Paper 37. Vancouver: Institute of International Relations, University of British Columbia, June 2001.

Harvey, Frank P. *Smoke and Mirrors: Globalized Terrorism and the Illusion of Multilateral Security.* Toronto: University of Toronto Press, 2004.

Hawes, Michael K. *Principal Power, Middle Power, or Satellite?* Toronto: York Research Programme in Strategic Studies, 1984.

Haydon, Peter T. *The 1962 Cuban Missile Crisis: Canadian Involvement Reconsidered.* Toronto: Canadian Institute for Strategic Studies, 1993.

Hegel, G.W.F. *Elements of the Philosophy of Right.* Ed. Allen Wood, trans. H.B. Nisbet. New York: Cambridge University Press, 1991.

Hermann, Charles F. "International Crisis as a Situational Variable." In *International Politics and Foreign Policy.* Edited by James N. Rosenau, 409-21. New York: Simon and Schuster, 1969.

Heston, Alan, Robert Summers, and Bettina Aten. *Penn World Table Version 6.2.* Center for International Comparisons of Production, Income and Prices at the University of Pennsylvania, September 2006. http://pwt.econ.upenn.edu/php_site/pwt_index.php.

Hilliker, John, and Donald Barry. "Uncomfortably in the Middle: The Department of External Affairs and Canada's Involvement in the International Control Commissions in Vietnam, 1954-1973." Paper presented at the Biennial Meeting of the Association for Canadian Studies in the United States, Seattle, WA, 15-19 November 1995.

Hillmer, Norman. ed. *Partners Nevertheless: Canadian-American Relations in the Twentieth Century.* Toronto: Copp Clark, 1989.

Holmes, John. "Geneva: 1954." *International Journal* 22, 3 (1967): 457-83.

–. *The Shaping of Peace: Canada and the Search for World Order, 1945-1957.* Toronto: University of Toronto Press, 1979.

Ikenberry, G. John, ed. *America Unrivaled: The Future of the Balance of Power.* Ithaca, NY: Cornell University Press, 2002.

–. "Liberalism and Empire: Logics of Order in the American Unipolar Age." *Review of International Studies* 30 (2004): 609-30.

Jervis, Robert. "Understanding the Bush Doctrine." In *American Foreign Policy: Theoretical Essays,* 5th ed. Edited by G. John Ikenberry. New York: Pearson-Longman, 2004.

Jockel, Joseph. *Canada in NORAD, 1957-2007: A History.* Montreal and Kingston: McGill-Queen's University Press, 2007.

–. *Security to the North: Canada-U.S. Defense Relations in the 1990s.* East Lansing: Michigan State University Press, 1991.

Johnson, Lyndon Baines. *The Vantage Point: Perspectives of the Presidency, 1963-1969.* New York: Popular Library, 1971.

Kaplan, Morton. *System and Process in International Politics.* New York: Krieger, 1975.

Keeble, Edna. "Immigration, Civil Liberties, and National/Homeland Security." *International Journal* 60 (Spring 2005): 359-72.

Keenleyside, H.L. "The Canada-United States Permanent Joint Board on Defence, 1940-1945." *International Journal* 16, 1 (1960-61): 52.

Keohane, Robert. "Neoliberal Institutionalism: A Perspective on World Politics." In *International Institutions and State Power.* Edited by Robert Keohane, 1-20. Boulder, CO: Westview, 1989.

–, ed. *Neorealism and Its Critics.* New York: Columbia University Press, 1986.

Kirton, John J. *Canadian Foreign Policy in a Changing World.* Toronto: Thompson-Nelson, 2007.

Kissinger, Henry. *Ending the Vietnam War: A History of America's Involvement in and Extrication from the Vietnam War.* Toronto: Simon and Schuster, 2003.

Krepon, Michael. *Cooperative Threat Reduction, Missile Defense, and the Nuclear Future.* New York: Palgrave, 2003.

Kupchan, Charles. *The End of the American Era: US Foreign Policy and the Geopolitics of the Twenty-First Century.* New York: Vintage, 2003.

Lake, David A. "Anarchy, Hierarchy, and the Variety of International Relations." *International Organization* 50, 1 (1996): 1-33.

–. "Escape from the State of Nature: Authority and Hierarchy in World Politics." *International Security* 32, 1 (Summer 2007): 47-79.

Langguth, A.J. *Our Vietnam: The War, 1954-1975*. Toronto: Simon and Schuster, 2000.

Langille, Howard Peter. *Changing the Guard: Canada's Defence in a World in Transition*. Toronto: University of Toronto Press, 1990.

Larson, David L., ed. *The Cuban Crisis of 1962: Selected Documents and Chronology*. Boston: Houghton Mifflin, 1963.

Lawson, Robert. "The Ottawa Process: Fast-Track Diplomacy and the International Movement to Ban Anti-Personnel Landmines." In *Canada among Nations, 1998: Leadership and Dialogue*. Edited by Fen Osler Hampson and Maureen Appel Molot. Toronto: Oxford University Press, 1998.

Lentner, Howard H. "Foreign Policy Decision Making: The Case of Canada and Nuclear Weapons." *World Politics* 29, 1 (1976): 29-66.

Levitt, Joseph. *Pearson and Canada's Role in Nuclear Disarmament and Arms Control Negotiations, 1945-1957*. Montreal and Kingston: McGill-Queen's University Press, 1993.

Lyon, Peyton. *Canada in World Affairs, 1961-1963*. Toronto: Oxford University Press, 1968.

–. "Defence: To Be or Not to Be Nuclear." In *Canada in World Affairs, 1961-1963*. Edited by Peyton Lyon. Toronto: Oxford University Press, 1968.

Lyon, Peyton, and Brian W. Tomlin. *Canada as an International Actor*. Toronto: Macmillan, 1979.

Maloney, Sean. "Canada's New and Dangerous Mission in Afghanistan." *Policy Options* (March 2006): 98-103.

–. *Learning to Love the Bomb: Canada's Nuclear Weapons during the Cold War*. Washington, DC: Potomac Books, 2007.

Mann, Robert. *A Grand Delusion: America's Descent into Vietnam*. New York: Basic Books, 2001.

Martin, Lawrence. *Iron Man: The Defiant Reign of Jean Chrétien*, vol. 2. Toronto: Viking, 2003.

–. *The Presidents and the Prime Ministers*. Toronto: Doubleday, 1982.

Mason, Dwight N. "US-Canada Defence Relations: A View from Washington." In *Canada among Nations, 2003: Coping with the American Colossus*, edited by David Carment, Fen Osler Hampson, and Norman Hillmer. Don Mills, ON: Oxford University Press, 2003.

McCall, Christina, and Stephen Clarkson. *Trudeau and Our Times. Volume 2: The Heroic Delusion*. Toronto: McClelland and Stewart, 1994.

McClelland, Charles A. *Theory and the International System*. New York: Macmillan, 1966.

McDonough, David S. "The Paradox of Afghanistan: Stability Operations and the Renewal of Canada's International Security Policy?" *International Journal* 62, 3 (Summer 2007): 620-41.

McLin, Jon B. *Canada's Changing Defense Policy: The Problem of a Middle Power in Alliance*. Baltimore: Johns Hopkins University Press, 1967.

Mearsheimer, John. "Back to the Future: Instability in Europe after the Cold War." *International Security* 15, 1 (1990): 5-56.

–. *The Tragedy of Great Power Politics*. New York: Norton, 2001.

Meredith, P.L. "The Legality of a High-Technology Missile Defense System: The ABM and Outer Space Treaties." *American Journal of International Law* 78, 2 (1984): 418-23.

Minifie, James. *Peacemaker or Powder Monkey: Canada's Role in a Revolutionary World*. Toronto: McClelland and Stewart, 1970.

Molgot, Daniel. "The Sequel: Canada Does It Again in Vietnam, April 1968–May 1973." In *Canadian Peacekeepers in Indochina, 1954-1973*. Edited by Arthur E. Blanchette. Ottawa: Golden Dog, 2002.

Munton, Don. "Going Fission: Tales and Truths about Canada's Nuclear Weapons." *International Journal* (Summer 1996): 506-28.

Murray, Douglas. "NORAD and U.S. Nuclear Operations." In *Fifty Years of Canada-United States Defense Cooperation: The Road From Ogdensburg*. Edited by Joel J. Sokolsky and Joseph T. Jockel. Lewiston, NY: Edwin Mellen Press, 1992.

Myers, Deborah Waller. "Does 'Smarter' Lead to Safer? An Assessment of the US Border Accords with Canada and Mexico." *International Migration* 41, 4 (2003): 5-44.

Naftali, Timothy, and Philip Zelikow, eds. *The Presidential Recordings, John F. Kennedy: The Great Crises,* vol. 2. New York: Norton, 2001.

Nash, Knowlton. *Kennedy and Diefenbaker: Fear and Loathing Across the Undefended Border.* McClelland and Stewart, 1990.

National Commission on Terrorist Attacks upon the United States. *The 9/11 Commission Report: Final Report of the National Commission on Terrorist Attacks upon the United States.* Authorized ed. New York: Norton, 2004.

Newman, Peter C. *Renegade in Power: The Diefenbaker Years.* Toronto: McClelland and Stewart, 1963.

–. *The Secret Mulroney Tapes: The Unguarded Confessions of a Prime Minister.* Toronto: Random House, 2005.

–. *The True North: Not Strong and Free.* Toronto: McClelland and Stewart, 1983.

Nicholson, Patrick. *Vision and Indecision.* Don Mills, ON: Longman, 1968.

Nossal, Kim Richard. "Mission Diplomacy and the 'Cult of the Initiative' in Canadian Foreign Policy." In *Worthwhile Initiatives? Canadian Mission-Oriented Diplomacy.* Edited by Andrew F. Cooper and Geoffrey Hayes. Toronto: Irwin, 2000.

–. "Pinchpenny Diplomacy: The Decline of 'Good International Citizenship' in Canadian Foreign Policy." *International Journal* (Winter 1998-99): 87-105.

–. *The Politics of Canadian Foreign Policy,* 3rd ed. Scarborough, ON: Prentice Hall, 1997.

Ørvik, Nils. "The Basic Issue in Canadian National Security: Defence against Help/Defence to Help Others." *Canadian Defence Quarterly* 11, 1 (1981): 8-15.

Pachter, Henry M. *Collision Course: The Cuban Missile Crisis and Coexistence.* New York: Frederick A. Praeger, 1963.

Pearson, Geoffrey. *Seize the Day: Lester B. Pearson and Crisis Diplomacy.* Ottawa: Carleton University Press, 1993.

–. "Trudeau Peace Initiative Reflections." *International Perspectives* (March/April 1985): 3-6.

Pearson, Lester B. "Extracts from an Address by the Right Honourable Lester B. Pearson, Prime Minister of Canada, to the Canadian Club of Ottawa, February 10, 1965," Canada, Department of External Affairs, Statements and Speeches, 65/3.

–. *Mike: The Memoirs of the Right Honourable Lester B. Pearson. Volume 3, 1957-1968.* Edited by John A. Munro and Alex I. Inglis. Toronto: University of Toronto Press, 1975.

Pope, William Henry. *The Elephant and the Mouse: A Handbook on Regaining Control of Canada's Economy.* Toronto: McClelland and Stewart, 1971.

Posen, Barry R., and Andrew L. Ross. "Competing Visions for U.S. Grand Strategy." *International Security* 21 (Winter 1996-97): 5-53.

Reford, Robert. *Canada and Three Crises.* Toronto: Canadian Institute of International Affairs, 1968.

Rhinelander, John B. "Implications of US and Soviet BMD Programmes for the ABM Treaty." In *Space Weapons and International Security.* Edited by Bhupendra Jasani. Toronto: Oxford University Press, 1987.

Richter, Andrew. "A Question of Defense: How American Allies Are Responding to the US Missile Defense Program." *Comparative Strategy* 23 (2004): 143-72.

–. "From Trusted Ally to Suspicious Neighbor: Canada-U.S. Relations in a Changing Global Environment." *American Review of Canadian Studies* (Autumn 2005): 471-502.

–. "North American Aerospace Defence Cooperation in the 1990s: Issues and Prospects." Department of National Defence, Canada, Operational Research and Analysis Establishment (ORAE) Extra-Mural Paper 57. Ottawa: Department of National Defence, 1991.

Roach, Kent. "Did September 11 Change Everything? Struggling to Preserve Canadian Values in the Face of Terrorism." *McGill Law Journal* 47 (2002): 893-947.

Robinson, H. Basil. *Diefenbaker's World: A Populist in Foreign Affairs.* Toronto: University of Toronto Press, 1989.

Ross, Douglas A. *In the Interests of Peace: Canada and Vietnam, 1954-1973.* Toronto: University of Toronto Press, 1984.

Ross, Douglas A., and Christopher N.B. Ross. "From Neo-Isolationism to Neo-Imperialism: Grand Strategy Options in the American International Security Debate and the Implications for Canada." In *The Dilemmas of American Strategic Primacy: Implications for the Future of Canadian-American Cooperation,* edited by David S. McDonough and Douglas A. Ross. Toronto: Royal Canadian Military Institute, 2005.

Rudd, David. "Muddling through on Missile Defence: The Politics of Indecision." *Policy Options* (May 2005): 30.

Ruggie, John Gerard. "Continuity and Transformation in the World Polity: Toward a Neorealist Synthesis." In *Neorealism and its Critics.* Edited by Robert O. Keohane, 131-57. New York: Columbia University Press, 1986.

–. "What Makes the World Hang Together? Neo-Utilitarianism and the Social Constructivist Challenge," *International Organization* 52, 4 (1998): 887-917.

Saywell, John T., ed. *Canadian Annual Review for 1962.* Toronto: University of Toronto Press, 1963.

–. *Canadian Annual Review for 1965.* Toronto: University of Toronto Press, 1966.

Schmidt, Brian C. *The Political Discourse of Anarchy: A Disciplinary History of International Relations.* Albany, NY: SUNY Press, 1998.

Schneider, Barry R., and Colin S. Gray. "Defending versus Avening: A Critical Assessment of SDI and MAD Policies." In *Space Weapons and International Security.* Edited by Bhupendra Jasani. Toronto: Oxford University Press, 1987.

Seaborn, J. Blair. "Mission to Hanoi: The Canadian Channel, May 1964–November 1965." In *Canadian Peacekeepers in Indochina, 1954-1973.* Edited by Arthur E. Blanchette. Ottawa: Golden Dog, 2002.

Sharp, Mitchell. *Foreign Policy for Canadians.* Ottawa: Department of External Affairs, 1970.

–. *Which Reminds Me ... A Memoir.* Toronto: University of Toronto Press, 1995.

Shore, Sean M. "No Fences Made Good Neighbors: The Development of the US-Canada Security Community, 1871-1940." In *Security Communities.* Edited by Emmanuel Adler and Michael Barnett. Cambridge: Cambridge University Press, 1998.

Sigler, John H., and Dennis Goresky. "Public Opinion on United States-Canadian Relations." *International Organization* 28, 4 (1974): 662.

Sokolsky, Joel J. "Arms Control Negotiations: Confronting the Paradoxes." In *Canada among Nations, 1985: The Conservative Agenda.* Edited by Maureen Appel Molot and Brian W. Tomlin. Toronto: James Lorimer, 1986.

–. "Canada and the Cold War at Sea, 1945-68." In *The RCN in Transition, 1910-1985,* edited by W.A.B. Douglas. Vancouver: UBC Press, 1988.

Soward, F.H., and Edgar McInnis. "Forming the United Nations, 1945." In *Canadian Foreign Policy: Selected Cases.* Edited by Don Munton and John Kirton, 4-18. Scarborough, ON: Prentice Hall, 1992.

Stairs, Denis. "The Political Culture of Canadian Foreign Policy." *Canadian Journal of Political Science* 15, 4 (1982): 667-90.

Stancati, Bernard. "The Future of Canada's Role in Hemispheric Defense." *Parameters* 36 (Autumn 2006): 103-16.

Stein, Janice Gross, and Eugene Lang. *The Unexpected War: Canada in Kandahar.* Toronto: Viking, 2007.

Stewart, James. *Seven Years of Terrorism: The FLQ. A Special Report by the Montreal Star.* Richmond Hill, ON: Simon and Schuster, 1970.

Stursberg, Peter. *Diefenbaker: Leadership Lost, 1962-67.* Toronto: University of Toronto Press, 1976.

–. *Lester Pearson and the American Dilemma.* Toronto: Doubleday, 1980.

Taylor, Charles. *Snow Job: Canada, the United States and Vietnam [1954 to 1973].* Toronto: Anansi, 1978.

The Senator Gravel Edition of The Pentagon Papers: The Defense Department History of United States Decision Making on Vietnam, vols. 2 and 3. Boston: Beacon, 1971.

Thompson, John Herd, and Stephen J. Randall. *Canada and the United States: Ambivalent Allies,* 3rd ed. Montreal and Kingston: McGill-Queen's University Press, 1994.

Tremblay, Col. Alain. "The Canadian Experience in Afghanistan." In *The New World of Robust International Peacekeeping Operations: What Roles for NATO and Canada?* Edited by Brian S. MacDonald and David S. McDonough. Toronto: Royal Canadian Military Institute, 2005.

Trudeau, Pierre Elliott. *Lifting the Shadow of War.* Edmonton: Hurtig, 1987.

–. *Memoirs.* Toronto: McClelland and Stewart, 1993.

Turner, Barry, ed. *The Statesman's Yearbook: The Politics, Cultures, and Economics of the World.* New York: Palgrave, 2004.

Van Evera, Stephen. *Causes of War.* Ithaca, NY: Cornell University Press, 1999.

Van Rooy, Alison. "Civil Society and the Axworthy Touch." In *Canada among Nations, 2001: The Axworthy Legacy.* Edited by Fen Osler Hampson, Norman Hillmer, and Maureen Appel Molot. Don Mills, ON: Oxford University Press, 2001.

Vasquez, John A., and Colin Elman, eds. *Realism and the Balancing of Power: A New Debate.* Upper Saddle River, NJ: Prentice Hall, 2003.

Von Riekhoff, Harold, and John Sigler. "The Trudeau Peace Initiative: The Politics of Reversing the Arms Race." In *Canada among Nations, 1984: A Time of Transition.* Edited by Brian W. Tomlin and Maureen Molot. Toronto: James Lorimer, 1985.

Walt, Stephen. "Keeping the World 'Off Balance': Self-Restraint and U.S. Foreign Policy." In *America Unrivaled: The Future of the Balance of Power.* Edited by G. John Ikenberry, 121-55. Ithaca, NY: Cornell University Press, 2002.

–. *The Origins of Alliances.* Ithaca, NY: Cornell University Press, 1987.

Waltz, Kenneth. *Theory of International Politics.* Toronto: McGraw-Hill, 1979.

Warnock, John P. *Partner to Behemoth: The Military Policy of a Satellite Canada.* Toronto: New Press, 1970.

Welsh, Jennifer. *At Home in the World: Canada's Global Vision for the 21st Century.* Toronto: HarperCollins, 2004.

Wendt, Alexander. "Anarchy Is What States Make of It: The Social Construction of Power Politics." *International Organization* 46, 2 (1992): 391-425.

Wendt, Alexander, and Daniel Friedheim. "Hierarchy under Anarchy: Informal Empire and the East German State." In *State Sovereignty as Social Construct.* Edited by Thomas J. Biersteker and Cynthia Weber, 240-77. Cambridge: Cambridge University Press, 1996.

Yao Wenbin. "The Impact of SDI in International Security." In *Space Weapons and International Security.* Edited by Bhupendra Jasani. Toronto: Oxford University Press, 1987.

Newspaper and Magazine Articles

Alberts, Sheldon. "Liberal Rift Delays Entry to Arms Plan." *National Post,* 8 May 2003, A1.

–. "PM Maintains War in Iraq Is 'Not Justified': 'Case Was Not Made.'" *National Post,* 19 March 2003, A12.

–. "Powell Urges Canada to Join Iraq Coalition." *National Post,* 15 November 2002, A16.

–, with files from Chris Wattie. "War Planners Get Cold Feet: Canada Reconsiders Role." *National Post,* 20 November 2001, A01.

Allen, Mike. "Cheney Reaches Out to Iraq War Critics; Anti-Terror Efforts Need 'Many Hands.'" *Washington Post,* 25 January 2004, A17.

Apple, R.W. Jr. "No Middle Ground." *New York Times,* 14 September 2001, 1.

Baker, Peter. "Bush Doctrine Is Expected to Get Chilly Reception." *Washington Post,* 23 January 2005, A1.

Blackwell, Tom. "Contract 'Takes Canada into Missile Program': $700,000 Radar Testing: Defense Accused of Pushing Ahead before Issue Debated." *National Post,* 16 February 2004, A2.

Blanchfield, Mike. "Canadian Soldiers Based in Baghdad: Senior Officers Part of NATO Training Program." *National Post,* 19 February 2005, A6.

Chase, Steven. "Spend More on Military, Ottawa Told." *Globe and Mail,* 8 October 2001, A13.

Chrétien, Jean. "Don't Act Alone," *Globe and Mail,* 14 February 2003, A17.

Dawson, Anne. "Budget to Add $2B for Military: Forces Pushing for Major Role in Iraq War." *National Post,* 8 February 2003, A1.

Den Tandt, Michael, and Paul Koring. "Opposition Rakes Liberals over Missile-Defence Coals; but 'Unprecedented Spectacle' of Confusion on Issue Causes Little Stir in Washington," *Globe and Mail,* 24 February 2005, A4.

Den Tandt, Michael, and Daniel Leblanc. "PM Set to Reject Missile Defense: After McKenna Says Canada Is in, Martin Will Announce that It's out." *Globe and Mail,* 23 February 2005, A1.

Fife, Robert, with files from Paul Wells. "Canada to Back Missile Shield: Chrétien Cabinet Prepares Public Opinion for Policy Switch on High-Tech Defense." *National Post,* 14 May 2001, A1.

Fife, Robert, and Peter Morton. "Missile Plan Splits Canada, U.S.: Shock in Washington: Putin Nominates Ottawa as Mediator in Shield Stand Off." *National Post,* 19 December 2000, A1.

Freeman, Allan. "Canada Shuns Minor Peace Role." *Globe and Mail,* 4 January 2002, A1.

Gee, Marcus. "Canada's Peacekeeper Image a Myth." *Globe and Mail,* 4 January 2002, A6.

Goodspeed, Peter. "Ottawa Will Support Missile Defense: Experts: 'It's Just a Question of Timing,' Seminar Told." *National Post,* 12 May 2001, A11.

Green, Howard. "Caribbean Area Vital to Canada." *Ottawa Journal,* 12 October 1963, 10.

Grey, Walter. "Ottawa Reaction on Cuba One of Cautious Moderation." *Globe and Mail,* 28 October 1962, 16.

Hébert, Chantal. "Quebecers Have Moved on." *Toronto Star,* 15 April 2003, A1.

Immen, Wallace. "85% Want U.S. to Pay for Tragedy." *Globe and Mail,* 22 April 2002, A1.

Knox, Paul. "Cellucci Urges Canada to Hike Defence Budget." *Globe and Mail,* 3 October 2001, A8.

Koring, Paul. "Bush Adds $2-Billion to Border Pot." *Globe and Mail,* 26 January 2002, A13.

Koring, Paul, and Daniel Leblanc. "Canadian Will Run Persian Gulf Naval Task Force." *Globe and Mail,* 11 February 2003, A1.

Krauss, Clifford. "Divergent Paths: Canada Breaks with U.S. Over Missile Shield." *New York Times,* 27 February 2005, 3.

Laghi, Brian, and Jill Mahoney. "Troops Won't Go if They're 'Unwelcome.'" *Globe and Mail,* 20 November 2001, A1.

MacCharles, Tonda. "Air Travelers Face Screening." *Toronto Star,* 17 January 2004, A1.

–. "Small Countries Look to Canada – Feeling Pressured over Iraq Stance Council Members Want Compromise." *Toronto Star,* 3 March 2003, A1.

MacGregor, Roy. "Mixed Signals on Star Wars." *Maclean's,* 8 April 1985, 10.

MacKinnon, Mark. "For Canadian Serving in Iraq Is a Source of Pride," *Globe and Mail,* 21 March 2008, A3.

–. "Secrecy Surrounds Canadian Missions." *Globe and Mail,* 7 February 2002, A15.

Mayer, Jane. "The Experiment." *New Yorker,* 11 July 2005.

McKenna, Barrie. "U.S. Praises Security Blueprint." *Globe and Mail,* 26 April 2004, A7.

"Missile Defence Approval Expected. U.S. Ambassador Optimistic Canada to Join Shield Plan." *Winnipeg Free Press,* 10 January 2005, A1.

Morton, Peter. "U.S. Citizens at Odds with World on War: Nearly 60% of Americans Support Attack on Iraq." *National Post,* 12 March 2003, A15.

Perkel, Colin. "U.S.-Canada Relationship Could Suffer, Cellucci Says." *Globe and Mail,* 1 March 2003, A9.

"Powell's Address, Presenting 'Deeply Troubling' Evidence on Iraq." *New York Times,* 6 February 2003, 18.

Preston, Julia. "Security Council Votes, 15-0, for Tough Iraq Resolution." *New York Times,* 9 November 2002, 1.

Pugliese, David. "U.S. Thanks Canada for Role in Iraq War: But Ottawa Insists It Did Nothing to Help." *National Post,* 14 June 2003, A1.

Purdy, Matthew. "A Nation Challenged: The Law; Bush's New Rules to Fight Terror Transform Legal Landscape." *New York Times,* 25 November 2001, 1.

Roche, Douglas. "How Canada Bucked the U.S. Line on Nuclear Arms." *Globe and Mail,* 23 November 1998, A21.

Rowswell, Ben. "McLellan's U.S. Challenge." *Toronto Star,* 18 December 2003, A31.

Rusk, James. "PM Support on Star Wars Pleases US." *Globe and Mail,* 2 February 1985, 1.

Russo, Robert. "Canada Feels Heat to Back Star Wars II." *Winnipeg Free Press,* 16 March 2000, B1.

Sallot, Jeff. "Axworthy Blasts U.S. on Nuclear Policy." *Globe and Mail,* 23 October 1999, A12.

–. "U.S. Subs to Sail in Strait: Nuclear Vessels Cause Uproar." *Globe and Mail,* 31 October 1991, A1.

–. "U.S. Wants Troops for Iraqi War." *Globe and Mail,* 15 November 2002, A1.

Sanders, Richard. "Who Says We're Not at War?" *Globe and Mail,* 31 March 2003, A15.

Schiller, Bill. "The Road to Kandahar." *Toronto Star,* 9 September 2006, F01.

Simpson, Jeffrey. "The Canadian Connection." *Globe and Mail,* 16 January 1985, 6.

–. "Trying to Make Love and War in Afghanistan." *Globe and Mail,* 7 March 2006, A15.

"Star Wars Endangers Peace Role, Tories Told." *Globe and Mail,* 17 July 1985, P1.

Struck, Doug. "Canada Rejects Missile Shield Plan; Decision Is a snub to Bush, Who Had Sought Partnership." *Washington Post,* 25 February 2005, A18.

Taber, Jane. "Ottawa Torn by Turbulent Elections; Iraq; Martin Says Yes to Training Workers, but No to Troops." *Globe and Mail,* 6 December 2004, A1.

Thompson, Allan. "Can Canada Still Lay Claim to Being Glorious and Free?" *Toronto Star,* 9 September 2002, A6.

–. "Canada Lines Up Military Muscle for War on Iraq." *Toronto Star,* 9 January 2003, A1.

Trickey, Mike. "Canadian Destroyer Nabs Two al-Qaeda Suspects: Gulf of Oman Chase." *National Post,* 16 July 2002, A6.

"U.S. Admits Its Mistake over Canada's Role in War." *Toronto Star,* 23 June 2003, A18.

"U.S. Backs Away from We-Won't-Protect-You Stance of Admiral: Anti-Missile Shield: 2's Comments Do Not Reflect Official Policy, Washington." *National Post,* 4 May 2000, A11.

Wattie, Chris. "Canada's Homeland Defence Team Names Its First Commander." *National Post,* 29 June 2005, A6.

Weston, Greg "Fix Leaky Borders: U.S." *Toronto Sun,* 20 September 2001, 7.

White, Scott. "Canadian Soldiers in Afghanistan Top Story – CP Members Pick 1 News Event; Four Deaths Touched a Nerve." *Toronto Star,* 2 January 2003, A18.

Internet

Canada. Department of Foreign Affairs and International Trade. "Canada and the World: A History, 1968-1984: The Trudeau Years." http://www.dfait-aeci.gc.ca/depatment/history/canada9-en.asp.

–. "Notes for an Address by the Honourable John Manley, Minister of Foreign Affairs, to a Special Session of Parliament." 17 September 2001. http://w01.international.gc.ca/minpub/Publication.asp?FileSpec=/Min_Pub_Docs/104518.htm.

–. "Nuclear Disarmament and Non-Proliferation: Advancing Canadian Objectives." http://www.dfait-maeci.gc.ca/nucchallenge/POLICY-en.asp.

–. "Statement by the Government of Canada on Iraq's Parliamentary Elections." 15 December 2005. http://w01.international.gc.ca/MinPub/Publication.asp?Language=E&publication_id=383558.

Canada. Department of National Defence. "Backgrounder – Canadian Operational Support Command." 31 January 2006. http://www.forces.gc.ca/site/newsroom/view_news_e.asp?id=1853.

–. "Letter from Minister Pratt to Secretary Rumsfeld." 15 January 2004. http://www.forces.gc.ca/site/Focus/Canada-us/letter_e.asp.

–. "Reply from Secretary Rumsfeld to Minister Pratt." http://www.forces.gc.ca/site/Focus/Canada-us/letter_e.asp.

–. "Canada-.U.S. Amend NORAD Agreement." 5 August 2004. http://www.forces.gc.ca/site/Newsroom/view_news_e.asp?id=1422.

–. "Operations Briefing – Defence Minister Art Eggleton and Chief of Staff Ray Henault Give a News Conference on Deployment of Canadian Forces in Afghanistan. 7 January 2002. http://www.forces.gc.ca/site/Newsroom/view_news_e.asp?id=352.

Canada. Privy Council Office. *Securing an Open Society: Canada's National Security Policy.* April 2004. http://www.pco-bcp.gc.ca/docs/information/publications/natsec-secnat/

natsec-secnat-eng.pdf, viiCanada. Standing Senate Committee on National Security and Defence. *Managing Turmoil: The Need to Upgrade Canadian Foreign Aid and Military Strength to Deal with Massive Change.* Interim Report of the Standing Senate Committee on National Security and Defence (October 2006), http://www.parl.gc.ca/39/1/parlbus/commbus/senate/com-e/defe-e/rep-e/RepOct06-e.pdf.

Canada Border Services Agency. "Canada-United States Integrated Enforcement Teams." http://www.cbsa-asfc.gc.ca/general/enforcement/ibet-eipf-e.html.

–. "The Free and Secure Trade Program." http://www.cbsa-asfc.gc.ca/import/fast/menu-e.html#what.

Canadian Association of University Teachers (CAUT). Letter to Senators Expressing Concern over Bill C-7: Public Safety Act, 4 March 2004. http://www.caut.ca/en/issues/civil_liberties/2004mar_CAUTbillc7.pdf.

Canadian Bar Association. Office of the President. "Re: Bill C-7 – Public Safety Act, 2002." http://www.cba.org/CBA/submissions/pdf/04-09-eng.pdf.

Canadian Embassy (Havana) Dispatch. CONFIDENTIAL, "Cuba – Final Impressions." 15 June 1961. http://www.gwu.edu/~nsarchiv/bayofpigs/19610615.pdf.

Canadian International Development Agency. "Iraq Overview." http://www.acdi-cida.gc.ca/iraq.

Cellucci, A. Paul. "Speech to the Economic Club of Toronto." 25 March 2003. http://ottawa.usembassy.gov/content/content.asp?section=embconsul&document=cellucci_030325.

Centre for Research and Information on Canada. "Canadians Oppose US Missile Defence System by a Small Majority." 4 November 2004. http://www.cric.ca/pdf/cric_poll/portraits/portraits_2004/eng_can_us_2004.pdf.

"Chrétien Government Rejected Military's Advice on Afghan Deployment: Ex-Army Chief." CBC News, 18 October 2006. http://www.cbc.ca/canada/story/2006/10/18/afghan-military-advice.html.

Doyle, Charles. "The USA Patriot Act: A Sketch." CRS Report for Congress, 18 April 2002. http://www.fas.org/irp/crs/RS21203.pdf.

Edited Hansard, 37th Parliament, First Session, Number 126, 6 December 2001. http://www.parl.gc.ca/37/1/parlbus/chambus/house/debates/126_2001-12-06/han126_1135-E.htm.

Eland, Ivan, with Daniel Lee. "The Rogue State Doctrine and National Missile Defense." Cato Institute Foreign Policy Briefing 65 (29 March 2001). http://www.cato.org/pubs/fpbriefs/fpb65.pdf.

Hildreth, Steven A. "Ballistic Missile Defense: Historical Overview." CRS Report for Congress. 22 April 2005. http://www.fas.org/sgp/crs/weapons/RS22120.pdf.

In-depth Afghanistan: CBC-Environics Public Issues Poll. November 2006. http://www.cbc.ca/news/background/afghanistan/afghanistan-survey2006.html.

Islamic Republic of Afghanistan. *Afghanistan National Development Strategy, Summary Report: An Interim Strategy for Security, Governance, Economic Growth and Poverty Reduction.* http://www.unama-afg.org/news/_londonConf/_docs/ANDS-SummaryReport-eng.pdf.

Jockel, Joseph. "After the September Attacks: Four Questions about NORAD's Future." *Canadian Military Journal* (Spring 2002). http://www.journal.forces.gc.ca/engraph/Vol3/no1/pdf/11-16_e.pdf.

Kennedy, President John F. "Radio and Television Report to the American People on the Soviet Arms Buildup in Cuba." The White House, 22 October 1962. http://www.jfklibrary.org/.

London Conference on Afghanistan. "The Afghanistan Compact." London, 31 January – 1 February 2006. http://www.unama-afg.org/news/_londonConf/_docs/06jan30-AfghanistanCompact-Final.pdf.

Manley, John, Derek H. Burney, Jake Epp, Paul Tellier, and Pamela Wallin. *Independent Panel on Canada's Future Role in Afghanistan.* January 2008. http://dsp-psd.pwgsc.gc.ca/collection_2008/dfait-maeci/FR5-20-1-2008E.pdf.

Mason, Dwight N. "A Flight from Responsibility: Canada and Missile Defense of North America." Center for Strategic and International Studies, 25 February 2005. http://www.csis.org/americas/canada/050225_Mason.pdf.

Missile Defense Agency. "Ballistic Missile Defense Approach." Fact Sheet, March 2002. http://www.acq.osd.mil/bmdo/bmdolink/pdf/approach.pdf.

Moseley, T. Michael, Lt. Gen. USAF. *Operation Iraqi Freedom – by the Numbers.* 30 April 2003. http://www.globalsecurity.org/military/library/report/2003/uscentaf_oif_report_30 apr2003.pdf.

Office of the Auditor General of Canada. "National Security in Canada – The 2001 Anti-Terrorism Initiative." Chapter 3 in *Report of the Auditor General to the House of Commons.* March 2004. http://www.oag-bvg.gc.ca/internet/English/parl_oag_200403_e_1123.html.

Pena, Charles V. "Missile Defense: Defending America or Building Empire?" CATO Institute Foreign Policy Briefing 77. 28 May 2003. http://www.globalpolicy.org/empire/intervention/2004/0528missdef.pdf.

Project for a New American Century. "Rebuilding America's Defenses: Strategy, Forces and Resources for a New Century." September 2000. http://www.newamericancentury.org/RebuildingAmericasDefenses.pdf.

Public Safety and Emergency Preparedness Canada. "About Us." http://www.psepc-sppcc. gc.ca/abt/index-en.asp.

–. "Canada-United States Cross Border Crime Forum." http://www.psepc-sppcc.gc.ca/prg/le/oc/cbc-en.asp.

–. "Integrated Border Enforcement Teams." http://www.psepc-sppcc.gc.ca/prg/le/bs/ibet-en. asp.

Rashid, Ahmed. "Who's Winning the War on Terror?" *YaleGlobal,* 5 September 2003. http://yaleglobal.yale.edu/display.article?id=2384.

Romalis, Coleman. "What Is Star Wars Doing to Canada?" *Peace Magazine,* June 1985. http://www.peacemagazine.org/archive/v01n4p11.htm.

Roosevelt, President Franklin. Address at Queen's University, Kingston, Ontario, Canada. 18 August 1938. http://www.ibiblio.org/pha/7-2-188/188-09.html.

Senate Committee on Intelligence. "Report on the U.S. Intelligence Community's Pre-War Intelligence Assessments on Iraq." 2004. http://www.gpoaccess.gov/serialset/creports/iraq.html.

Transport Canada. "Public Safety Act Receives Royal Assent." 6 May 2004. http://www.tc.gc.ca/mediaroom/releases/nat/2004/04-gc004ae.htm.

United States Navy. *A Cooperative Strategy for 21st Century Seapower.* October 2007. http://www.navy.mil/maritime/MaritimeStrategy.pdf.

US. Department of Defense. "Report on Progress toward Security and Stability in Afghanistan." 27 June 2008. http://www.defenselink.mil/pubs/Report_on_Progress_toward_Security_and_Stability_in_Afghanistan_1230.pdf.

US. Department of Homeland Security. "Fact Sheet: Security and Prosperity Partnership." 27 June 2005. http://www.dhs.gov/xnews/releases/press_release_0695.shtm.

–. "US-Canada Smart Border/30-Point Action Plan Update." 6 December 2002. http://www.dhs.gov/dhspublic/display?content=128.

US. Office of Homeland Security. *The National Strategy for Homeland Security.* July 2002. http://www.dhs.gov/xlibrary/assets/nat_strat_hls.pdf.

US. White House. "President Discusses Strong Relationship with Canada." Halifax, 1 December 2004. http://www.whitehouse.gov/news/releases/2004/12/20041201-4.html.

–. "Summary of the Smart Border Action Plan Status." 9 September 2002. http://www.whitehouse.gov/news/releases/2002/09/20020909.html.

–. *The National Security Strategy of the United States of America.* September 2002. http://www.whitehouse.gov/nsc/nss.pdf.

–. "U.S.-Canada Smart Border/30-Point Action Plan Update." 6 December 2002. http://www.whitehouse.gov/news/releases/2002/12/20021206-1.html.

Index